REASONABLE CAUSE
TO SUSPECT

REASONABLE CAUSE TO SUSPECT

A Mother's Ordeal to Save Her Son from a Kurdish Prison

Sally Lane

DUNDURN
PRESS

Publisher: Kwame Scott Fraser | Acquiring editor: Russell Smith
Cover designer: Laura Boyle
Cover image: city and explosion: shutterstock.com/unlu; barbed wire and sky: Unsplash .com/FachyMarin

Library and Archives Canada Cataloguing in Publication

Title: Reasonable cause to suspect : a mother's ordeal to free her son from a Kurdish prison / Sally Lane.
Names: Lane, Sally (Mother), author.
Identifiers: Canadiana (print) 20220432015 | Canadiana (ebook) 20220432139 | ISBN 9781459750944 (softcover) | ISBN 9781459750951 (PDF) | ISBN 9781459750968 (EPUB)
Subjects: LCSH: Lane, Sally (Mother) | LCSH: Letts, Jack, 1995- | LCSH: Mothers—Canada—Biography. | LCSH: Political prisoners—Syria—Biography. | LCSH: Syria—History—Civil War, 2011- | LCGFT: Autobiographies.
Classification: LCC HV9777.5 .L36 2023 | DDC 365/.45092—dc23

We acknowledge the support of the Canada Council for the Arts and the Ontario Arts Council for our publishing program. We also acknowledge the financial support of the Government of Ontario, through the Ontario Book Publishing Tax Credit and Ontario Creates, and the Government of Canada.

Dundurn Press
1382 Queen Street East
Toronto, Ontario, Canada M4L 1C9
dundurn.com, @dundurnpress 𝕏 f 📷

For Tayab Ali, human rights warrior and friend

Twitter exchange, 2020:

Me: Sometimes I wonder if I'm going crazy, or if the world is

"The Londonistani": Defo the world

Introduction

Soon after being captured by the YPG (the Kurdish People's Protection Units) in northern Syria in May 2017, our son, Jack Letts, was kept in solitary confinement in a cell he described as a dungeon. There was no ventilation and only a tiny window with two layers of bars at the top of the wall. It was here that he spent thirty-five days, with only his brain for company, fearing he was going insane.

Abandoned by both his governments (he was a dual British/Canadian citizen) and believed by the world to be a fearsome jihadi — based on a sensation-seeking media that printed lies and assumptions — Jack was trying to come to terms with his fate. "This sounds weird," he told a Canadian consular officer ten months later, in January 2018, "but in solitary, I wrote letters to the management. The last one I signed with my own blood, after scratching my face, thinking someone is going to listen. But no one listened.... I knew I was going out of my mind."

When Jack was first captured, he was allowed to speak to us, his parents, via a phone app, for half an hour every other day. It was then we learned that initially the Kurds had treated him well, offering him cigarettes and telling him they were negotiating his freedom with Britain. They had their own spies in Raqqa, they told him, who had reported back that he was "one of the good guys." They knew he had stood against ISIS — even refuting them in religious arguments in the street, right outside the police station — and told him he would be freed in three days' time.

Over five years later — 2022, at the time of writing — this assertion seems like a sick joke. Britain, it seemed, and then Canada, had no interest in letting back any of their nationals to their home countries, preferring they remain indefinitely — in legal limbo, and in cramped, squalid conditions — where they were. After two months of frequent contact with Jack, all communication suddenly ceased. We didn't know if he was alive or dead, and no one seemed to be able to help us find out. "We advise against all travel to Syria," was the Foreign and Commonwealth Office's reply to our desperate pleas. "We have no consular access in Syria, and are unable to assist Jack Letts while he remains in that country." FCO staff, it appeared, were even incapable of picking up a phone to speak to Jack's captors, whose contact details we had provided them with.

How did any of this happen to a bright, lively, linguistically talented teenager from Oxford — only eighteen when he went to Syria — who had a love of the Arabic culture, language, and religion? Astonishingly, even a YPJ fighter, whose childhood friend worked in the prison Jack was in, and with whom I was in sporadic correspondence, described him as "charming." How could it be that he went from being the class clown with a sense of fun and a wide circle of friends to being the world's "most wanted" in the space of under a year?

Official sources of help, such as human rights NGOs or the Labour party opposition, which, in normal circumstances, could be relied upon to challenge the government's intransigent position, also professed an inability to do anything. Jack, it seemed, was "politically difficult." In an age of mass and instant technology, no one in the world seemed able to reach a British youngster, who had gone to Syria believing he was assisting the Syrian people against a brutal dictator, but had ended up locked in a foreign jail, and then forgotten.

As Jack's parents — his only supporters, apart from a small circle of friends — we were prevented from running a full-scale, public campaign to negotiate his release, by strict contempt-of-court rules. In January 2016, we had been arrested under a charge of fund-raising for terrorism after we'd tried to send Jack £1,000 to escape Raqqa, Syria, with the help of a people smuggler. Three and a half years later, we were still on bail, and newspapers and broadcasters were threatened with a hefty fine for contempt of court if they published anything revealing what we knew about Jack's activities in Syria. Ostensibly, this was to prevent the possible prejudicing of a jury in our forthcoming trial (although the newspaper stories about "Jihadi Jack" had done that very well already). In actuality, the threat of contempt of court acted as a gag order on us so that we were unable to defend Jack against the lies that had been circulated about him, or campaign vigorously for his release.

Eventually securing a meeting with the Foreign Office in June 2017 — after screaming uncontrollably down their "emergency" phone line — I asked the Head of Special Cases how he would feel if it were his own son.

"I can see that it is very distressing for you," he said.

"And how would you feel if it was your own son, and you were faced with someone like you?" I pursued.

"At least you would know you had done all you could do," was his reply.

The Head of Special Cases was wrong. We were nowhere near saying that we had done all we could do. Our battle for justice for Jack had only just begun.

Chapter 1

Reasonable cause to suspect

On January 26, 2016, Detective Inspector *T* and Detective Sergeant *M* from the South East Counter Terrorism Unit (SECTU), Thames Valley Police, visited our home in Oxford to discuss the terrorism charges on which John and I had been arrested three weeks earlier. In many ways, this visit was no different from the dozens of "informal chats" we'd had with the police since they'd first visited us in December 2014, enquiring about the whereabouts and activities of our son Jack, who, in May 2014, at the age of eighteen, had gone on a ten-day trip to Jordan to visit a friend from Oxford.

We had arranged the holiday for Jack, hoping that it would positively channel his academic interest in Islam and allow him to practise his spoken Arabic, which he'd managed to master to a surprisingly high degree in a short time. His dedication to the language showed itself in the piles of Arabic grammar books that lay around the house, in the endless hours he spent in Oxford coffee shops speaking in Arabic to his new university student friends from

Kuwait, Qatar, and Turkey, and in the frustration of his sixth-form college teachers, who declared he did no work at all on the end-of-year exams he was having to repeat that year.

When Jack had phoned from Jordan, just before his ten-day holiday was up, to say that his friend was going to Kuwait for a three-month course in Arabic and Islamic Studies at Kuwait University and to ask if he could go, too, John, my husband, and I agreed that he could. Jack had been investigating Middle Eastern universities online before he left and hadn't been able to decide which would suit him best. In the circumstances, his being able to do a short course and being accompanied by someone he knew, and whose family we knew of in Oxford, seemed to us to be a reassuring option. The boys would be living in a nice, spacious apartment close to the university on Jamal Abdul Nasser Street. Would I be able to send him the money for his ticket and his first month's rent? In light of what happened later, it appears naive of us that we didn't question Jack more closely about his possible long-term plans ("She even paid for his ticket!" declared the Westminster court magistrate nearly two years later), but hindsight, of course, is a luxury we did not possess at the time.

Our January 26, 2016, visit from Detective Inspector T and Detective Sergeant M was supposed to clarify some of the issues surrounding the charges against us. By then, it was known that Jack had continued on to Syria after studying in Kuwait for a couple of months, and any money we sent to him while he was in Syria could be viewed as being "suspicious." The official charges were that *"we entered into or became concerned in an arrangement as a result of which money or other property was or was to be made available to another person, knowing or having reasonable cause to suspect that it would or might be used for the purposes of terrorism."* These charges had been brought under sections 17 and 22 of the Terrorism Act.

The relevant wording of the act, upon which the whole edifice of our arrest, surveillance, and prosecution was based, was the phrase "reasonable cause to suspect." John and I felt confident then and now that, for a myriad of reasons, we did not have reasonable cause to suspect Jack was a terrorist or that the money sent to him would be used for terrorist purposes. The whole notion was absurd: the money had been to get him away from terrorism. It all seemed simple and self-explanatory, and since the police had access to the same information about Jack and his activities as we did, we couldn't understand why they didn't reach the same conclusion. Only a month before we sent the money, in November 2015, we had been informed by Detective Constable N that there was "no evidence that Jack has done anything wrong." And if there was any "secret intelligence" information to the contrary, it was not available to someone at the pay grade of a detective constable, and certainly hadn't been made available to us. In fact, nearly three years after this 2016 meeting — i.e., in September 2018 — we discovered, following a disclosure request by our lawyers, that, in fact, no secret intelligence information existed at all.

Over tea and panettone, as with all our other "informal chats," the detectives, John, and I discussed what "reasonable cause to suspect" actually meant. The police's contention was that Jack was a suspected terrorist because he had expressed a number of anti-Western government views on Facebook, and was believed to be living in Raqqa, the Syrian capital of "The Islamic State of Iraq and al-Sham," the self-styled caliphate commonly referred to in English as ISIS. John and I didn't dispute either of these contentions; it was what they amounted to that formed the crux of our difference of opinion with the police.

"Are you saying that anyone living in Raqqa is guilty of supporting ISIS?" asked John. "Does that mean that it is actually impossible to do humanitarian work if you're living in the city?"

"Yes," said DS *M*. "If you're living and working in the city, you are by definition supporting the state by paying taxes and by participating in the caliphate."

"What if you're a kebab seller?" continued John. "And you've been living in Raqqa all your life and you pay taxes on your kebab business, and perhaps on a Friday you give a free kebab to an ISIS fighter just to keep in with them so they don't target and murder your family. Is that considered supporting the state?"

"Yes," said *M*. "Absolutely."

"What else is the kebab seller supposed to do?" John pursued. Like Jack, he could never be accused of dropping an argument. "He doesn't know anything else."

"He could get another job," said *M*. "Or move."

"But tens of thousands of them are trying to move at the moment," I joined in. "And Europe won't let them in."

"What about a doctor doing humanitarian work in Raqqa?" asked John. "Is he a suspected terrorist?" (We didn't know it at the time, but a British trauma surgeon, David Nott, who had operated at gunpoint on an ISIS fighter in Aleppo in 2013, was similarly called upon to justify his actions in June 2016 by Kirsty Young on *Desert Island Discs*. When asked whether he should have saved the life of an ISIS fighter, who would no doubt go on to take many more lives, David Nott replied, "There was a chance that the [fighter] would have a change of heart because his life had been saved." Additionally, of course, Dr. Nott had had a gun to his head throughout the whole operation, so had not really been in a position to calmly debate the ethics of his situation.)

"Yes, he would be considered a suspected terrorist," said *M*.

Much later — i.e., more than three years after this particular conversation with the counter-terrorism unit — John discovered that this was indeed the case. At the promotion of Dr. Nott's book, *War Doctor: Surgery on the Front Line*, at the 2019 Oxford Literary

Festival, John managed to have a chat with the heroic doctor himself. Despite the fact that by this time Nott had been awarded an OBE for his courageous war-time surgery, he revealed to John that he was on a police list of four thousand terror suspects because he had spent time in Syria.

I took the opportunity at this point in the conversation to ask about the fate of Mashudur Choudhury, a Briton who had had a civilian job in a laundry and a nursery in Syria for just over two weeks in October 2013, and who had been sentenced for four years for "preparing acts of terrorism." He was one of a group of five young men from Portsmouth who were among the first to leave the U.K. to fight in Syria. Four of them were dead by July 2015. After Jack told us in September 2014 that he was in Syria, I had followed the case of the Portsmouth five closely, as it was clearly having a large influence on British attitudes to suspected Islamic terrorists, and on the likely prison sentences such suspects could expect to receive. *M* told me that he had been personally involved in the Choudhury case, and that, although it wasn't widely reported, Choudhury had ended up serving less than half his sentence.

Getting back to our discussion on our son's activities, John and I explained once again what we believed Jack had been doing in Iraq and Syria, based on the Facebook and phone conversations we'd had with him over the past year and a half. Jack had told us that he had worked a bit in a hospital and had also helped out a friend some mornings in a school. Not long after he'd first arrived, he'd said that he wanted to do "sheik training" (training to become a religious teacher) but he needed the permission of the local imam to do so, and obtaining this seemed to be taking a long time. He was very well versed in the Qu'ran, and professed embarrassment that his close friend was able to recite much more from memory than he was. He had told us he wasn't a fighter, and we had gone to some lengths to find out from external sources whether his pattern of activities — moving between towns in Syria and Iraq — fitted that of an ISIS fighter being sent to different parts of the front line, or whether civilians moved around in a similar way. Our primary concern was about his chances of staying alive. Part of the evidence that he wasn't a fighter seemed to be that he had been there for nearly two years and had somehow escaped being one of the 350,000 Syrians who had already been killed.

I suspected, from my following of the Portsmouth case, where even a laundry and nursery worker could be convicted of the preparation of terrorist acts, that Jack would be considered a terror suspect by the British state even if he was working in a school or hospital. I was secure in my own belief that someone who was working in a civilian capacity should not be classified as a terrorist, even if that differed from the official British view. When the story about Jack broke on January 24, 2016, two days before our present meeting with the two detectives, I'd countered the erroneous press reporting by saying that, before he left, Jack had talked about doing humanitarian work with refugees in Syria, and was now integrated into the local population (the latter assertion based on my knowledge of his school and hospital work). The papers translated this into my saying that Jack was "doing humanitarian work" in Syria, and I was asked to provide the name of the organization he was working for. When I replied that he wasn't working for an organization as such, it looked as if I was either being evasive or deliberately hiding the truth.

Listening to *M*'s comments about the kebab seller, John was incredulous. He'd had no idea that the British state believed it was impossible to do humanitarian-type work in Raqqa, and that a doctor could be tarred with the same brush as a brutal ISIS fighter who believed it was acceptable to cut the heads off disbelievers. It appeared that, under current terrorism law, there was no distinction between the doctor and the fighter, which was what led me to conclude that it was the law itself that was at fault, given that its imprecise wording, referring to something that might or might not happen in the future, could be applied in such widely disparate cases.

Another aspect of our academic-seeming discussions around our dining room table concerned the actual trajectory of funds that found their way to Syria. According to *M*, even if £10 ended up as a bribe, say, to an ISIS border guard, those funds could be defined as money destined for terrorism. In other words, the intention for how those funds should be used was not important. Even if the funds had been intended for an entirely different purpose — for making a hostage payment, for instance, or for trying to extract someone from a war zone — there was always a chance that some of the money could end up elsewhere. All that was required was the fact that there were "reasonable grounds to suspect" that money could potentially be used for terrorist purposes. It was difficult to know where this argument ended.

To take it one step further, you could postulate that anyone who put gas in the car while on holiday in Turkey could well be paying some money to ISIS, since much of the oil ISIS produced was smuggled across the border into Turkey. And even further, that anyone paying taxes to the British government was supporting the sending of arms and finance to Saudi Arabia, a country suspected by many of directly supporting terrorism in Syria, Iraq, and Yemen. (Indeed, this suspicion was officially confirmed in October 2016, with the Wikileaks release of Hillary Clinton's emails from 2014, which included her statement that both Saudi Arabia and Qatar were providing "clandestine financial and logistic support to ISIS.")

Our discussions with the detectives would be merely intellectually diverting if it weren't that their practical application in our case could land us in prison for a very long time. We couldn't believe that British justice would allow this to happen. And how could it be illegal to try to save our son's life when there wasn't even any evidence he had done anything wrong? None of it made any sense.

The detective inspector, *T*, appeared to be getting impatient with the theoretical nature of our conversation. She was there to talk about what would happen next, and what the police recommendations were if Jack wished to extract himself from Syria. So far, their advice in this regard had been woefully lacking, apart from giving us the addresses of the British consulate and embassy in Turkey. We knew they must have people on the ground in Syria, in addition to the whole network of intelligence operations that were shared among the "Five Eyes" security services in the U.S., U.K., Canada, Australia, and New Zealand, as well as in Europe. However, advice for Jack was contingent on his agreeing to talk to the U.K. police from where he was. Knowing Jack's distrust of the police and knowing that he was well aware of the fifteen-year prison sentences that were being handed down to people who had gone to Syria, I was very doubtful about the chances of this happening. Our suggestion was that any negotiations with the U.K. police could be mediated by us, but this idea wasn't received with any enthusiasm by the two police officers in front of us, and the conversation quickly turned to other topics.

Uppermost in our minds was the crucial issue of how we were going to rescue Jack from a war zone, a feat that would require us to be out of jail if we were to be fully functional. At that point, at the end of January, we had been arrested but not charged, and the decision as to whether we would be charged or not rested with the Crown Prosecution Service (CPS). Detective Inspector *T* mentioned that our case was very political and this decision "would be made at ministerial level." Why our case was so different from other cases of families being caught up in the horror of their children going to Syria I couldn't fathom. Was it because we weren't Muslim? Or because we were white and supposedly "middle class"? (Although, even if we were middle class by education and aspiration, we were definitely working-class poor by income, dependent as we were on the proceeds of John's as yet unprofitable business and my paltry earnings as an administrator at a publicly funded hospital. We certainly didn't own our own £600,000 home, contrary to what the *Daily Mail* implied.)

We hoped that the CPS would see that it was nonsensical to charge us, as we were merely parents trying to protect our child. The payments we sent him hadn't even gone through. The CPS, it turned out, had a completely different agenda, the wisdom of which we couldn't even guess at.

Chapter 2

"I'm here now"

Jack was an irrepressible torrent of energy, intensity, and curiosity from the second he was born. I say this in good faith, since my viewing position of that whole business was, of course, at the wrong end. It was later that I heard the account of his popping out and gazing round at the assembled crowd with a look of wondering appraisal on his face, as if to say, "So, this is the outside world. Well, I'm here now, so we can begin."

And from then on, he never stopped. He craved attention, people, activity, movement, and being in the centre of everything. He was funny, fearless, dramatic, and exhausting. At the age of five, he introduced himself with, "I'm the famous Jack Letts" (little did he know how prophetic that was). By the age of eight, he was doing school assembly performances of his own rap songs that he improvised on the spot. He had clearly inherited his father's gene for confidence and showmanship. My family struggled to see in him my more reflective and bookworm side — we came from a long, sober line of vicars and bank managers — and I had to convince them that, since I had evidentially been there at the time of his birth, he was definitely mine.

Throughout his childhood, Jack went through a series of passionate interests. Each one he would take up with the same intensity, then blaze through whatever it was until he had extracted every last drop of substance from it, and then, suddenly, the interest would be dropped as if it had never been. His first all-consuming passion around the age of four was Pokémon, and it seemed he knew every single element, characteristic, strength, rating, score, and special power, of every single Pokémon character in the trading card pack. He would act out all the various combinations of battles between the characters and would try to get me to play the opposing sides. I wasn't much use, though, since I could only ever remember the characteristics for Pikachu because he was the small, fluffy one they made into toys, and Jack could never understand how I didn't know each character as he did.

When Jack first went to primary school, the teachers were struck by his exceptional verbal skills. The head teacher even brought in an Oxford professor, who was a poet as well as a psychologist, to test him. All I remember is that they said he was on the very high end of the spectrum of verbal reasoning and ability, and we should keep an eye on him, whatever that meant. He loved music and used to climb out of the first floor window of our house to stand on the conservatory roof to sing "Hound Dog" or "Johnny Be Good" while John played the guitar. I found it hard to understand how he could hear a song once or twice and instantly know all the words. Any excuse he could get to perform — friends' weddings or anniversaries, for instance — he would ask if he could get up on stage and sing. (This wasn't always welcomed by the hosts, who didn't necessarily like the idea of being upstaged by a seven-year-old with a big mouth.) One of the saddest things of his later Islamic conversion was, I thought, his refusal to engage with music of any kind. At that stage, he would leave the room if John started playing the guitar, or if I had the radio on. The only music he allowed himself during this period was the music of the recitations from the Qu'ran.

At the age of ten, Jack got the chance to have a starring role at Wembley stadium in London. The occasion was the international horse show, a stunning musical, dance, and dramatic extravaganza, where the finest horses in the world — Arabian, Spanish, and Russian — performed feats, stunts, and spectacles in front of eighty thousand people. A friend of ours knew one of organizers and had recommended Jack to play the role of the young boy who accompanies the narrator as he strolls around the arena. Jack took to the concept instantly and became firm friends with the narrator, who was kind to him backstage as well as onstage. Jack also fell in love with one of the Russian singers, who had an amazing, operatic voice and an intimidating presence. He wanted to tell her how beautiful her voice was, but didn't quite dare. I told him she'd probably love to know she had a young fan, and sure enough, after he'd plucked up the courage to approach her and declare his admiration, she wrapped him into her capacious bosom, covered him in kisses, and made loud, Russian utterances of hearty appreciation.

Jack's grand passion around the same time, as with many small boys, was football. This meant footballs and football gear all over the house and frequent conversations about Michael Owen, the Liverpool striker. Jack was forever doing kick-ups, practising special moves, dribbling, heading, and doing push-ups. By this time he had a younger brother to play with, so, fortunately, I wasn't expected to join in. Jack was determined to be the best footballer ever, not for the fame or the money, which didn't seem to interest him, but because he was convinced his special moves on the pitch needed to be seen to be believed. Once it became clear that there were boys on his local football team who were better than he was, he suddenly dropped football and started going to basketball practice several times a week instead. After basketball came boxing; then rap music; then graffiti (Banksy replaced Michael Owen as his hero); then being part of the rebellious gang at school, who were disrespectful to teachers, and who loped late into lessons, arms round each other's shoulders and trousers halfway down their backsides. Low-bagging fashion seemed nonsensical to me, since surely it just hobbled the wearer like a tied-up camel? I guessed the point was that parents weren't supposed to understand.

Throughout this latest phase — when he was the "worst kid in Year 9" according to the Head of Discipline — Jack still did well in most of his subjects, excelling in some of them, such as English and drama, and even getting an A in maths and physics exams. His teachers seemed to either love him and find him entertaining, or find him difficult and infuriating. When, for instance, Jack wrote "Abducted by aliens" under "Reason for lateness" in the late book, his form teacher laughed, and the Deputy Head gave him an extra detention.

Sometimes mixed feelings about Jack would occur within the same department. At one parent-teacher meeting, the drama teacher took the opportunity to vent his obviously long-pent-up anger about Jack's wisecracks during lessons, his failure to stick to the script, and his general feeling that the rules didn't apply to him. The teacher concluded by saying he would be very reluctant to have Jack in his class the following year. During his tirade, I noticed that his young deputy seemed to be trying to signal something to me with his eyes, and sure enough, a little while later, this younger man sidled up to me, saying Jack had a definite talent, and he would be personally very sorry if he didn't continue with his drama studies. It seemed that none of the school's authority figures was entirely sure how to handle our son, but even the most strident detractors amongst them never expressed the idea that there was ever any malice in Jack's behaviour.

Around the age of fifteen, Jack's energies seemed to be bursting out in more unusual ways. He developed strange tics and mannerisms, such as moving his neck sideways to stare in one direction for a few seconds and then turning to do the same on the other side. When we asked him what he was doing, he would brush off the question. He became obsessed with washing, spending hours in the bathroom and spreading wet towels around the house, and often making his brother late for school. He knew himself that there was something wrong and told me one day that he found himself having to do everything in fours, then eights, and then sixteens. One incident that occurred while he was playing football convinced him that he couldn't control these strange obsessions any longer: he could see the ball coming toward him and knew that if he didn't move, it would hit him. Yet he still felt compelled to complete an all-important stepping ritual in sequences of sixteen, and sure enough, as he was in the middle of his steps, the ball struck him square-on.

John and I were alarmed and scared by what was happening to him. We put it down to the stress of his exams, and took him off to the doctor. After hearing Jack's account that he was now having difficulty reading as the words jumped about the page, the doctor referred him immediately to the Child and Adolescent Mental Health Services (CAMHS) near the Churchill Hospital. CAMHS soon diagnosed him with severe obsessive compulsive disorder, or OCD, 9 out of 10 on the scale, and recommended a course of cognitive behaviour therapy (CBT).

The information sheets that Jack brought back with him detailing the techniques he was supposed to practise in between his CBT sessions seemed to consist mainly of breathing exercises, where he was encouraged to focus on the breath in a calming, yogic manner whenever he felt compelled to carry out one of his rituals. What triggered the rituals themselves remained a secret to us — other than the fact that they were "bad thoughts" — and this secrecy/ confidentiality was part of the treatment itself. Since his parents were presumably part of the problem, and since Jack needed to be reassured that whatever he said remained between him and the psychologist, we were not privy to the actual content of the sessions. We were, however, induced to undertake separate couples therapy in order to reveal the effect we were having on Jack's anxiety. The primary conclusion of this, as I remember, was that John was a "dog" (extrovert, demonstrative), and I was a "cat" (reserved, self-contained), the usefulness of which I wasn't sure.

During this time, Jack still had a large group of friends, was loud and popular, and was considered to be the class clown. His humour never had a tinge of nastiness to it; he was still rueful and gentle-natured, with a sweet smile that disarmed old ladies on the street, who said he was a "lovely boy." He was unusual in that, despite being in the popular crowd, he would surprise his social circle by befriending people on the margins of other, less popular, social groups. For instance, he purposefully walked to the bus stop with one of the new girls at school — who lived in the travellers' camp at the edge of town and who "looked rough" — because no one else wanted to walk with her. Or he deliberately befriended the autistic boy who everyone else thought was weird, because he thought he was interesting and had things to say. Anyone who has been to school understands the intricacies and pitfalls of school social groups and the need to jostle for position in order to be identified as "in" one group or "out" of another. I wouldn't experience the same fear of adolescent social death until I ended up in Bronzefield prison nearly forty years later and had to negotiate the terms of my own social survival all over again. Jack's approach to friendship was perhaps unusual for someone his age, and was probably confusing to his peers and teachers, who generally expect teenaged social hierarchies to be more predictable.

When he was sixteen, Jack's behaviour changes became more pronounced. Always a passionate arguer, he was becoming very engaged in his "Ethics and Philosophy" course and had long classroom discussions with his teacher, an intelligent and socially conscious man, a Quaker, I later found out. For his special project for his course, Jack chose to write about Islam, influenced as he was by some of his close friends at school, who were smart, popular, and Muslim. This group of friends I particularly liked, as they were thoughtful and respectful and didn't find it awkward to discuss contemporary issues with their friends' parents. They had all worked together on their final year drama project that counted toward a third of their mark. Deciding to do things differently, they had performed the piece as a clever subversion of contemporary racist perceptions, so that the Black kids in the group played the parts of the white, working-class characters, and the white kids played the Black gangsters. Their performance was screamingly funny (I had little excerpts played to me in the kitchen), and it was to be the only performance in the whole year group that made the examiner laugh out loud.

I had great ambitions for their group, and tried to encourage them to write their own stuff in a similar, subversive, multicultural fashion, and perform at that year's Edinburgh festival. With their white/Black reversal, I believed that Jack and his friends would be doing something completely innovative and daring. Indeed, seven years later, in 2018, my optimism for their potential success was validated by a panel of comedy experts: one of these friends, Mamoun Elagab, now aged twenty-two, was nominated as one of the six best newcomers at the BBC New Comedy Awards.

In Jack's case, unfortunately, my idea that he might try to put his performing talents to good use at the age of sixteen came nowhere near to fruition: not long after their school performance,

Jack decided that comedy itself was petty, trivial, and a display of Western indulgence and complacency, and nothing I said could make him change his mind.

Other opinions and habits of his were changing, too. He had started to follow his interest in Islam by meeting with a local discussion group headed by one of the sheiks in town, who prided himself on being the face of tolerant, interfaith dialogue in Oxford. I had been surprised to see this particular sheik at a mass at Christchurch College cathedral a couple of Christmases earlier: it had seemed incongruous to see a Muslim representative at a Christian festival. Upon reflection, I'd decided that interfaith worship could only be a good thing and that perhaps it should happen more often. Presumably, it was the same God for both faiths.

I had lost my own faith as a teenager; to me, rejecting the Church of England had been like forgoing roast beef and Yorkshire beef on Sundays, or rejecting the doctrine of knitted doilies on toilet rolls. It was all too narrowly English and reminiscent of my suburban Ruislip roots (or "pink-cake land," as John called it). I hadn't taken up any other faith as a replacement, so was left with a sort of wishy-washy spiritualism with overtones of Christian morality. John was much the same, except that his overtones were more strongly French Canadian Catholic. In any event, we had not forced religion on either of the boys, and their religious experience had been confined to the nursery nativity play and singing the odd religious song in primary school.

Under the influence of his new group, Jack took to occasionally wearing a long, Islamic-looking gown around the house, given to him by one of his new university student friends. He was meeting people older than him through the Muslim network in Oxford, where he was mixing with students from Kuwait, Qatar, and Turkey in coffee shops on the Cowley Road. He also became more concerned about what he was eating. At this stage, he didn't insist on eating only halal food and instead would quiz me on how Christian I was, exactly, since apparently it was acceptable for him to eat food "prepared by a Christian." For the sake of unified family meals, I let it be understood that I was more Christian than I really felt. After all, I knew most of the Bible stories even if I disputed whether they had been directly inspired by God. However, as time went on, Jack found more and more excuses not to eat with us, even when his aunties, "the regulars," came round. As John and I didn't have immediate family in England, our families being in Canada or the States, we had formed our own "friendship family" in Oxford, made up mostly of single mothers with boys whom we had met through the nursery or school: the so-called aunties. Jack used to love going to the aunties' houses, mainly because they were much better cooks than I was.

Later on, I was to ask him if his attraction to Islam stemmed from the fact that the food at his Muslim friends' houses — the lamb biryanis and stuffed vine leaves — was so much tastier than the food he got at home. This was to be only one of the sticks I used to beat myself up with when he rejected not just my food, but everything we stood for, including our "Western" lifestyle.

One Saturday evening as Jack was preparing to go to his discussion group, he announced, "Mum, I'm going to convert to Islam."

"What!" I said. "You can't just waltz out the house casually saying something like that. This is something we have to talk about."

"But there's nothing to talk about," he replied. "It's really easy. You just have to say that there is no God but Allah and you have to confirm that no one has forced you to say so."

"But this is a life-changing decision," I said. "You should discuss it with your parents. What it means. How it changes things. You could at least delay it until you've talked to us properly."

"Well, okay," he said. "But since I'm going to do it anyway, I don't see how delaying for a few days is going to make any difference."

In the end, John and I realized that we didn't really have a strong argument against Jack's conversion to Islam. The fact that it wasn't in our cultural experience wasn't a good enough reason, and even went against the position of tolerance and cultural understanding we'd both preached throughout our working lives. I had worked at the Oxfam headquarters in north Oxford for eight years, and then worked as a charity fundraiser and book editor, and John had dedicated his life to understanding the science behind the evolution of wheat varieties and its practical application to organic farming. He'd been growing ancient wheat varieties such as Egyptian emmer wheat, which was not grown commercially in the U.K., and had started an organic flour business that was attracting national press coverage. There were even plenty of cultural arguments in favour of Jack's converting to Islam. He had, for instance, become much more helpful around the house, putting away the shopping instead of being slumped in front of the computer, or thinking about what it meant to "honour one's parents." I even enjoyed an elevation in status due to the Qu'ranic phrase, "Paradise lies at the feet of the mother," a tribute that I secretly believed John resented, since why was the mother more honoured than the father? Jack also started helping out the neighbours with various unpaid errands: cutting down the overgrown ivy of the lady next door who had severe MS; helping another neighbour plant her allotment; taking a book to the elderly lady down the street who was lonely after her husband went into hospital.

After some discussion, John and I didn't raise serious objections to his conversion. Sure enough, a few days later, Jack became Muslim.

Although there were outward changes to Jack's behaviour, in many ways he was the same old Jack. One of his friends from school (let's call him *A*), who was temporarily homeless, stayed with us for a few months. *A* quickly became a welcome part of our household as he entertained us with long dramatic stories about his large and eccentric family. For *A*'s part, he found it amusing that Jack still cuddled up to me on the sofa at the age of sixteen — although after his comment on this, Jack, sadly, never did it again.

Later on, when Jack was in Syria telling the world how much he hated his parents, I thought of this sweet-natured boy who used to chatter to his mum about his day. During the time of *A*'s stay, Jack was still funny and voluble, and did hilarious impersonations of his teachers and workmates at his new part-time taxi-rank job. He had adopted a comic Indian immigrant accent — like that of a lovable and wacky Indian uncle — which he did so often I forgot it wasn't his real voice.

His new teachers at the local further education college, where he was having to repeat his end-of-year exams, didn't always find him so comical, unfortunately. I was called in to a meeting with the learning support staff who wanted to address the fact that he didn't seem to be able to focus on his work in any way. On the last day of term, he had refused — politely, he told me — to watch the film version of *The Great Gatsby* because he found it onerous to watch a bunch of spoiled, nouveau-riche wasters at play when there were serious problems in the world, and watching a film wasn't doing work, anyway. In this case I had sided with the school: he couldn't expect special treatment just because he felt ideologically opposed to the film, and he should just voice his opinion in the discussion afterward.

At one point in the learning support meeting, Jack perked up. The topic was how to accommodate his OCD difficulties. By this time, his consultant doctor's advice on his condition had changed, from suggesting he be heavily medicated (which he had adamantly refused, with me taking his side), to saying John and I should simply accept him for the way he was. The rituals and practices of his new faith, the doctor had advised, provided him with a structure and channel for the ritualistic obsessions of his medical condition. At this college meeting, Jack was told by the well-meaning support officer that if he was having difficulty writing during the exam because of his OCD, he could have a scribe.

"A scribe?" asked Jack. "What's that?"

"Someone who can write for you if you can't manage it yourself," came the reply.

"Ah, someone who can write down my thoughts," said Jack, tickled by the concept. He went into skit mode: "Toby, I feel a thought coming on," he spoofed, putting a hand to his temple and puckering his brow in a look of intense concentration. "Yes, I think it's a good one." Then, pointing dramatically to the desk, he added, "Toby, write this down!"

I laughed, despite myself. The learning support staff, however, were unmoved and didn't crack a smile. I wondered if they thought Jack's problems stemmed from his over-liberal parents who hadn't taken a firm enough hand with him. Later on, judging from the comments from the *Sun* and *Daily Mail* readers, a portion of the general public certainly believed this to be the case. I've wondered this myself many times during my constant internal discussions. Over and over again, I've raked over all the incidents of his childhood where I could have been better, or acted differently, or followed, or not followed various pieces of advice. Did we deprive him of an extended family by living several thousand miles away from our immediate families so that he sought another, larger family in a Muslim network? Did I not take his OCD seriously enough, believing it to be a stress response and not a serious mental condition? Did I indulge his comic and dramatic side so that he didn't understand that life is serious, real, and cruel? Was he given too much agency at an early age so that he grew up with the belief that he could, as an individual, change the world? Or, perhaps, had he been traumatized when, at the age of three, his father and I separated for a couple of years and he had spent formative years in a chaotic household that he, his younger brother, *E*, and I shared with a group of lodgers, including an aggressive heroin addict whose friends regularly robbed the place? All these guilty thoughts and doubts I have lived with daily. At one point in the whole self-recrimination process, I decided it didn't really matter what the reasons were; I had to deal with the here and now and think through the strategic remedies that were available to us.

Chapter 3

The misnomer of "Jihadi Jack"

Two days before Detective Inspector *T* and Detective Sergeant *M* came to our house to talk about kebab sellers and ISIS border guards, the story about "Jihadi Jack" exploded across the globe. The print version of the story first appeared in the *Sunday Times* on January 24, 2016, and then online versions spread like an aggressive form of cancer across the internet. Online stories based on the same background information, with extra scurrilous bits added for spice, appeared almost instantly on the *Daily Mail* and the *Sun* websites, and then rapidly moved to Europe, North America, Australia, and the Far East. By the time the story got to China, the facts had been so distorted that "Jihadi Jack" had become a girl.

Gossip from our neighbours, Jack's school friends, and "associates of the family" suddenly became front page news. Concerned sources unknown to us gave quotes to the papers about how the past two years had been "anguish" for us, and how we "just wanted Jack home." Anyone who had had even a passing connection to Jack was sought out and quoted, including the football coach he'd

---

had at the age of ten, who said he "was just one of the boys." What else, really, did people expect? Was a ten-year-old who spent all his time practising kick-ups and dreaming of playing for England really going to display jihadi tendencies that would cause him to become the talk of the globe ten years later?

It was the *Mail Online* version of the story that made us question our own knowledge of Jack and his activities. Jack was now known as "Abu Mohammed," stated the article, and had a son called Mohammed. Soon after reaching Syria, Jack (alias Abu Mohammed) had reportedly met "fellow British ISIS fighter, Omar Hussain, also known as the supermarket jihadi." John and I didn't have a clue who Omar Hussain might be and found out much later by searching online that he was a former security guard at the Morrisons supermarket in High Wycombe, reputed to have travelled to Syria with the same aid convoy as Alan Henning, who had been beheaded by ISIS. Omar had joined ISIS, it was claimed, and had become "notorious after threatening attacks on the U.K. in a number of videos." Further articles in the *Daily Mail* stated that Jack had "posted several photos of himself posing with weapons, thought to have been taken near the Tabqa dam in Syria."

Coincidentally, we were able to question Jack on the truth of these "revelations" when he phoned home the day the story broke. He was aware of all the stories that were being flung around the world about him and seemed rather bemused by it all. I asked him if we were now grandparents and he had somehow omitted to tell us, and he laughed and said, no, he didn't have a son — the media just made stuff up. He said his name wasn't Abu Mohammed, he had never owned a weapon in his life, and he had never met Omar Hussain. In typical Jack style he added, "He looks very handsome in the photos, though."

We knew from our reading of the vicious online comments from the trolls on the *Daily Mail* website that such levity from suspected jihadis would not go down well. The trolls had already made up their minds that Jack was a bloodthirsty jihadi who was hell-bent on slitting their throats, and vehemently expressed their desire for him to be obliterated, droned, killed without mercy, tortured, you name it. This without knowing any of the facts and being manipulated by the media with unsubstantiated claims. We, his parents, were portrayed in the comments either as gullible fools who couldn't bring themselves to believe their little boy was a rapist and a murderer, or complicit, by virtue of our liberal, wishy-washy attitudes, in allowing him to rape, murder, and blow people up. The fact that even the articles that called him "Jihadi Jack" provided no evidence he was involved in violence or in threatening violence didn't deter these commentators. It seemed that the trolls didn't see the irony in the fact that they themselves were indulging in hate speech by calling for unspeakable violence to be visited on someone they didn't know and had no evidence about. The mob had been stirred up and the mob was determined to get its vengeance in advance, no matter what the truth might be.

As the phone rang off the hook with calls from journalists, and as men with large cameras patrolled our street seeking out talkative neighbours who enjoyed the limelight, we tried to assess the damage. Luckily, Jack's reaction had been one of incredulity at the over-reaction and misrepresentation by the media rather than fear of the consequences. We had been worried that now he was in the spotlight he might be seen by ISIS as a valuable commodity and might be forced to carry out acts for their propaganda purposes. When I asked him if the media attention had presented him with any difficulties, he said that he "didn't think he was famous [there] yet." With regard to the impact on our own safety, given the viciousness of the trolls' comments, we were afraid we might be attacked by right-wing extremists, particularly since the homepage of the English Defence League — a far-right anti-immigrant group — featured a direct link to the *Daily Mail* article. This article had included a picture of our terraced house, complete with caption giving the full address.

Although the address was removed the following day, the caption then instead helpfully identified our house with the words *green door* in brackets. Presumably, this information was given out to make sure that whoever might be thinking of fire-bombing us would get the correct house. The police safety officer advised us to block up our letter box and get an external one as a precaution. We also managed, after some wrangling with the *Daily Mail*, mediated by the Press Complaints Committee, to get the photo and its "green door" caption removed. We decided that the articles' lies, as well as the hate speech in the comments section, could be tackled at a later stage if we wanted to consider taking court action for libel.

Most of the journalists' calls we ignored, choosing only to talk to the *Oxford Times* and later on the *Guardian*, both of which countered some of the mistruths that had been reported. Despite our agreement not to sound off to other journalists for fear of further misreporting, John slipped up on the day the story broke by telling one journalist that the story was a product of a "right-wing conspiracy." His comment referred to the unhealthy relationship between the defence services, government sources, and the global newspaper empire owned by Murdoch. I myself lost my temper the following day and ended up ranting at an *Evening Standard* journalist who phoned early in the morning. I informed him that Jack had talked about working with Syrian refugees before he left, and that he was currently doing work in a social capacity. When the journalist asked if we had opposed Jack's conversion, I replied that Jack was "entitled to choose his own religion."

It may have been this last comment that prompted one Oxford imam to declare that the "thoughts and prayers [of this Muslim community] were with the Letts family in Oxford, at what must be a very difficult and distressing time for them." It would appear, however, that the real message the Oxford Muslim community wanted to convey to the public was contained in the second part of this statement: mosques in Oxford, continued the imam, had "measures in place to promptly report any form of extremist and suspicious behaviour" and that these measures would "continue to be developed and implemented in liaison with, and following advice and guidance from, local law enforcement authorities."

Clearly, Jack was toxic to the Oxford Muslim community, who were, and still are, keen to distance themselves from him as far away as possible. As non-Muslims we had tried rather unsuccessfully to engage with representatives at the mosque Jack used to go to. The imam I spoke to soon after we discovered Jack had gone to Syria had been kind when I'd burst into tears in front of him, and had listened to me for some time as we sat on the floor together in one of the bare, carpeted side rooms. However, I had taken exception to his response after I'd explained that Jack had some mental health problems.

"Ah, yes," he had said. "It is always the retarded ones they target." I had indignantly explained through my sobs that Jack was actually very clever; he had taught himself Arabic and was now fluent, and he was always striving to be a devout Muslim. I was also taken aback by the imam's illustration of his point that Muslims were obliged to treat non-Muslim parents such as John and me with tolerance, i.e., one of the companions of the Prophet himself had parents who were *kuffar*, nonbelievers. *What if this hadn't been the case?* I thought. *Where was the natural law that said that all of God/Allah's souls were entitled to equal respect?* Clearly, however, the imam and I were entering into semantic territory, and there were, of course, numerous instances in history, such as the Crusades, or the more recent example of the violence against the Rohinga Muslims in Burma, where Christians and Buddhists had demonized and persecuted people not of their own faith.

At the end of the conversation, the imam stressed that the mosque had a very good relationship with the police, and that they were duty bound to report any incidences of suspect behaviour, and did he have my permission to tell them about what we'd discussed? At the time, I didn't grant him permission, saying I would tell the police myself.

John's experience with another imam at the same mosque was less cordial. We had received reports from one of Jack's Muslim friends in Oxford that a teacher at the mosque was an ISIS sympathizer and that he may have influenced Jack. John was determined to confront this teacher and extract from him everything he knew about where Jack might be and how he had got there. All he knew about the teacher was that he was Somali, and that when Jack's friend had been distributing anti-ISIS leaflets outside a mosque in London, the teacher had torn up a leaflet in front of him, accusing him of being in the pay of the Saudi government and declaring that when the "retribution began" he would be "the first he would come for." The friend had duly reported him to the police and to the mosque (and also later decided to become the chief prosecution witness in John's and my trial, but that is another story). It made us sick to think that this teacher could have had a brainwashing effect on Jack and had caused him to end up in a war zone.

When John first approached the imam just before evening prayers to ask if he knew the Somali teacher, the imam said that no Somalis worshipped at that particular mosque. As groups of people started to gather on the pavement outside, one taxi drew up and several Somali-looking men piled out. "I'm looking for someone called B," persisted John. "No one of that name here," said the imam, looking the other way. One onlooker, however, who had heard the exchange, surreptitiously approached John. "I know B," he said, quietly. "I'll tell him you want to talk to him." After the prayers, as people started to filter out, his contact came up to him.

"*B* doesn't want to speak to you," he said. "Well, I'm going to wait here until he gets out," John replied. After a few minutes, a small, Somali-looking man came up to him. Yes, he knew Jack, he told him, and yes, Jack had come to some of his classes; Jack hadn't participated much but had just sat in the corner and listened. He didn't know where Jack was and he had never discussed anything to do with jihad with him.

John came back home frustrated, and not much further ahead than when he left. We found out later that *B* had been raided a few times by the police, but nothing had come of it. *B* was, however, sacked from any teaching responsibilities at the mosque on the strength of the testimony of Jack's friend about the threats he had made outside the London mosque.

Both these incidents demonstrated how the general climate of fear and suspicion surrounding Muslims and their activities was causing Muslim leaders to become inward-looking, but also fearful and uncertain about the need to report any "suspicious" activity to the police, whether that activity was indicative of an offence or not. The general message seemed to be that anything that could possibly be viewed as suspicious should be reported, and then the police would decide whether these suspicions should be acted upon. The problem lay in the fact that it was extremely difficult to know what constituted suspicious "extremist" behaviour and what didn't, since there didn't seem to be a definition of what extremist meant. If it meant being extremely religious — for instance, being overly concerned with beard length or how many inches off the ground one's robe was supposed to be — then several people per day could be reported for extremist behaviour. In the public mind, extremism seemed to have become synonymous with terrorism, even though the dictionary definition of terrorism included the element of violence or intimidation, and the dictionary definition of extremism made no mention of violence.

The difficulty of interpretation was compounded by the fact that it was no longer just a civilian's sense of duty to report suspicious activity; it was *now a crime not to*. The relevant section in law, for anyone who wanted to look it up, was to be found in section 38(B) of the Terrorism Act 2000, which made it "an offence not to disclose information which may assist the apprehension, prosecution or conviction of somebody involved in terrorism." The Counter-Terrorism and Security Bill 2015 further stated that "a specified authority must, in the exercise of its functions, have due regard to the need to prevent people from being drawn into terrorism." Relevant authorities included not just local council officials and probation officers, but also universities, schools, and even nursery schools. These authorities have to have proper procedures in place, through which they are obliged to work with the police officers of Prevent, the government's anti-radicalization program, who investigate any claims of suspected extremist behaviour among staff, students, pupils, or nursery children. Not since the days of Nazism or McCarthyism has the police devolution of responsibility to the general populace been so widespread, so sinister, and so fear-mongering.

When John and I questioned the Prevent officers who visited us a year after Jack had left about what the government definition of extremism was, they said that it was "active opposition to fundamental British values." It was difficult to see how a child in nursery school could exhibit extremism as defined thus (when the punishment for violating the British value of the rule of law usually meant having to sit on the naughty chair), but this was obviously something the proprietor of that child's nursery school would need to think about if they didn't want to fall foul of anti-terrorism legislation.

In the case of Jack, John and I have asked ourselves whether he could have been prevented from going to Syria if the Prevent program had investigated him earlier. After much soul-searching, we still think that no one could have known that Jack's hypothetical discussions about helping out in Syria were anything but that: hypothetical discussions. He was a seventeen-year-old kid who loved to talk and debate important issues. We believed we had persuaded him he would be of no use to the Syrians and their ravaged country until he had studied more and got himself a profession: in medicine, say, or humanitarian affairs. The Prevent officers would no doubt have uncovered the same information. In hindsight, of course, we have cursed ourselves that we didn't hide his passport, but we also know that he could easily have applied for another, and that someone else would have provided the money for him to go.

The issue of disclosing information about Jack to the police became a minefield for our friends, associates, employers, official contacts such as doctors, and neighbours. People were vaguely aware that knowing anything could implicate them and could make them liable to prosecution. People I considered close friends begged me not to tell them anything about Jack, even when I told them that the police knew where Jack was and that we were in constant contact with them about what he was up to. The environmental charity I had been working for as a fundraiser when we'd first discovered Jack had gone to Syria was atypical in that it was very supportive. I reassured the director that he was not at risk of prosecution if he didn't report my conversations with him to the police, as the police had already been informed about Jack's whereabouts. I did, however, have to explain that I was in no fit state to continue my fundraising job, since funding strategies and targets to save the freshwater ecosystem had ceased to have any meaning for me when all I could think about was Jack and how to keep him alive.

Other official contacts took a different, more nervous tack. My doctor, for instance, was aware that even doctor-patient confidentiality was "trumped" by anti-terrorism legislation, and was wary about anything in my medical notes that showed she was aware of my situation. Conscious that we didn't want to put our friends and neighbours in a difficult situation, John and I deliberately isolated ourselves from a larger social circle and spoke only to our closest friends. I stopped using social media for any public purposes, and only kept my Facebook account in order to communicate privately with Jack. Muslim contacts have since said to us, "Now you know what Muslims go through all the time," and it is true that I now have an understanding of the fear and suspicion that drive the relationship between those who are considered to be the "other" and those who feel threatened by the "other." The resultant malaise is insidious, manifesting itself first in a withdrawal from open society (our self-isolation from our larger social group), and leading to a more widespread societal discrimination in which it is no longer possible to rely on established official relationships (with, for instance, doctors or welfare officers). It is easy to see how this isolation of groups leads to further radicalization of individuals, since the targeted individuals no longer have access to mainstream society, develop a feeling of victimhood, and start to band together to try to fight back. In other words, the government's Prevent program risked creating the very radicals it was designed to protect society against.

Chapter 4

Jack in Syria

Jack's phone call from Syria, September 2, 2014

In the early evening of September 2, 2014, I was alone in the house when the phone rang. As I answered it, I could only just hear Jack's voice above the very loud crackles on the line, as if he were standing in the midst of a violent gale. "Mum," he said. "I'm in Syria." I began screaming at him, "You promised you wouldn't go. You'll get killed. You'll get beheaded. What the hell do you think you're doing? You stupid, stupid boy." Jack never replied to any of my questions as the line then went dead. He didn't contact us again for another three weeks — the worst three weeks of my life.

After this short and horrifying conversation, I couldn't contact John, as he didn't answer his phone, so I contacted Jack's friend, *C* (the later prosecution witness), who was at work but said he would leave straightaway and come over. When *C* arrived, he came in and tried to calm me down, making me go over every single detail of the conversation and asking me if I knew where Jack was, what else

I could hear in the background, what was his tone of voice, etc., but I had no helpful answers to any of his questions. When John came home a couple of hours later, we all sat down with our map of Syria spread out in front of us and tried to overcome our shock and fear in order to work out what we could do now that our world had been blown apart.

When I remember this now, I am both angry and astounded that one of the main thrusts of the subsequent police investigation against us has been the idea that we knew about, and even encouraged, Jack's departure for Syria. Here was the most devastating thing that had ever happened to us, and the police seemed bound and determined to prove that we had known about it all along. Why any parent would want their child to go to a war zone is absolutely beyond me, whatever their faith, creed, belief, or political outlook. To this day, I cannot work out what police achieve by criminalizing the victim. We were horrified, heartbroken, bewildered, and terrified that at any moment our son could be killed, yet the police seemed desperate to seize upon any shred of evidence to show we had somehow connived in Jack's plan: evidence such as my desperate emails to my friends, or the research books on Islam that John had downloaded onto his computer. The fact that, on the day before Jack was due to fly to Jordan, we had dismissed the claims of Jack's friend C that Jack might be planning to go on to Syria, was one of the central planks of the police's case against us. According to the police, we had been warned by C about Jack's plans, yet failed to act, whereas we believed we knew our son better than C did, and if Jack had promised he wasn't going to Syria at that particular time, then he wasn't.

When Jack finally contacted us again by phone three weeks later, he apologized for his twenty-second phone call, saying he hadn't expected it to cut off so quickly and since then he had been travelling so it had been difficult for him to contact us. He was fine and was living with a group of people and was helping out with translation. We shouldn't worry about him as he was in a safe place. He was thinking about doing "sheik (religious) training." He was no longer in Syria, but was now in Iraq. He had been ill for a while (the thought of which sent us into panic), but one of his friends had helped to look after him, and he had now recovered. He was happy and had lots to eat, so we should "resume our lives."

Every couple of weeks or so, he would update us with similar bulletins while we were desperately trying to contact everyone we could think of who could help get him out, or help us work out what he was doing if he wasn't a fighter, which he told us he wasn't. We assumed he was on the civilian side of things because of his language skills, and Jack's British Muslim friends reassured us that, because of these skills and because he was a white convert, he would have a certain value to the group he was with and therefore was not likely to be used, for instance, as a suicide bomber. By the time Jack had contacted us after the first three weeks, I had done my reading and had asked him on the phone what group he was with — was it ISIS, or al Nusra, or the Free Syrian Army? He had replied "no" to all of these, saying there were "loads of groups" and the situation wasn't how people in England imagined it to be. When I asked him how he was supporting himself, he again said how the situation was very unlike England in that people looked after each other by sharing everything, and it was possible to get by on very little as things were cheap. He mentioned that he used to go with a group of his friends to the market (it wasn't safe to go on his own, apparently), and that people were friendly to them and were pleased to be no longer living under the oppressive, Iran-backed, al-Maliki government, which came to power in 2006 and had vastly favoured the minority Shiites over the majority Sunnis.

It was important to us to ascertain what group he was with so we could know what we were facing. As Jack wasn't always very expansive in his answers, we tried to piece together information from the bits and pieces he did say. Often, we would ask him about things we read about in the news and were struck by how much he didn't seem to know. When John tackled him in a phone conversation on the question of the Yazidis, for instance, hundreds of whom were massacred by ISIS in August 2014, with thousands of women and girls being captured as sex slaves, Jack said he hadn't heard anything about it and couldn't answer for the actions of the perpetrators. He added that it was absolutely forbidden in Islam for a girl or woman to be forced to have sex against her will, and how could we think he would be in agreement with such things? He was, he said, "the same person he was when he left." I remembered that previously, when I had taken Jack to task about the position of women in Islam (when he had been involved in an Oxford conference that had separated the female and male delegates), he had maintained that men and women were "separate but equal." He told us that Khadija, the prophet's first wife, had been a wealthy businesswoman in her own right, having inherited her father's trading business, and that all the Muslim women he knew would be insulted by the idea that I thought them oppressed. He wanted me to meet his female friends so I could debate such issues with them. With regard to the current plight of the Yazidis in Iraq, we thought that perhaps even though Jack was living in the country where this was taking place, we were better informed about global news than he was, as his access to the internet was limited by poor electricity supply, and much of the news he received was via word of mouth.

Around this time — September and October 2014 — little was known about ISIS and how they had miraculously and swiftly come to take over "vast swathes" of Iraq and Syria. Rumours abounded; for instance, the group had been funded by the United States, to provide the latter with an excuse to invade the Middle East again (the weapons and the white sneakers of the ISIS fighters in the photographs looked suspiciously squeaky clean). Another rumour was that hundreds of political prisoners had suddenly and secretly been released from prisons in Qatar and Kuwait on the orders of the highest levels of their governments, and all these prisoners had converged on Iraq in order to bring down the corrupt al-Maliki government (which fell in 2014 after eight years in power). When ISIS took over Fallujah and Ramadi in January 2014, they were seen as just one Sunni group amongst many taking on the Shiite-led government. However, with the fall in June 2014 of Mosul — Iraq's second-largest city, with an estimated 2014 population of two and a half million — the world suddenly sat up and took notice. It seemed inexplicable that thirty thousand Iraqi soldiers could be defeated by only fifteen hundred ISIS soldiers in six days of fighting, with many Iraqi soldiers simply fleeing the city.

The fall of Mosul proved to be a massive boost to ISIS's power, as not only were they now in control of a major city, they had also captured a huge cache of U.S.-made missiles, machine guns, tanks, and ammunition, as well as 2,300 Humvees (the latter fact admitted by Iraqi Prime Minister Haider al-Abadi in an interview with Iraqiya state TV in May 2015). The U.S. moved quickly to replenish the weapons and equipment stocks, but ISIS were now well on their way to taking over further areas of Syria and Iraq. It was on June 29, 2014 — during the same month as Mosul's fall — that Abu Bakr al-Baghdadi, ISIS's leader, declared a caliphate, the so-called Islamic State in Iraq and Syria.

Raqqa — the capital of the Islamic State in Syria — had initially fallen to the rebel forces Ahrar al-Sham Brigade and al-Nusra in March 2013 during the fighting between Syrian government forces and the opposition. It was the first city to be liberated from Assad's regime and was declared by local activists to be an "icon of the revolution." The organization known, in English, as "Raqqa Is Being Slaughtered Silently," which is heavily relied upon by the

Western press as a source of information about conditions within the city (often smuggled out at great personal risk to its members), is perhaps one legacy of this opposition in Raqqa. However, after many months of political infighting between the various factions in the city, ISIS was able to take advantage of the lack of unity and managed to wrest Raqqa from al-Nusra control in January 2014. As a result, al-Nusra, which is affiliated with al-Qaeda, became cast in the role of the more "moderate" faction, known in the region for its soft approach in delivering handouts and working through the local imams, compared to ISIS, which became known for its torture and arbitrary detentions.

With so much focus currently on the atrocities of ISIS and the spread of its power, it is sometimes difficult to remember that the initial impetus for the war in Syria was the 2011 Arab Spring uprising against the repressive rule of Assad, and that many of the first foreign fighters who went out to Syria were motivated to join the movement for freedom for the Syrian people. Many of these became disillusioned very quickly with the infighting between groups, saying they had not gone to Syria with the intention of "killing other Muslims."

John and I struggled to work out what Jack's role was in all this. Even in the early days of his time in Iraq and Syria, around September–October 2014, he denied being a fighter, and the only things he did tell us about how he spent his time were, as we told the police later, that he had worked in a school and a hospital.

In October 2014, he casually mentioned to us in a phone conversation that he had got married to an Iraqi girl who was the same age as him, and that since she had grown up during the Iraq War, she "wasn't naive." He had become friends with her father first, and it was her father who had suggested the marriage. They had recently got a place together. We hoped that since he seemed to be integrating into the local population, he wasn't with a group of foreign fighters and wasn't going to be sent to the front. We knew, however, that whatever he was doing, in Britain he would be assumed to be a terrorist by virtue of where he was, and the onus was on us and on him to prove otherwise.

Although it was, and still is, British government policy to work toward the removal of Assad as president of Syria, the situation is complicated by the fact that Assad's government is still considered the legitimate government of Syria, which means that any foreign individual who actively opposes his regime is automatically considered a terrorist. The so-called Syrian moderate rebels — i.e., those on our side who are anti-Assad — are, however, *not* considered terrorists, because they are locally based and, well, on our side. The difference between "moderates" and "terrorists," I assume, is that the latter have an Islamic agenda, wanting to impose their version of sharia on their territory, and are sustained by anti-Western rhetoric. However, I would guess that many of the so-called moderates are also governed by conservative Islam and are anti-Western, so this distinction seems to quickly fall away. David Cameron, in his address to Parliament in November 2015 arguing for the use of air strikes in Syria in the wake of the Paris attacks, maintained that there were seventy thousand "moderate rebels" in Syria who would support the RAF by following up air strikes with "boots on the ground." He was not able, however, to say who these moderate rebels were, and admitted that he was "not arguing that all of these seventy thousand are ideal partners" but they were "people we can work with."

For John and me, and for Jack, these distinctions were not mere academic quibbles. Jack has been termed a potential terrorist because of some mouthy Facebook quotes condemning the British government's actions in Syria, as well as some unintelligible postings from the Qu'ran (unintelligible to me because of their bad Google translation from the original Arabic). He was called "Jihadi Jack" by a *Sunday Times* journalist who pandered to the British public's liking for alliteration, and who published the false information that Jack had "admitted to his parents that he was with ISIS in Syria in September 2014" (something the journalist himself knows is untrue, since he taped the entire interview we had with him). Jack never identified himself as belonging to any group, saying only that "there are loads of groups." The defence correspondent of the *Guardian*, Ewen MacKaskill, backed up Jack's assertion in his November 2015 article analyzing David Cameron's estimate of seventy thousand "moderate" opposition fighters in Syria, stating: "There are at least 100–120 different groups, with various aims, and differing in size from thousands to just 100–200 members. They are splintered, with some limited to a narrow geographical area. And some are far from moderate, sharing the ideology of al-Qaeda." Certainly, since Syria's population is 89 percent Muslim (with 68 percent being Sunni Muslim), it is likely that many of these groups in question are Islamic in character. The political aims of the vast majority of them are anti-ISIS as well as anti-Assad.

The only reference Jack has ever made so far to working with any group was in his interview with the *Independent* on January 30, 2016, when he stated, "I've spent efforts to take down the Syrian government. That's all I want to say." Since, therefore, it had still not been possible to ascertain the identity of the group Jack was with, and since for all we and the government knew, he could be with one of the so-called moderate rebels opposing Assad, it seemed premature, to say the least, to call him a terrorist. And, by extension, even more premature to put John and me on trial for being fundraisers for terrorism.

When I screamed at Jack in our phone call of September 2, 2014, that he was a "stupid, stupid boy and would get himself killed or beheaded," I was referring to the news that had already hit the Western press about the killing of American and English journalists and aid workers. In August 2014, James Foley, a war correspondent, was the first American citizen beheaded by ISIS. This was followed by Steven Sotloff, also an American journalist, who was killed in September 2014. David Haines and Alan Henning, both British aid workers, were killed in September 2014 and October 2014 respectively, both beheaded by Mohammed Emwazi, called in the English press "Jihadi John." The horror and brutality of the cold-blooded killings shocked the world, and the West's reaction to those killings has formed the basis of its foreign policy in the region ever since. "Degrading and destroying ISIL," in the words of President Obama, using the alternate English name for ISIS, is what has managed to unite America and Russia, despite these countries' differences in achieving this goal.

It is easy to see how the world's fear and revulsion at these despicable events have clouded rational public debate about the complexities of the situation on the ground, and why the original objective of countering Assad's atrocities against his own people seems to have been forgotten. It is also easy to see why the UN-led peace talks with representatives of any other groups in Syria seem to be doomed to failure. It explains the scared look on the bank teller's face when she sees that my account is being closed "for security reasons," and also explains the words of the National Health Service manager, who said there was no further employment for me because "other staff might believe I present a danger to them." Or my Oxfam "friend" who told a mutual friend she didn't want to meet up for coffee with me as she "didn't want MI5 scrutiny in her life." There is no point explaining that I am just as afraid of bomb attacks on the tube as they are. I am, in fact, more afraid about bomb attacks in general, since my son could be killed or maimed in one any second. I have no idea what the karmic reason is that I find myself in this unreal situation after having lived a fairly uneventful and law-abiding life for fifty-four years. I just want to wake up and find out it's not really happening.

Chapter 5

East Timor and West Papua: *"La luta continua"*

Jack's brother, *E*, is two years younger than he is. When they were small, their home was often filled with people from East Timor and West Papua. The reason for this was twofold: first, I had moved out of the family home in 1998 and rented a house in Oxford for me and the boys while John and I were separated for a couple of years. John had then needed lodgers to help pay the bills at the family home. The second reason was that John had become involved with two political support groups based in Oxford: one that campaigned for the independence for East Timor from Indonesia, and the other for the independence of West Papua. Tensions had been bad between me and John since the birth of the boys: I'd had severe postpartum depression after each of them and had mentally gone off the rails, John was spending long periods abroad at the time working on archaeological digs, our families couldn't help out as they were in Canada or America, Jack was a high-intensity and demanding child (with *E* being mercifully laid back in comparison), and I was struggling as a new mother trying to keep myself sane and the children alive. I thought that by living in a communal house with other single mothers I would have both company and help (I had advertised through the local "Daily Information" bulletin to find sharers). It didn't actually work out that way, as most of the people who moved in were young and irresponsible, and either didn't pay the rent or ran up large telephone bills to overseas and then skipped town. The heroin addict whose friends regularly robbed the place didn't help, either.

Between the two houses, therefore, the boys probably had an unusual and somewhat chaotic upbringing. The East Timor lodgers were young political activists whose families had been killed fighting against the Indonesian occupation of their country. (Indonesia had invaded in 1975 and then stayed for the next twenty-five years. During this period, over a hundred thousand East Timorese were killed, either in the resistance, or from disease or starvation.) Two prominent East Timor campaigners had come to Britain to study law, politics, and journalism at university, to improve their own professional knowledge and to raise awareness of their country's plight. The father of one of them had been a guerrilla fighter in the mountains, and their family had had to survive in the jungle while the resistance fighters made excursions against the Indonesia troops. On one occasion, he explained to me, he, his mother, and his sisters had to drink water from a stream that was streaked with blood from a massacre that had occurred upriver. They had had no choice: it was either that or die from thirst.

The West Papuans had similar stories. West Papuan villages were regularly bombed by Indonesia jets, resisters were shot, and women were raped by Indonesian troops. Benny Wenda, a prominent activist, had managed to escape, and had obtained refugee status in the U.K. He had his wife, Maria, set up home in Oxford, where they started to raise children while running the Free West Papua campaign. John became involved in the campaign, hosting meetings at the house, organizing campaigning events and meetings with U.K. and European politicians. John had even managed to get into the London offices of the lad mag *Zoo* to complain about a competition the publication was offering, where the prize was a "cannibal sex holiday" in Papua. Objecting to the ignorance and casual racism of the piece, the Free West Papua campaign had publicly protested, and John had talked his way past security to get into *Zoo*'s offices, where he refused to leave until he had spoken to the managing editor. After the editor nervously agreed to speak to their group, Benny was finally granted an apology and promised a follow-up piece that would "set the record straight" (although this never actually happened).

The effect on Jack and *E* of this politically active household was probably more profound than I realized at the time. Both the East Timorese and the Papuans made a big fuss over both boys, the Papuans making them beautiful headdresses of pheasant feathers and playing jungle skirmishes in the back garden; the East Timorese giving them each a guerrilla fighting name, incorporating them into their group and into their struggle ("*La luta continua*"). Both cultures were greatly centred round children, partly because they were seen as the hope for the future, and partly because children were expected to be integral members of the community who had a responsibility toward their family and their tribe. In Timor, for instance, children were vital participants in the resistance, carrying messages between groups and running errands for the fighters.

When Jack and *E* were exposed to the world of these activists at a young age — beginning at two and four years old — I valued the fact that they had access to a rich, cultural experience that opened their eyes to worlds beyond Oxford. Jungle skirmishes in the garden were surely just another form of cowboys and Indians; and having tribal names bestowed upon them was another form of make-believe, like pretending to be Buzz Lightyear, or a Pokémon, or a dragon. I can't help wondering now, though, whether the early exposure to the Papuans and Timorese fighting for a just cause — i.e., the liberation of your country against an invader — somehow became lodged in Jack's consciousness when he was too young to tell the difference between make-believe and reality. And that this aspiration somehow later became translated into his desire to fight for justice for Muslims, whom he had been told by his new friends were the "most oppressed people on earth," and who, in his mind, had the whole might of the U.S. army and its partners against them.

I will never know what the influence of his early upbringing was, and I rationalize to myself that the same influence could have pushed him to work for the UN, or to become a doctor or lawyer. All we could do was appeal to his brain and his heart so that he got a chance to put other life goals into action, and to achieve good in the world, despite what the rest of the world appeared to think of him. In 1999, East Timor did indeed gain independence from Indonesia, and the activists who stayed in our house are now important figures in the new government. West Papua is still struggling for independence, but Benny Wenda is still in Oxford, leading the European wing of the campaign.

Chapter 6

In search of British Islam

In those first three horrible weeks of September 2014 after Jack's phone call informing us he was in Syria, John and I contacted as many people as we could think of who might be able to help. This period is all a bit of a haze now, as we weren't sleeping very well, and during the night the phone was always beside the bed in case Jack contacted us or we got a phone call telling us the worst news imaginable.

We started with Jack's friends and contacts in England (the ones we didn't know personally we traced through his Facebook account), and also the friends he'd been staying with in Jordan and Kuwait. Among the other people and organizations we contacted were the imams of both the Oxford mosques Jack used to go to; the anti-radicalization charity, Inspire; the British Muslim website, 5pillarsuk.com; a youth worker who advised the government's anti-radicalization Prevent program; and the film-maker Robb Leech, who had made a documentary, *My Brother the Islamist*, about the conversion to Islam in 2009 of his stepbrother, Richard Dart. Anjem Choudary, the British Muslim political activist, who was the spokesperson for Islam4UK before it was banned as an

organization in 2010, played a large part in Richard Dart's conversion. As I watched Robb's film, I felt my heart breaking at the
contrast between the old photograph of him and his brother as
lively young boys, and the later camera footage of Richard with his
blank-eyed look.

When I spoke to Robb, it had been difficult to hear him as he
was in an internet café and the reception on his mobile seemed particularly bad, for some reason. However, I managed to piece together bits of what he said. I told him I had seen his documentary the
evening before, and I had surprised myself at the pure hatred I felt
for the smiling, smug, odious Choudary during his interview with
Robb. Never in my life before had I felt like punching someone in
the face, and I'm sure I wouldn't be much good at it, but Choudary's
face definitely seemed to invite it. This man, and people like him,
were responsible for turning young brains such as Richard Dart's
and Jack's and were the reason Richard was now in prison and Jack
was now in mortal danger. I told Robb he was to be commended
for allowing Choudary to speak for himself, with little interfering
comment; I'm not sure I would have been able to keep my temper
in the same situation. Robb said that a hands-off approach was
his method of documentary-making, so that people could judge
for themselves the real personality behind the interviewee's public
persona. One of Choudary's comments, for instance, that I found
particularly telling was his response to the contention that he might
be brainwashing young minds: "Some brains need washing," was
what he had said, with a self-satisfied smirk.

It was a mystery to Jack's Muslim friends in Oxford how
Choudary had managed to get away with his hate speech for so
long. He had appeared to praise those responsible for the September
11 and July 2005 attacks, and had made threatening statements
about "capital punishment" to Pope Benedict XVI after the latter appeared to insult the Prophet. Robb's explanation was that

Choudary had trained as a solicitor and was always very careful about treading the line between free speech and hate speech. My Muslim friends' explanation was that he was useful to the British government in that he helpfully personified the Muslim threat — i.e., he was hateful, dangerous, extremist — thereby providing a visible justification for the government's all-out response to the Islamist terror threat. Our modern version of "Reds under the Beds," as it were. I certainly found it ironic that the Crown Prosecution Service had not been able to find enough evidence to charge Choudary after ten years of his activities, whereas they managed to find enough evidence to charge John and me after mere months, when we had simply been trying to get our son away from terrorism. In July 2016, however, Choudary finally went too far, and was arrested under the Terrorism Act 2000 for allegedly urging his thirty-two thousand followers on Facebook to join ISIS. He was sentenced in September 2016 to five year's imprisonment.

As Robb and I chatted, it became evident that there were not a lot of similarities between his stepbrother and Jack. Although both of them had OCD (which seemed to feed into the washing and praying rituals), Jack had never expressed a desire for sharia in Britain and had not revealed any political aims other than justice for Syrians. He also didn't seem lost, angry, or alienated, as Richard seemed to be. He had never criticized me for not covering up my bare arms or legs or for drinking alcohol. For him, his religion was all about having personal relationship with Allah and having appreciation for the creation of the universe. In the months before he left, he used to marvel at the amazing display of the natural world in our neighbours' front gardens as we walked along the street. "How can you not believe this was made by a Creator?" he would say. "All this beauty and wonder, it can't have come from nothing." It didn't matter if I talked about one-cellular slime and billions of years of evolution; he was too caught up in his own rapture to take any notice.

✳   ✳   ✳

Z was one of the advisers we went to in search of help. He was the boss of a friend of ours and he ran a community college in Oxford that helped improve the employment prospects of ethnic minorities in the area. He also acted as a youth adviser for the government's Prevent program, although he assured us that everything we said to him would remain confidential. (This, we found out later, was a false promise, since soon after our visit he supplied a witness statement to the police.) One Saturday morning in November 2014, he generously, we thought, gave up his free time to listen to our tale of anguish. As part of our discussion, and as a Muslim, he was able to give us examples from the Qu'ran that discussed the concept of jihad. The word *jihad*, he explained, had been hijacked by the media and other groups so that it had come to refer only to "violent jihad," or "holy war." In fact, the word *jihad* merely meant "struggle," and could apply equally to spiritual struggle as to violent struggle, e.g., striving to become a better person through prayer, or good works, or fasting during Ramadan. Violent jihad was actually very rare in Muslim history and there were strict rules governing it: for instance, the war had to be defensive, and it had to be declared by a proper authority and supported by scholars.

In the months before he'd left, when he had determined to be the best Muslim he could be, Jack had read a lot about jihad and what it meant. I believe, for instance, that his sudden concern for the welfare of the elderly neighbours on our street was probably part of his efforts to comply with the Muslim imperative of jihad. However, we were now concerned that he might have decided to go further and had alighted on the idea that it was also his duty as a Muslim to oppose Assad, an unjust ruler who had declared war on his own people.

After our conversation with *Z*, I did some of my own reading on the concept of jihad and looked up what the Islamic Supreme

Council of America had to say on the matter. At this stage, we conducted all our internet searches somewhat gingerly, knowing that this activity was closely monitored by the police for signs of extremism. Searching *jihad* was bound to ring alarm bells; however, our need to know was stronger than our desire not to arouse suspicion.

I discovered on the Islamic Supreme Council of America's website an example of the Prophet's view on the distinction between violent and spiritual jihad. After returning from a military campaign, Muhammad is quoted as saying, "This day we have returned from the minor jihad to the major jihad." According to the Council, "minor jihad" in this quote refers to the armed battle, and "major jihad" refers to the peaceful battle for self-control and betterment. Earlier, when Jack had first shown an interest in the definitions of jihad, John had done his own reading and had printed off "Constants on the Path to Jihad" in order to research the subject fully. This publication was of great interest to the police when they subsequently discovered it during their search of our house, although, in the end, it was to form part of the mass of "unused" evidence against us.

Z also gave us advice on how best to communicate with Jack as we were desperate not to lose contact with him yet found his messages to us so strange and religion-filled, and with such a worryingly dismissive attitude toward the *kuffar* (disbelievers), that we weren't sure how to respond. Jack's contempt for the *kuffar* seemed to have spread from being directed at the government of Assad, to including anyone who didn't believe the "truth" as he did. John and I also seemed to be on the receiving end for this contempt, as we were increasingly identifying ourselves as atheist in the midst of all the religious intolerance, and Jack appeared to think that atheists were the worst of all groups since they had the arrogance to believe they were above Allah.

I had tried to tackle Jack's increasing intolerance during my Facebook conversations with him. I'd told him that I knew he wanted us to convert to Islam so that we could be in Paradise together. However, I believed that on any Judgment Day people would be judged on their actions, not their beliefs, and I didn't believe I would be condemned to hell as I didn't think I was a bad person. I even tried to explain to him with an anecdote concerning a friend of mine (whom Jack knew and respected), how insulting the word *kuffar* was. This particular friend had been the only Black student at a private school in Shaftsbury, Dorset, and was regularly greeted in the corridor by another student, a white South African boy, with the words "Alright, *kaffir*?" I told Jack that *kaffir* was an insulting term for Black people under apartheid in South Africa and had probably derived from the language of the Arab slave traders who shipped slaves from African shores.

Jack was scornful in his reply, saying this was a completely different situation: Islam wasn't racist, and one of the Prophet's companions, Bilal, was Black and an ex-slave. "Yet he was from the best of mankind and became a leader for all the believers," he added. Later on, these conversations between Jack and me would form the core of the evidence that the police had against me, as surely I had "reasonable grounds to suspect" Jack was a terrorist, given that I knew about his intransigent beliefs and about his disdainful attitude toward those who didn't share them.

The conclusion *Z* came to was that our communication with Jack should be centred around home, warm, loving, and noncontentious. That way, we would run less risk of losing communication altogether and reassure Jack that he always had a home to come back to. Both John and I took his advice to heart, although John stuck to it longer than I did. After a while, it seemed to me fatuous that I should be telling Jack how much his favourite cat missed him when he was surrounded by horror and slaughter, and when he seemed to be being drawn ever deeper into the extreme beliefs of those around him. I started to tackle him on subjects that we heard about on the news — the imprisonments, the booby-trapped buildings, the killing of dissenters. We also mentioned the stories smuggled out of Raqqa — about girls as young as ten being forced to veil their faces; or about the religious police, men and women, who would arrest you if your gown was too long or your beard not long enough, if you were a man, or for being unchaperoned or not covered sufficiently, if you were a woman. Jack rarely, if ever, responded to these statements or questions. Sometimes, he would retaliate with contentions of his own about the ills of the West, although sometimes he tried to say that it was not the West's sense of regional identity that was at fault; rather, it was its failure to embrace Islam. One early message of his read:

> I hate all disbelieving Americans and love all Muslim Americans and none of this is because they are American. Their Americanism is irrelevant in the basis of this love and hate. On top of that, most of the American population are steeped in either bad ideologies, racism, alcoholism and drug addictions, abuse of many sorts, ignorant nationalism, support of their criminal government and army, ignorance in a general sense, arrogance etc.

The second part of that message, I thought as I read it, rather seemed to negate the first, although I was aware that Jack's declared opposition to modern American hegemony is not an uncommon view, shared as it is by many people and many nations throughout the world. Such negative comments, however, coming from a young, religious English person based in Syria are, of course, going to take on a rather different significance, and the fact that many people say such anti-American things every day suddenly becomes irrelevant.

As I was conversing with Jack about such topics, I knew that MI5 and MI6 were taking a keen interest. In the early days, the police denied to us that they had full access to anyone's Facebook account whenever they felt like it. We were suspicious of their denial, mostly because a friend of ours based in Birmingham had told us that when his sister had gone missing for a few days, the police had accessed her Facebook account within seconds. By March 2015, in any case, we knew the police were able to access my, John's, and Jack's accounts, as the police had told us that they had obtained a warrant in order to do so. Apparently, this had been a long process, involving requests to Facebook headquarters in California and various court orders. What it meant for us was that we knew every word we said to Jack could be used in evidence against us, without our having been read our rights first. It is astonishing to me how the generation that has grown up with Facebook has no appreciation of what a massive abrogation of our human rights this is, and how an unaware and careless population are merrily doing the police's work for them every single day. I knew that if I did get convicted for aiding a suspected terrorist, I would have been very largely hanged by my own words, in conversations that were desperate attempts to talk reason into my recalcitrant and misguided son, eavesdropped upon by terrorist-seeking government agents. If John and I had had the attitude that Jack had made his bed, now he had to lie in it, or had written him off, or disowned him — as some contacts and friends had told us we should do — we would not find ourselves in the position we were then in — i.e., facing possible conviction and several years' imprisonment under the Terrorism Act 2000.

Fortunately, in the early months after Jack's bombshell departure, we did have supporters as well as detractors. Many friends who are parents have told us that in the same situation they would have acted exactly as we had done, and these personal messages of support became very important to us. I came to see some of the expert advice as just that — expert advice that sometimes fitted our situation and sometimes didn't.

I was reminded of a situation that had arisen when I was a very insecure new mother: Jack had been a week or so old, and I was still receiving home visits from the midwife. Somehow, I'd got it into my head that each cry of a newborn baby signified a different need — hunger, needing a nappy change, etc. (I think this idea originated from long-ago conversations with a zoologist friend, who'd told me that bird calls are not fixed according to species but change according to circumstances, e.g., mating, raising alarm, etc.) In any case, on this occasion, as the midwife was entering the house, I asked her what sort of cry Jack was making. "I don't know," she replied, incredulously. "He's your baby!" For me, that was the best thing she could have said. I stopped believing there was a particular science to looking after babies; all I needed was to follow my instincts and care for him like a normal human being. With regard to Jack's present situation, I felt we should use our instincts in communicating with him, as much as follow any expert advice. After all, we knew him better than the experts, and Jack maintained he was still the same person he had been when he'd left, albeit somewhat brainwashed, in our view. We just needed to get his brain working coherently again and get him away from the unholy mess he'd got himself into. And, soon enough, we discovered that much of the expert advice we did receive depended to a large extent on the hidden agenda of the person or organization giving it.

Chapter 7

Thames Valley Police and the Mounties

Police visit, December 2014

Early one morning in December 2014, while I was having my breakfast at the sitting room table, the doorbell rang. The ring was unusual for two reasons: I wasn't expecting anyone so early in the morning, and the ring tone itself was unusually loud, prolonged, and insistent, as if someone had rested their entire weight behind the doorbell button to show they had no intention of going away.

When I opened the door, I found three very tall, plain-clothed men on the doorstep, behind whom was a small woman, also in plain clothes. I stared at them as they stared at me.

"Mrs. Lane?" the lead tall one asked. "We're from Thames Valley Police. We'd like to talk to you about Jack."

"Come in," I said, as I led him and his retinue into the living room. "I'm surprised it took you so long."

My latter comment was ill-advised. Although I was vaguely aware that one was supposed to report people going to Syria, I didn't know it was an offence not to report someone you suspected might be going there. The law is complicated by the fact that it is not illegal to go to Syria, but since it is assumed that everyone who goes to Syria is going with the intention of engaging in a terrorist act, then you are *de facto* committing an offence by not reporting it. It was not until we engaged our first lawyers several months later that we learned more about this issue: the vast majority of the terrorist-related cases before the courts were "non-disclosure" cases, i.e., relatives or friends were being prosecuted for not reporting people leaving the country who might be going to Syria. To this day, the police have not actually accused us of "non-disclosure," although a lot of their investigation has focused on the premise that we knew in advance that Jack planned to go to Syria, and that his holiday in Jordan was just a ruse. Perhaps because our main charge was fundraising for terrorism, the non-disclosure charge took second place.

"We'd just like a chat," said the lead officer as we went into the living room. "We have had reports that Jack has gone to Syria, and we'd like to know what you know about this."

I then proceeded to tell him about the information I had, about Jack's phone call on September 2, and that we were in utter shock, but we were trying to communicate with him and get him back. I asked him who had told them about Jack, and he said he couldn't tell me. I asked if they had any more information about him, and he said no. When I asked if they would pass on any information they did find out, he said we could have a mutually beneficially arrangement — i.e., we would tell them what we knew, and vice versa. (To date, it is only us who have kept our side of this bargain.) During our conversation, the other officers didn't say a word, and the female officer wrote down notes.

This initial meeting with the police was fairly brief. They left, saying we would all be in touch. Strangely, I felt relief. It had been hard keeping the whole thing secret, with our friends, relatives, and colleagues not wanting to know too much about the situation in case they were implicated in the secrecy. Now I could go to my boss and explain that the police knew all about it, and ask if I could go down to two days a week after my period of sick leave, as I needed to concentrate on getting Jack back. My workplace was very understanding, but I ended up leaving a month later.

My prime suspect in guessing who had reported Jack to the police was the imam at the Oxford mosque. The imam had told me they "had a very good relationship with the police," and no doubt, they wanted to cover their own back. It turned out, however, that it was John's family in Canada who had provided the report. When John had told them about the situation, his sisters had apparently been so terrified that Jack would somehow creep into Canada to commit terrorist acts, they had informed the Mounties. They had done this without telling us, and despite having had Jack stay with them the summer before, when they had found him soft-hearted, amiable, and helpful. At the time, John's sister had declared herself touched by the fact that Jack had even chastised her teenaged daughter (his cousin) for being rude to her mother, pointing out, "She did give birth to you, you know." The U.K. police told us that, yes, they did have a close relationship with the Canadian authorities, so we guessed the man on a horse had passed the sisters' message on.

By the time of that first police visit, I had already learned about the circumstances of Jack's journey to Syria from my phone app conversations with *Y*, who had been Jack's housemate in Jordan and Kuwait, and who was still studying in the Middle East. *Y* told me that Jack had been talking more and more about the civil war in Syria and was angry that no one seemed to be doing anything

about it. *Y* and his friends began to suspect that he might be thinking of going there himself and became more suspicious around the
time they all needed to renew their visas. In Kuwait, a visit visa
lasts thirty days, and if the visitor wants to stay longer, the Kuwait
Ministry website recommends that "a pleasant solution is to obtain
a second visit visa to Kuwait." The easiest way to do this is to "travel
to Bahrain on a morning flight and re-enter Kuwait in the evening
round trip (40 minutes flying time)." This is what the boys planned
to do, although according to *Y*, Jack had other ideas. Instead of
flying to Bahrain, Jack said he would fly to Turkey to visit a friend
and renew his visa at the same time. Smelling a rat, on the day of
Jack's departure, the boys drove him the long way round to the
Kuwait City airport so that he missed his flight. Apparently, Jack
had been incensed by their deception, so that the second time he
tried, he didn't tell anyone and took very little with him in the way
of possessions. *Y* had kept in touch with him sporadically after this
but was wary because of his own security situation: it could cause
trouble for him if it were known that he was in contact with someone in Syria.

I told the police about my conversation with *Y*. It seemed that
this route to Syria via Turkey was the most common one, as the
border between the two countries was very long (about five hundred
miles) and "very porous." It was easy to slip across, particularly if
you had contacts. The Turkish government didn't seem to be doing
much to stop it, and some said that it was deliberately turning a
blind eye to the crossing of foreign fighters, as it, too, was opposed
to Assad's regime.

I became obsessed with finding out who Jack's contacts were.
I had planned on putting pressure on the mosque to give me the
names of possible contacts, but then I had ruined my own plans by
bursting into tears and sobbing in front of the imam instead. I did
have one more promising lead, however. This had come about as a

stroke of luck when I'd signed into my Facebook and Jack's email sign-on address had popped up. I knew that all I then needed was his password in order to hack into his account. One of Jack's friends told me it would be easy to reset his password as we were still paying for Jack's mobile phone contract, and the code to change the password could be sent to Jack's mobile phone. All we needed to do was get a replacement SIM card from the mobile phone shop, which again was very easy to do. I was unexpectedly becoming much more technically proficient, and was also suddenly able to access Jack's private messages on his account. I admitted to the police that I frequently accessed Jack's account to find out what he was up to.

My unforeseen infiltration of Jack's account yielded something of a bonanza. I was able to click onto his new friends' accounts and read their comments. One of them, a university student, had posted a picture of himself and about five of his friends, all standing grinning with their arms around one another's shoulders. The caption below read, "I hope we can all meet like this in Paradise." *What is wrong with these people?* I thought. *Why are young men in their twenties already making plans for their time after death, and why is it such an everyday preoccupation for them? And how had Jack come to be so influenced by them?*

John's explanation for this was that Jack was abnormally terrified of death: when he was about thirteen, Jack had poured out his fear of the blackness that lay beyond. In the same conversation, Jack had even told him about an incident that had scared the life out of him when he was three years old. It had been during the time he was living with me in the shared house in Oxford, and a young Bulgarian tenant had told him a bedtime story about the "naughty children who were abandoned on an island where no one could ever reach or speak to them ever again." When I heard this story from John, I became furious at the heedless callousness of the long-ago Bulgarian babysitter. Even as I did so, however, I realized there were no doubt numerous incidents that had produced Jack's anxiety, and I would never be sure what exactly had produced the fear inside him that only religion could cure.

More revealing information was to be gleaned from Jack's private messages to and from his friends, particularly those his friends had urged him to delete, and which Jack, being slapdash, had not. The most relevant of these had come from a university contact of Jack's, whom I'd already been warned about by Jack's Muslim friends, who believed him to be a bad influence. I had taken their warnings with a pinch of salt, as their concern seemed to be based on the fact that this person was studying politics, something they felt detracted from religion (although, thinking about it now, perhaps I had misunderstood them, and they were worried about the application of revolutionary politics to religion). In any case, it was clear from the messages from this student that he had put Jack in contact with various people soon after his arrival in Jordan, whom he said would be able to help him with "the path." Some of these contacts had pseudonyms and seemed to have connections to rebel groups. I felt ill that this university student was some sort of armchair revolutionary, who influenced boys like Jack who were much younger and more naive than him, to carry out his brand of politics.

When I confronted the student via Facebook, he was initially charming and denied everything, until I said I had written evidence of his involvement, at which point he turned nasty and told me not to contact him again. The police also told me not to contact him again (I was somewhat loathe to in any case, as I'd had a terrifying dream involving him and an acid attack), and said they were conducting their own investigation into his activities. Much later, we discovered that the student had been arrested but released without charge. Perhaps he was more useful to the police in helping them with their enquiries.

Chapter 8

Police raid

Charlie Hebdo shooting, January 7, 2015

On January 7, 2015, Paris experienced the first of two serious terrorist incidents in which mass shootings were carried out in the
name of Islam (the second was to take place in November 2015 in
several coordinated suicide bombings and shootings, including at
the Bataclan theatre, where eighty-nine concert-goers were killed).
In the January incident, two brothers, Saïd and Chérif Kouachi,
stormed the offices of the French newspaper *Charlie Hebdo* in the
centre of Paris, shot dead twelve people, and injured several others.
Nine of those shot dead were cartoonists, with the attackers claiming they were acting on behalf of al-Qaeda in Yemen. Witnesses
reported that the gunmen shouted that they were "avenging the
Prophet Mohammad," and the killings were seen by the world's
media as a revenge attack on the newspaper for its publication
of cartoons mocking the prophet. Two days after the attack, the
brothers were killed by police after a nine-hour siege at a printing

works, and two days after this, on January 11, 2015, forty world leaders gathered in Paris, linking arms amid a crowd of 1.5 million people in a show of solidarity with the French people. *"Je suis Charlie"* became the slogan of people demonstrating their support for the principles of free speech as well as their respect for those who died.

The terror incident sparked huge debate in the Muslim and non-Muslim world about democratic values and religious fundamentalism, as well as about the increased threat posed by Islamic terrorism. Controversy raged as to the right of freedom of expression in opposition to the laws against hate speech. The Muslim world overwhelmingly expressed its condemnation of the attacks, including the governments of Saudi Arabia, Iran, Jordan, and Qatar, and the leading Sunni institution based in Cairo, Al-Azhar University, which stated that violence was never appropriate, regardless of "offence committed against sacred Muslim sentiments." A minority of commentators appeared to justify the attacks (including Anjem Choudary, who maintained that he was quoting the Prophet by saying that "those who insult prophets should face death").

Noam Chomsky attempted to give the incident some sort of historical context when he pointed out the hypocrisy of the world leaders' demonstration of sympathy for the *Charlie Hebdo* journalists when there had been no such outpouring when NATO killed sixteen employees in Radio Television Serbia's headquarters in 1999.

Around this time, Jack posted his two cents' worth on his Facebook page, following Chomsky's line that the display of outrage by Western leaders was hypocritical. I was fully aware that the same sentiment coming from a world-renowned American academic and a young, firebrand, Islamic convert would be viewed very differently, and told him to remove the post if he had any sense and didn't want his Facebook page shut down. When Jack asked me in a personal message how "people had received the operations in France," I responded in typical outraged fashion, saying, "How do you think people have received the news in France??? They are horrified, of course, that people could be mown down for a mere drawing." We then had a discussion about hate speech and blasphemy laws, and Jack replied with an unintelligible diatribe about man-made laws, which seemed completely bizarre and unlike any views he had ever expressed before, and made me extremely worried about the influence of the people who must be surrounding him. His private Facebook message to me read: "The legal route you've mentioned is taking legislation to man-made law. Taking legislation to Allaah alone is an act of worship therefore taking it to other than him is worshipping other than Him and polytheism. I declare my disassociation from the advocates and promoters of these laws and my disassociation from the laws themselves." I assumed this must be his definition of a caliphate, where, if everyone acted according to the law of Allah, a sort of theological utopia in which everyone acted morally would ensue. A later message of his in the same conversation stated, "If anyone thinks for about 5.34 seconds, they can establish there is a difference between what a deep [religion] teaches and the actions of its adherents when they oppose the religion's teachings. Allaah is All-Powerful and he is able to eliminate his enemies but he leaves some of them and makes apparent with them who His friends are," which also seemed to represent an alien, nonsecular way of thinking, but which, at least, seemed to show that he made a distinction between the "truth" of the religion and the actions by which some religious adherents distorted this truth.

Throughout February and March 2015, Jack and I, and sometimes John via his own Facebook account, had similar frustrating conversations, where we tried to penetrate the religious fog that appeared to form the core of his new personality, but which meant nothing to us, and tried to ascertain what his strange and unfathomable beliefs actually meant in real life. It turned out that the police were keen to explore the same question, and at the end of March 2015, four police officers, including DS *M*, who nearly a year later was to discuss with John the fate of the Raqqa-based kebab seller, knocked on our front door early in the morning, complete with warrant, ready to conduct a raid of our house.

Police raid, March 31, 2015

On the morning of March 31, 2015, I heard again that loud, insistent, drawn-out doorbell ring that meant only one thing: the police. Sure enough, when I opened the door, there were four of them standing on the doorstep. Ever since Jack had been in Syria, we'd lived with our hearts in our mouths, fearing at each moment that the next phone call, the next Facebook login or doorstep visit would mean the worst news possible.

"Is Jack okay?" I asked.

"He's fine," said the officer. "You might want to invite us in as you might not want the neighbours to see." He brushed past me (rudely, I thought) in the narrow hallway, followed by the others.

"There's nothing to worry about," he said, as we entered the living room.

"What, four of you, and nothing to worry about?" I said.

He ignored this and we sat down, with a couple of the officers remaining standing.

"We have concerns about Jack, and we've obtained a warrant from the CPS [Crown Prosecution Service] to search the property," he said. He handed me a piece of paper. "We've come in plain clothes and we haven't parked a police car outside your house."

I realized I was supposed to feel grateful that they hadn't embarrassed us in front of the neighbours by arriving in riot gear and smashing down the front door.

"Do you know where he is? Have you found out anything?" I asked.

"We've got no evidence he's done anything wrong," said the officer, "we are just conducting our inquiries." I now know this officer, *M*, was to prove to be one of our most significant betrayers in the months to come. At this stage, however, he was still presenting himself as the kindly officer we could rely on. Embarrassingly, I even told him on this particular occasion that we trusted the police. I also sympathized with him over the ailment he was suffering from, which he mentioned later on that day — i.e., frozen shoulder — as I myself had had the same condition a few years before and knew how debilitating it was. Given what was to come, I can hardly believe I wasted my fellow feeling on someone who ended up devoting a large portion of his life to destroying us in every way possible.

M then gave the order to search our house. The other officers snapped into action, donning plastic gloves and starting to go through our bookshelves, bedroom drawers, and desk papers. I watched them as they went through Jack's box of soft toys and tried not to cry. I had no idea what they expected to find amongst his teddy bears, his fluffy Pikachu, and his Tweety Bird puppet.

It wasn't until late afternoon that they were satisfied they had everything they needed. *M*'s subordinates had carted off boxfuls of papers, books, manuals, my dilapidated address book, as well as our computers (including *E*'s) and phones. They told us that in order to save us embarrassment (those nosy neighbours again), they were putting our computers in plastic sacks to disguise what they were. John told them he wasn't worried about the neighbours, and I told him he should be more worried than I was, since no doubt the neighbours would think he was a pedophile if they saw it was our computers that were being carried off. All in all, it seemed incongruous that the police seemed so concerned about our standing amongst the neighbours while being so unconcerned about the impact the absence of our computers and phones would have on our lives.

This was particularly concerning for *E*, as he was in the middle of his end of year exams and he was severely disadvantaged without his computer, which had all his revision notes. In the end, after a couple of weeks of downloading material, the police gave back *E*'s computer, and then after a few more days, they gave back John's. Mine they kept as evidence, as that was the computer that Jack had used and that I had mostly used to message him. I would get it back — with all the other items they confiscated over the coming months — only when the investigation into Jack was over. Which, of course, means never.

✳   ✳   ✳

Taking stock at this point of what we knew about Jack's activities, allegiances, and plans, our summary was that we knew he had moved from Syria to Iraq (the country code on his mobile phone confirmed this); he was married; and that he said he was welcomed by the local people in the markets. He had also met someone who had been imprisoned for five years in Camp Bucca, the U.S. military prison in southern Iraq that had brought together hundreds of insurgents during the American occupation, including Abu Bakr al-Baghdadi, who some years later was to become the leader of ISIS. The camp itself, in fact, was credited by several Western journalists for creating the environment in which ISIS was forged, since these Sunni insurgents, confined together, were able to organize themselves around their grievances against the American imposition of power and its favouring of Iraq's larger Shiite population. We realized that Jack was no doubt being influenced by a powerful figure who had reason to harbour severe resentment against the former Western occupiers of his country. In addition, in one phone conversation, Jack had told us that he had spent some time in Fallujah, a city forty miles west of Baghdad, which had been a centre of resistance to American troops during the occupation and which had suffered bombardment by American shells containing white phosphorus, a chemical weapon that causes severe birth defects in children. During our conversation, Jack broke off in order to relay to us a comment made by someone in the room with him; children with genetic abnormalities were still being born, said this person, as the heavy metals are still embedded in Fallujah's soil.

The bits of information we gleaned from such telephone conversations, together with explanatory articles we read in the British press — most notably by Martin Chulov, who seemed to be that vanishing type of journalist, i.e., an investigative one, and who was determined to put the phenomenon of ISIS into context — formed the backdrop of our communications with Jack. We knew that Jack had married into a Sunni family, and we also knew that it was the large Sunni tribes that were in a position to most influence the balance of power between the Iraqi government and ISIS, i.e., tribes such as the large al-Jabouri tribe from the Tikrit area, could hugely bolster the ranks of ISIS if they chose to ally themselves with them, or alternatively, could provide a significant political and military force if they chose to resist them.

My Facebook conversations with Jack around this time reveal something of both his and our reactions to his first six months in Syria and Iraq. Looking over these now, I see that most of them relate to our differing opinions on democracy and religion, and convey little of the politics of the region. On March 11, 2015, for instance, he expressed his views on the fundamental tenets of his religion:

> I've made my position clear on my love and alliance and on hate and disassociation, there aren't exceptions. Do not get me started on the

ridiculousness and falsehood of giving the right of legislation to whoever happens to be the majority. I've debated this point with dad to the point that he admitted if 99% of a society agrees with baby murder then it should be accepted (this was essentially the result of the conversation).

... The true safety is in Tawheed. Tawheed is the fundamental principle of Islam, that all worship is for Allaah alone. From that worship is going to Allaah alone for legislation. True safety in this legislation is that the rights of people and their cases are brought to the book of Allaah and the sunnah of his messenger علي الله صلى وسلم ه.

... If you knew the history of the group of believers who remained on the way of the prophet صلى الله عليه وسلم then you would see how much struggle and oppression they have been through. If you knew how brothers and sisters were and still are treated in Iraq, Syria, Britain, America Burma Somalia Morocco Saudi Arabia Holland Nigeria etc., purely because they stick to the way of the prophet صلى الله عليه وسلم and the first Muslims ... I've lived with people who have been in prisons for their religion, with people who most of the world consider amongst the worst people on the planet. There are international agreements that the solution to these people is to exterminate them. With that, they are the nicest people I've known.

When I remonstrated with him that his chosen way of life was selfish and he was going to get himself killed, his reply on April 18, 2015, was this:

If your [*sic*] convinced I'm selfish then that's your own problem, you don't how I love my life. It's selfish for me to decide I want the safety of England while the Muslims of this part of the world are systemically raped tortured and abused with the help of your beloved country and it's [*sic*] friends from the 'modern and developed countries, heroes of democracy and freedom'. If you knew 1.3% of what you side with (democracy, those that propagate it and want to establish it in Iraq and Syria) have done here you would probably cry till you have eye problems. I've seen the children with shrapnel in their tiny bodies and I've seen them cry. I've witnessed the systematic bombardment of civilians by American funded battalions of subhuman thugs. Yes, I don't love and don't respect you due to your differing with that which truly deserves love, devotion and loyalty. As long as you stay upon disbelief then I'm disassociated from you and from your disbelief. The day we stand before my creator and your creator, He alone will judge between us.

My reply on the same day was designed to point out to him that we didn't support American policy in the Middle East either (which, as everyone knows, is, and always has been, to supports its oil interests), but that his presence there would not change things for the better; if anything, it would make matters worse:

I find it hard to believe that you think we would side with bombardment of civilians by Americans, or anyone else. We don't agree with the shelling by

Assad, or the massacres by the Iraqi government or the Shia militias. Just because we live here doesn't mean we agree with what our government does, just like the people of Syria don't agree with what their government is doing to them. Democracy doesn't always work, and dictatorship (by religious leaders or civil leaders) doesn't always work either.

I can understand your not wanting to be associated with people (even your own parents) because of their actions or what they support in their opinions, but not because of what they believe. When you weren't a Muslim you weren't a bad person — we are not bad people simply because we don't believe in God. This is what I mean by your selfishness — that you can't see things from anyone else's perspective. We can't all run off to Iraq to show our solidarity with oppressed people. There are oppressed people all over the world and all most people can do is charitable actions or political actions or live their own life in a way that is not oppressive.

A couple of weeks after I sent this message, I followed it up with a message updating him on our police raid:

I thought I would update you on the situation here — the police still have my computer and seem unlikely to give it back — apparently, they can seize it as "evidence." As it contains all my data for my work, my contacts, friends, etc. this has posed certain difficulties for me; however, this is ... an irritation rather than a huge problem. Basically,

under the Terrorism Act, you can be charged on
two counts — i.e., either if you had "the intention
to fight" by going abroad, and if you can be seen to
be "glorifying terrorism." However, the police did
say that if the political situation changes — e.g. if
the government in Syria or Iraq changes — then
the way the Act is interpreted changes too. All a
bit vague, I know, but no-one knows what is going
to happen so they can only say what the situation
is at the moment. And you know, of course, that
all your communications are being monitored so
I hope you bear this in mind when you message
people. The police are still saying that at present
there is no evidence against you.

Jack did not reply to this message for ten days, and I started to
think the worst. However, when he came back online he said that
he hadn't had access to the internet for a while, but was back now.
He told me that he and his wife had a new house. His subsequent
messages to us over the next few months seemed to follow a similar
pattern: he would often post an angry outburst about the victimiz-
ation of Muslims, and then follow this up with a "normal" message,
asking after his Oxford friends or saying he was thinking of getting
a cat. Our strategies, too, ranged from challenges to his powers of
reasoning to emotional appeals to his former affection for us. When
I told him that I had had tests for cancer and the results had come
back as a "3" (with "1" being benign, and "5" being cancer, "4"
being probably cancer, and "3" being a few abnormal cells), I was
hoping that this might elicit some sort of empathetic response from
him. I was pathetically grateful when he replied with the message,
"I'm glad to hear they didn't tell you you have number 5." It meant
there was still hope.

Chapter 9

Seeking an antidote

Recovery from Cults

Around this time, I began reading a book entitled *Recovery from Cults*, edited by Michael Langone. It had been recommended by a psychologist friend of John's, and I was hoping it would offer some psychological insights into Jack's mindset and give some clues as to the best way to communicate with him. Most of the advice we'd read on the internet said more or less the same things: reassure your family member or friend that you still love them, do not mention words like *brainwashed* or *cult*, ask gentle questions about their beliefs without attacking them, and above all, use every opportunity to maintain contact with them.

This seemed like sensible advice, and for the most part we followed three out of the four recommendations, i.e., we were not so good at gently asking questions about Jack's beliefs, and were much more likely to confront his beliefs, or our understanding of them, head on. I also slipped up by using the word *brainwashed* a couple of times, which as the internet advice explains, plays into the hands of the cult group, as the cult member will have been told that their family will criticize the group, and this criticism has the effect of reinforcing the group's solidarity. (One of the sad things about Jack's new allegiances was that when we told him we loved him, he was no longer able to say it back — this from a boy who, before he left the U.K., would tell us he loved us each time he left the house. As time went on, he was more likely to say he hated us for the sake of Allah.) I found it difficult not to make direct appeals to Jack's intellect, as I knew he was intelligent and used to thinking for himself, and not, as I ill-advisedly put it, used to "pretending he was living in the 7th century and being ruled by old men whose only qualification is being able to memorize passages from his holy book." In retrospect, this was a stupid thing to say and no doubt strengthened his allegiance to whatever religious group he was with; although, in my defence, I did fire it off in a fit of frustration before reading the Langone book's sensible advice.

Recovery from Cults was illuminating in that it included personal case studies from people who had left cults, as well as expert accounts from psychologists, educationalists, and therapists. These personal stories seemed to back up the academic analyses of the experts, i.e., cult "prospects" are initially showered with attention and positive reinforcement (like the "love bombing" of the Moonies); then there is a phase where dissent by cult members is called out as divisive and disruptive. As Michael Langone explains in his introduction, members become increasingly dependent on the group, and "to ensure continuation of the group's rewards (praise, attention, promise of future benefits …), members must implicitly, if not explicitly, acknowledge the group's authority in defining what is real, good, and true." Members are also gradually isolated from outside influences, until the group becomes their only form of support. One insight from the book particularly interested me as it seemed to directly relate to Jack's obsession with hour-long periods of praying that had so preoccupied him and had far exceeded the short prayers five times a day that Muslims were expected to engage in:

> Hours spent in practices that induce dissociative states (e.g., meditation, chanting, speaking in tongues, "criticism sessions") facilitate a psychological splitting that permits adaptation to the group's contradictory agendas and demand for subservience. Members who are tempted to object to or disagree with elements of the group's agenda may find themselves in a "loyalty/betrayal funnel" … If they remain loyal to their own perceptions about self and world, they betray the group on which they have become inordinately dependent; if they remain loyal to the group, they betray their own perception of what is real, good, and true…. The result of this process, when carried to its consummation, is a pseudopersonality … a state of dissociation in which members are "split" but not "multiple," in which they proclaim great happiness yet hide great suffering.

This passage of the book seemed to speak to me directly. It even used words that Jack himself used, as in his comment from April 2015: "As long as you stay upon disbelief then I'm disassociated from you and from your disbelief." Even the claim about "pseudopersonality" seemed to fit with Jack's pattern of assuring us that, since we were his parents, he was still obliged to "accompany us in this life with good" and "wanted [us] to know what it's like to have paradise to be in your heart wherever you go," alongside his comments about how much he hated us because of our disbelief. It might also explain why his vitriolic rants at us were followed up by "normal" pieces of conversation asking how we were, or how was the farm, or could we please send him photos of his old room. I knew that the son we loved was still in there somewhere, and that all we needed to do was remove the horrible pseudopersonality that had installed itself and which insisted on speaking to us in a bizarre, seventh-century dialect.

The one clear message that emerged from my reading of *Recovery from Cults* was that the impetus to break away from the group had to come from the cult member themselves. For change to occur, the cult member would need to start to see the hypocrisy of the cult leaders and the dissonance between their words and their actions. Our hope was that Jack, with his intelligence and strong aversion to hypocrisy of all forms, would start to see the disjunction between the fundamental tenets of his "beautiful religion," the basis of which was love, and the actions of the fundamentalist groups in Syria and Iraq that were spreading a bastardized form of that religion. This breakthrough did, in fact, happen, toward the end of 2015, by which time the police had decided we would not be permitted to enable him to leave Syria.

Radical, by Maajid Nawaz

Another book that I searched for clues as to how this moment of disillusionment could take place was *Radical*, the Amazon best-selling book by Maajid Nawaz. Nawaz's story is of particular interest, as he progressed from being a radical Islamist in his youth to becoming director of the Quilliam Foundation, a charity that has received extensive funding from the U.K. government and is the latter's think tank of choice when seeking advice on Islamic policy matters.

Nawaz was sixteen when he converted to Hizb al-Tahrir (HT), a radical Islamic group. Of Pakistani origin and from Southend, Essex, his story of recruitment to political Islam followed a narrative that was more familiar to the British public than "white boy from middle-class family leaves comfortable Oxford for a war zone," i.e., as a youth, Nawaz experienced discrimination, including from the police, as a result of his skin colour, and also experienced violence at the hands of the National Front and Combat 18 gangs. His radicalization was provoked by the conflict in Yugoslavia (the "Syria" of the 1990s) and the vicious treatment of the Bosnian Muslims by the Serb forces. In 2001, he was tasked with recruiting for HT in Egypt, but that same year he was arrested by the Egyptian police and remained in prison for five years.

During his time in prison, Nawaz renounced his former political beliefs and, after his release in 2006, began to campaign for a secular Islam, based on liberal values. The Quilliam Foundation, the think tank he co-founded with his friend Ed Husain in 2008, was set up to address Westphobic ideas at the same time as fostering a sense of belonging for all sectors of society. It is interesting to note that this admittance on the part of the British government that "poachers turned gamekeepers" — i.e., former jihadists who denounce their radicalism — can be useful in deradicalization policies, is at odds with the government's current dealings with disillusioned jihadis in Syria and Iraq. For example, when, in late 2014, a group of thirty disillusioned British fighters in Syria wanted to return home, they asked Shiraz Maher at the International Centre for the Study of Radicalisation, King's College, to negotiate with the Home Office on their behalf. The group was, however, given short shrift by the government. Instead, the Home Office, under the leadership of Theresa May, then Home Secretary, proposed exclusion orders preventing suspected British fighters from returning to Britain within two years of departure (perhaps hoping that most of them would be killed by then), and also recommended increasing security services' powers of data surveillance.

John and I were to meet Shiraz and his colleague, Nick, at his offices at King's College, London, in the summer of 2015 as part of our efforts to gain more background information on Jack's situation. I had identified Shiraz as a good potential source of assistance in this regard, as his name often seemed to crop up in news articles about British fighters in Syria. His involvement with the thirty disillusioned fighters had particularly caught my eye, since it showed that he had his ear to the ground at the same time as he was providing a political and social analysis of the situation that was given airtime by the media and taken seriously by the government. (I also heard from other sources later on, however, that Shiraz's connections to British fighters were closely watched by the security services so that his academic freedom was constantly under threat. On one occasion, his offices were even raided by the police, with [as in our case] his computers taken away. This seemed to be the stuff of the Stasi in East Germany, not of the Metropolitan police in London.)

Shiraz's position, which he often presented in media fora and to government committees, was that disillusioned fighters returning from Syria and Iraq could prove to be an extremely useful force for good in dissuading other idealistic young Britons from joining their brothers in the cause of jihad. Dangerous individuals would, of course, be separated from those who had renounced their former views, and a program of deradicalization would be implemented in prisons for those who were convicted. A Danish model for a similar deradicalization package was already in place and was achieving impressive results amongst returning fighters in Denmark. Despite the fact that Richard Barrett, the former director of global counterterrorism operations for MI6, supported Shiraz in his deradicalization proposals, the Home Office under Theresa May appeared to be turning a deaf ear to their potential benefits.

As it turned out, John's and my meeting with Shiraz in 2015 did not have a good result. A year later, in August 2016, when the evidence was served against us, we discovered that Shiraz had provided a witness statement for the prosecution against me and John, saying we were naive, didn't know anything about Islam, and refused to countenance the idea that Jack might be a fighter. One of the key questions we had asked him in our 2015 meeting was whether Jack's name appeared on his extensive database of British fighters, which formed the core of his research. Since Jack was a fair-skinned, blond convert, he would presumably be easily identifiable if he were a combatant. Although Shiraz said his name did not, in fact, appear, John and I should assume he was a fighter, since everyone who went there would be expected to fight. We were dubious about this assertion and were less than impressed with the rigour of his academic methods: for example, he had identified a Twitter account as belonging to Jack, even though factually it could not be (Jack was living in Oxford when the account was set up in Turkey); and also claimed that Jack was autistic, which he is not. We guessed that by submitting a witness statement, Shiraz was protecting his own Home Office funding by batting for the government's side. However, at the time of our meeting, we were obviously ignorant of this as a possible outcome, and still sought his advice as a possible "expert."

Nawaz himself is a good example of someone who was a radical Islamist as a youth but later managed to become a member of the British establishment, first as a Liberal parliamentary candidate in 2015, and then as a regular presenter for the cutting-edge, London-based, talk radio station LBC. His book offers a rare, first-person account explaining his intellectual and emotional awakening, in which he began to espouse a nonviolent and compassionate approach to human conflict. He was — in the language of academia — able to turn his experience into a useful anti-radicalization narrative.

I discovered, against my fond hopes, that his "change of views wasn't an overnight process." True to the analysis in *Recovery from Cults*, the initial point of his disengagement from the ideology of radical Islam came from disillusionment with the people in charge of his organization. And, as he says, he had "plenty of time to think about these events, lying awake in [his] cell." Reinforcing this change of viewpoint was Amnesty International's adoption of him as a "Prisoner of Conscience" and their campaign for his release. (This move was apparently controversial internally for Amnesty, as Nawaz's views at the time were considered unsavoury. However, Amnesty took Voltaire's view: "I disapprove of what you say, but I will defend to the death your right to say it.") Nawaz was deeply touched by Amnesty's support of him, saying that it signalled the beginning of his "rehumanization." He began to see events in terms of their human costs instead of their political significance. For instance, his view on the attacks on the London Underground on July 7, 2005, contrasted with his reaction to the events of 9/11, which he had seen as an understandable response to the deaths of half a million children during the American invasion and occupation. The subsequent American-led invasions of Afghanistan and Iraq after 9/11, he added, had only served to cement his feelings in this regard.

"Where the heart leads, the mind can follow" is a phrase Nawaz often repeats in this section of the book. After his rehumanization experience with Amnesty, he began to educate himself about Islam through intensive study of the Qu'ran, and also learned about moral complexity through studying English literature (provided to the prison by the British Consul in Egypt). His study of history made him question the Islamists' contention that the Turkish Caliphate, or Ottoman Empire, was the "last true example of legitimate government," as he discovered that the Caliphate never had a codified legal system in a unified state; rather, sharia law had been interpreted by local community tribunals. All of this newfound knowledge he discussed with his prison mates, among them bomb makers and theologians, some of whom came around to his revised point of view, i.e., it was possible for justice to be achieved by groups other than Islamists, even by communists (like his lawyer), and by liberals (like his fellow prisoner who had challenged the power of Mubarak).

One episode mentioned by Nawaz about this period of his re-awakening echoed some of the sentiments I had tried to convey to Jack. I, like nearly everyone I know, believe in the old adage that democracy isn't perfect but it's the best system we've got. This didn't mean I believed in imposing it, American-style, on other countries, but it did mean that I was unused to having to defend democracy itself as an institution. Jack's dismissal of democracy as a system which, he said, "would allow baby murder if 99 per cent of the population agreed with it," had forced me to refine my arguments about rule by the majority. The Iraq War was a prime example of the failure of democracy, where the protest of a million people in Britain did not dent the war-mongering determination of Bush and Blair. Even so, it is clear that the act of protest itself has symbolic and long-lasting value, if nothing else, as is evidenced by Nawaz's citing of the demonstrations against the Iraq War as having a huge impact on his conversion to liberalism while in prison. "These were human beings in London, campaigning for other human beings in Iraq," he told his fellow prisoners, showing them news clippings of the million-strong march of February 15, 2003, in London. As an eight-year-old, Jack had attended the Oxford version of this march alongside us, his parents. Nawaz had found himself touched by the fact that the largest demonstration against the Iraq War was not in Egypt, Saudi Arabia, or Pakistan, but in the U.K.

I had a reconnection to Nawaz's book some months after I read it when one of Jack's school friends turned up on our doorstep. He looked as if he had been sleeping rough, and, sure enough, he told us that his Muslim family had declared him an "apostate" after he'd announced he no longer believed in Islam, and had kicked him out of the house. After we invited him in, he told us that he was staying with friends until he could take up his place to study philosophy at University College London. He spotted Nawaz's book on our bookshelf and told us that he'd been greatly affected by it and had signed up as an anti-radicalization volunteer at the university on behalf of Quilliam. At this time — in 2015 — I was unaware of the controversy surrounding Quilliam — i.e., that it was used by successive prime ministers to push a governmental agenda of targeting and spying on Muslims. It was only later, as I deepened my knowledge of the heterogeneous Muslim community, and as John and I became subject to the same targeted suspicion ourselves, that I realized that Nawaz was seen by many as a convenient ally for those who believed that Islam itself was the problem.

In the grip of trying to save Jack from himself, however, I believed that a Nawaz-type re-examination of belief was what he needed. Furiously typed conversations with him in the short space of time he was online weren't doing the trick. And the government's position — that every young person who had gone to Syria was an unredeemable terrorist — was an additional, massive hindrance. To me, it seemed to be breath-taking hypocrisy on the government's part for them to commission anti-radicalization briefing papers from people like Nawaz, an ex-Islamist, while at the same time refusing to give the benefit of the doubt to disillusioned jihadists currently in Syria and Iraq. Particularly, since the government's intransigent position meant the difference between life and death to young people like our son.

Chapter 10

The Tabqa dam

Turkey, May 2015

In May 2015, our hopes were raised that we might be able to see Jack in Turkey. This was the first time since he had left a year before that he had made any indication that he might be able to meet us. Being hopeful was a new feeling, and I didn't want it to slip away. Jack had messaged me while I was at work at the Mindfulness Centre and had asked if I could send him money "for living, and for glasses." (He had lost his glasses some months before. His eyesight wasn't very poor, but he'd had his eyes tested shortly before he left, and the optometrist had said he should probably wear glasses occasionally.) I asked him if he could get to Turkey safely so we could give the money to him, and he replied, "Inshallah." It seemed that finally we would be able to lure him out of his dangerous situation, since once we had got him over the border, there was no way we were letting him go back in again. I asked him to message me again that evening when I wasn't at work so we could plan.

It turned out that our hope was short-lived, as Jack explained a few days later that he wouldn't be going to Turkey himself but would send someone. This wasn't what we'd counted on — there was no point giving him money if he wasn't going to use it to leave his location. The fragile plan collapsed before it had even begun, and our premature hopes were dashed. As if in recompense for the fact that we wouldn't be seeing him in person, Jack posted on Facebook a photo of himself standing on a rock at the Tabqa dam, on the Euphrates river, upstream from the city of Raqqa, in Syria. In the shot he was smiling and wearing a camouflage-type T-shirt, and appeared to be pointing one finger to the sky.

This photo has since been reproduced around the world, courtesy of the *Sunday Times*, which used it to accompany their article on Jack in January 2016. In the absence of much other data, the shot has been scrutinized for clues about Jack's activities in Syria. After our arrest months after it was posted, the police used an imaging expert to prove, via comparison with commercial satellite imagery, that the picture had been taken at the Tabqa dam (although since Jack had helpfully captioned the image "At Tabqa dam" himself, it didn't seem to require a great deal of expert effort to reach the same conclusion).

Newspaper commentators made a big fuss over the fact that Jack seemed to be wearing combat-type trousers, even though John had bought these for him at Sports Direct before Jack left Britain. With regard to the camouflage-type shirt, I imagine there are lots of these knocking about in second-hand markets in Syria. It was the finger pointing to the sky that most excited the speculation of media commentators: this was the sign of ISIS, they declared, as distinctive as the Nazi salute or the raised fist of Black power. For these self-appointed experts, this proved that Jack was with ISIS. Other Muslim commentators pointed out that this gesture is merely the sign of *tawhid*, or oneness of God, which is made on a daily basis by Muslims at prayer, in the same way that the sign of the cross is made by Christians.

When I commented to Jack that he looked happy in the photo, he replied that he had been the happiest he could remember in a long time; he had been swimming with his friends, and the water had been so clean. It seemed, however, that we were no closer to persuading him that he would be a more useful Muslim, making use of his language talents and his sincere commitment to his faith, in a location away from a war zone.

ISIS territory, June–August 2015

In June, July, and August of 2015, ISIS was still in a strong position with regard to the territories it either controlled or had influence over. Although the terror group had lost Kobane on the Turkish border in January 2015, Tikrit (Saddam Hussein's hometown) in March 2015, and was to go on to lose Ramadi in December 2015, in the summer of 2015 it still had logistical or administrative control over many of the most important towns and territories in Iraq and Syria, including the vitally significant oil and gas fields. It was estimated that around this time, ISIS was earning $40 million per month from oil revenues alone, 43 percent of its income, with the rest being derived from taxation, looted money from banks, and trafficking in drugs and antiquities. In one of the ironies of war, it was revealed by Adam Szubin, U.S. Treasury undersecretary for terrorism and financial intelligence, that the "far greater amount" of Islamic State oil was being bought by Assad. "The two are trying to slaughter each other and they are still engaged in millions and millions of dollars of trade," he said.

The territories that had fallen under ISIS's control comprised the "cradle of civilisation" itself, i.e., the fertile crescent between the

Tigris and Euphrates, known in ancient times as Mesopotamia. Key towns held or controlled by ISIS along the Tigris in Iraq included Mosul, Bajii, and Samarra. Along the Euphrates, they included the towns of Falluja, Ramada, Hit, and Haditha in Iraq, and Qaim and Deir ez-Zor, as well as the capital Raqqa, in Syria.

It was reported that during most of 2015, when the tax base of ISIS territory was extensive, ISIS fighters were paid good salaries, about $400 to $600 per month (compared to $200 per month earned by a public-sector worker in Iraq). It was only toward the end of 2015 that these salaries were cut by half, because the self-proclaimed "caliphate" had by then lost roughly 22 percent of its territory (and tax base) since the height of its powers in 2014. In addition, the price of oil had fallen drastically and was at its lowest point in twelve years.

The Caliphate

Given all the debate since ISIS's takeover about what a caliphate is, and what it isn't, I decided I should do some of my own research to find out. What I discovered was that the issue of a Muslim caliphate is a tricky one.

Generally, I dislike trawling through religious arguments. When religious callers like the Jehovah Witnesses come to the door, it is always John who engages them in hours of pointless debate, whereas I always firmly shut the door (after smiling apologetically, of course, since the press don't call me *middle class* for nothing). My research now, however, had a point to it. I found out that a caliphate is an Islamic State that is mentioned twice in the Qu'ran and is central to the Islamic faith. It is governed by a *caliph*, which means "successor to the Prophet Muhammad." Sunni Muslims believe that Abu Bakr, the father of Muhammad's wife Aisha, was

Muhammad's rightful successor, and that future caliphs should be elected by the Muslim community. Shia Muslims, on the other hand, believe that Muhammad divinely ordained his cousin and son-in-law Ali ibn Abi Talib to be the next caliph, making Ali and his direct descendants Muhammad's successors. This difference of opinion over the rightful successor to Muhammad after his death in 632 CE is the basis of the fundamental divide between the Sunni and Shiites, and at the heart of all the sectarian disagreements between them.

The caliph can be seen as the equivalent of the Catholic pope, i.e., a religious ruler who unites the world by virtue of their faith — no matter where its adherents reside globally. This comparison to a spiritual, rather than geographical entity, might explain why a 2008 YouGov poll revealed that 33 percent of British Muslim students supported the notion of a worldwide Islamic caliphate based on sharia law. Seen in this context, a caliphate seems rather less sinister than the rhetoric surrounding ISIS suggests; i.e., it can be viewed as a religious ideal that Muslims should strive for in a spiritual sense, similar to "creating the Kingdom of God on Earth," something I remember from my Christian Sunday School days.

Talking to Jack's British Muslim friends about a caliphate, I learned that, as pious Muslims, they believe they should strive to establish it on earth, but they are constrained by the constitutional realities of the countries they live in to create it in any legal or political sense. Although these friends are Wahhabists — the ultraconservative branch of Islam that is the state religion of Saudi Arabia — they recognize that establishing a political caliphate in Britain would require revolution, and that most people would, if given the choice, prefer to live under an unjust ruler (or one not compatible with their religious or political views) than to see their children die. Given the hundreds of thousands of deaths that have occurred in Syria and Iraq in the past five years, it is likely that many families, no matter what their religious, ethnic, sectarian, or political views, feel the same way.

Many of the young British people who were enticed to Syria by online recruiters stated they wanted to live a pure Islamic life in a caliphate. Some no doubt believed they were answering al Baghdadi's — the caliph's — call for "doctors, judges, engineers, and experts in Islamic jurisprudence to help develop the caliphate." One young woman who was inspired to leave for Syria in October 2014 was Tareena Shakil, the first woman from the U.K. to be convicted of joining the Islamic State, who later said that her decision had been based on her desire to "live a Muslim life" and "not to kill anybody." The court, however, was not convinced by her tale of disillusionment after less than three months in the country, and she was sentenced to six years in prison.

In his early messages to us, Jack, too, expressed a rosy view of the caliphate, as if he sincerely believed that it could be the Kingdom of God on Earth. He was obsessed with being a good Muslim, and had convinced himself that he needed to follow to the letter the teachings of Muhammad, as well as the early teachings of the first Muslims in the seventh century in order to save his own soul. After he left, I learned through my reading that the doctrine he adhered to was known as "Salafism," as it followed the example of the first three generations of Muslims, known collectively as the *salaf.* Salafism's relevant religious authority derived from a *hadith*, which quotes Muhammad as saying, "The people of my own generation are the best, then those who come after them, and then those of the next generation." A June 2015 article in the *Economist*, quoted on Wikipedia, explains: "The [Salafist] movement is often divided into three categories: the largest group are the purists (or quietists), who avoid politics; the second largest group are the activists, who get involved in politics; and the smallest group are jihadists, who form a small minority." Salafists are often associated with al-Qaeda and

ISIS, since they preach an ultraconservative version of the religion, so it was reassuring to learn that Salafist-jihadists actually make up only a small part of the movement as a whole.

We knew that when Jack had first started looking into Islam, he had researched several groups, and at different points had affiliated himself to various doctrines, such as Sufism. Why he finally settled on Salafism, I don't know, but John and I postulated that it was the austerity of the purist religion that appealed to him. The summer before he left, we had gone on a family holiday to Morocco, and Jack had been captivated by a rundown village of only a few, crumbling baked-earth houses, one tiny shop, and several skinny goats wandering about the dirt paths. Most teenagers would think they would die of boredom in a few minutes, but Jack decided it was the most interesting, wonderful place he had ever been to, and claimed he could stay there forever. Perhaps what we did wrong as parents was simply to give him too much: too many plastic toys, PlayStations, electric train sets, heaps of Christmas presents, when all he wanted was a crumbling village and a skinny goat.

Early versions of the ISIS caliphate were viewed very differently from later ones, both by their adherents and by the local people whose cities were taken over. Much illuminating information about this issue has come from the research of Patrick Cockburn, one of the best contemporary writers, in my view, on the story behind the rise of ISIS. Cockburn interviewed many people living in al Baghdadi's caliphate, providing on-the-ground information that has been sorely missing from most Western accounts. One interview caught my eye as it had taken place in an Iraqi town that I knew Jack had been to. The Iraqi interviewed, a farmer, recalled the joyous day that ISIS first entered the city: "At the beginning … we were so happy and called it 'the Islamic Conquest.'" Most of the people were offering them feasts and warmly welcoming their chief fighters. ISIS's sharia board of authority that was set up to resolve local problems at first was fairly lenient, encouraging people to go to the mosque, rather than — as happened later — forcing them to, and delivering forty lashes if they didn't. ISIS's reply to a group of community leaders concerned about the coercion and punishment was that "even at the time of the Prophet Mohamed, laws were not strict at the beginning and alcoholic drinks were allowed in the first three years of Islamic rule." As Cockburn explains, only after Islamic rule had become strongly entrenched were stricter rules enforced.

This description of an early caliphate, and its later descent into fascism and barbarity, followed Jack's early expressions of support for an Islamic system and his subsequent denunciation of ISIS's un-Islamic practices. As Jack had not stayed long in the Iraqi town mentioned in the article, I wondered if his situation had been similar to that of the farmer, who had left his home town with his family when military conscription was enforced (previously, families could avoid conscription by paying a heavy fine). With regard to the increasing repression and harsh punishments within ISIS's caliphate, I knew that, despite Jack's habit of seeing what he wanted to see, sooner or later, he would wake up to the brutal realities of the caliphate's rule. Sure enough, this did happen, but by this time, he had already sent to me several positive messages about the potential benefits of the caliphate ("Christians are treated better than before — you wouldn't believe how they used to be persecuted"). These messages came to be cited as direct evidence of his membership of ISIS, despite a mountain of evidence to the contrary, and the obvious fact that it is possible to believe in a spiritual caliphate at the same time as disowning the brutal rule of ISIS.

During this time, John and I were questioning Jack as to whether he was taking, or considering, an active combat role in Syria or Iraq. We were constantly terrified that he was going to get himself killed, and believed that if he was at least working in a civilian rather than a military capacity, his chances of remaining alive were increased. He had already denied to John during a telephone conversation in late 2014 that he was with ISIS but had made the more disturbing comment to *E* in a Facebook message that he "wasn't *currently* fighting." We were determined to get to the bottom of what this actually meant and sent him many anguished questions over Facebook asking him to explain himself. For this, we have been raked over the coals by the police, as they have used the mere fact that we asked him questions as evidence that we had "reasonable grounds to suspect" that Jack was indeed a terrorist and that any money we sent to him could therefore be seen as money to support terrorism. The fact that we were very careful to satisfy ourselves that the money we sent him would be used to *get him away from terrorism* and not for anything else, was, for the police, beside the point.

Our situation came to resemble more and more the witch scene in *Monty Python and the Holy Grail*. To paraphrase: if she looks like a witch, and witches are burned, just like wood is burned, then she must be made of wood. And since wood floats, the way to determine conclusively that she is a witch is to throw her into a pond to see if she floats. Whip up the mob to agree that this is a good idea. The same false logic was being applied to us: if we asked Jack if he was fighting or involved in jihad, then we must think that he was fighting or involved in jihad or we wouldn't pose the question. The way to definitively prove that he was a terrorist was to arrest us (who had implicated ourselves by asking the question) and whip up the mob (the British public) to make them believe that the only way to keep Britain safe from terrorism is to put us (and him, when he returns) in prison. With regard to Jack's actual answer to our question as to whether he was a fighter or not, was that if he were a fighter, he wouldn't need to ask us for money (since presumably he would be earning a fighter's comfortable salary of $400 to $600 a month).

Facebook account hacking, July 2015

Around July 2015, John and I began to suspect that another person was using Jack's Facebook account. For a period of about two weeks, the messages on his account were disturbingly extreme, expressing hatred for the *kuffar* and for the American and British armies, and calling for violence against them. Apart from their highly alarming content, which did not match sentiments he had ever expressed before, there were other indications that these messages were not coming from him. One was that they were posted on his public page, whereas during the whole time he had been in Syria or Iraq, he had only ever posted publicly twice, and that had been merely to change his profile picture. Another indication was that whenever I went on Facebook and the "chat" section indicated that Jack's account was online, the green light would suddenly go out, showing that this person had immediately logged off. Jack had never done this before. I also thought that the strange messages were remarkably similar in style and content to those posted simultaneously on one of his Facebook friends' account. This friend, I noticed later in the press, was one of the nine British Sudanese medical students who had travelled from Khartoum to Syria and was killed in combat against Assad in this same month of July.

These violent Facebook messages during this two-week period formed the core of the police's case against us. What compounded the distress for us was that the worst of these messages was a comment on the account of one of his former school friends, who had posted a photo of himself and the rest of his British army graduation class. The comment from "Jack's" account mentioned "performing a martyrdom operation" on the people in this photo, something that particularly struck me as strange, since Jack and I had had a phone conversation only a month before, in which he had said martyrdom operations were "un-Islamic." The school

friend's mother — who was from our same neighbourhood friendship circle, and with whom we used to go on annual camping trips
to Cornwall — reported the comment to the police. She was now
one of the key prosecution witnesses against us, and the next time
we saw her would not be on a beach in Cornwall but on the witness
stand at the Old Bailey.

It was only later that Jack admitted his account had been hacked
by "an extremist I stupidly gave my password to." At the time, however, he made no such denials when we questioned him, horrified,
about the messages. In fact, he did not give an answer one way or
the other when we asked if the comments were by him, which made
me think that either they weren't, or he was somehow under duress
and was being forced to write such postings. Either way, it showed
the perils of communicating with him when we didn't know who
was reading the messages on his end, and made us fear that the
things we said to him could actually be putting him in danger from
the people around him. It was toward the end of 2015 that this fear
really became relevant when Jack needed to send us messages he
definitely didn't want anyone else to see.

All we knew in practical terms about Jack's situation around
July and August 2015 was that he was in Raqqa and was waiting for his wife to join him. We knew he had seen bombings and
dead people in the street, including a taxi driver and his young
son, whom Jack said had been killed in a drone strike targeted at a
"British brother," who had been in the taxi at the time. What Jack
was actually doing in Raqqa we had no idea. I wondered if he was
perhaps part of the secret underground resistance forces against
ISIS, and that his angry Facebook messages against the *kuffar* were
part of his cover, as well as born out of genuine horror about the
coalition bombings that were killing civilians as well as fighters.

My probing questions to him around this time concerning his
role in the politics of the region were repeated back to me by the

police in their later interrogations (one of which was a marathon ten-hour session at the police station, relieved only by two five-minute breaks). "Do you know what Raqqa is?" they asked (yes, I did); "Why would he be there?" (I didn't know, but I really wished he wasn't); "Do you think it's possible to live there and not fully comply with what they say?" (I'm sure the situation on the ground is extremely complicated, but I imagine in order to survive you have to toe the line).

What I didn't say was that I'm sure the situation is not only beyond my own understanding; it is also beyond the understanding of a British police officer based in a provincial U.K. town. And since Jack was not there to defend himself, I was having to do it on his behalf, implicating myself in the process. The issue seemed to go back to John's initial conversation with Detective Sergeant *M* about the Raqqa-based kebab seller. The logic of this scenario had run thus: if the Syrian kebab seller is selling his wares to an ISIS fighter and paying taxes to the state authorities, then he is, de facto, supporting ISIS. The fact that he could possibly be killed by ISIS if he didn't sell them his wares was beside the point ("He could move," DS *M* had said). Although, of course, not to any European country, since, apart from the fact that there are checkpoints surrounding Raqqa preventing people from going anywhere, the Europeans were and are busy making sure no one enters their own place of safety (by, for example, sending international patrol boats to the Mediterranean to turn refugees back to Libya; building a wall in Calais to prevent asylum-seekers from boarding lorries; or introducing border controls in Hungary and Austria in breach of the Schengen agreement, which was set up to allow for the free movement of people through Europe). According to our lawyers, whom we contracted far too late for them to contribute to our many "cozy chats" with the police, the kebab-seller gambit has never been tested in court. And it is highly unlikely to be, since it greatly muddies the waters when considered within the present, simplistic terms of U.K. terrorism legislation.

Around the time we suspected Jack's Facebook account was hacked, strange things also seemed to be happening to our phones and computers. Calls to our mobiles would be mysteriously and immediately blocked (we tested this ourselves by calling our phones from the home phone; sure enough, the call was blocked each time). Sometimes, after we sent an email, our computers would go into suspension for an hour or so, for no apparent reason (our broadband was working fine). Once, immediately after one of Jack's friends phoned me at work, my phone turned Japanese, and not even my young, tech-savvy colleague could set the default setting back to English. *E* suggested to me later that perhaps someone had pressed the factory reset button on my Sony phone, and this reset button had returned it to the manufacturer's original Japanese.

Most tellingly, once, when I was having a Facebook conversation with Jack on my phone, the message space reserved for my messages suddenly and spontaneously started to fill itself in, without my touching the keypad at all. This happened on three occasions during the same conversation, and was always a string of letters that made no sense, almost as if someone had leaned on a keyboard. One of these spontaneous messages even forms part of the police evidence against me, as the letters at one point had composed themselves into the phrase "kkk," and Jack had replied in typical fashion by saying "What's this kkk? Don't tell me you hate Black people as well as us terrorists." The "us terrorists" part of his sentence greatly exercised the police. "Look, he's even admitting it," they said. No, he's mocking people who believe all Muslims are terrorists, I replied. "So Jack jokes about terrorism?" they said. I could see where they were heading with this line of questioning. "Mocking, not joking," I said. "There's a difference. And anyway, actual terrorists don't call themselves terrorists, they call themselves freedom fighters or something."

Daft as it may seem, because of this conversation I would now have to defend myself in court against the police accusation that I believe terrorists are actually freedom fighters.

Of course, since the police were conducting a full-scale investigation into Jack, it would be strange if unusual things weren't happening to our phones and computers. Some of our fears about things that seemed bizarre and inexplicable were backed up by independent research by academics, and we realized that online snooping at any time wasn't just a suspicion; it was even justified by Facebook officials and accepted as the "new norm" by the Facebook generation. In May 2016, for example, a professor of mass communications at the University of South Florida revealed that the smartphone Facebook app uses people's microphones to listen to what is happening around them. Facebook officials accepted that this is indeed the case, but denied that the information derived from listening was used to target advertising or news feeds. Instead, they said, it "promotes the feature as an easy way of identifying what you are listening to or watching, to make it easier and quicker to post about whatever's going on," and moreover, it is not "*always*" listening. Personalized ads were connected to "people's interests" (I assumed as related to internet searches) or users' "demographic information," the company said, but not to audio collection.

This assertion does not accord with the experience I had during this summer of 2015: I had been talking about some Druid friends of John's and, mysteriously, a link to the Druid Facebook page appeared on my news feed the next day. I had not searched on *Druids* or visited any sites connected to them. Under the "new norm," this does not seem sinister; when put into the context of a terrorism investigation into two completely innocent people, it is chilling. Orwell's Big Brother is now so utterly pervasive, with such long tentacles, that ordinary people, who are so wedded to using its services have lost the energy, capacity, or even desire to challenge it.

Chapter 11

Money for glasses

Police visit, November 3, 2015

On November 3, 2015, we received another visit from the police. Again, there were several of them. When I answered the door, they told me not to get John out of bed as it was me they wanted to speak to.

It had come to their attention via their checking of my bank account that I had sent a sum of money to Jack a couple of months before. I had the choice of either being arrested and taken to the police station where I would receive the services of a duty solicitor, or voluntarily giving an interview at home there and then. Since being arrested would mean the police taking our computers and phones all over again, just when we'd managed to replace the last lot, I agreed to the voluntary interview.

It has been remarked upon by several people how naive we were in our dealings with the police. Many other parents of children who had gone to Syria had hired lawyers right from day one, and it was these lawyers who gave statements to the press. We, on the other hand, apart from not having money to pay lawyers, had no reason to believe that we ourselves were under suspicion for terrorism, and believed that we were co-operating with the police in order to get Jack back.

When I was read my rights, therefore, in our upstairs room, and asked on tape why I had waived my right to a lawyer, I replied that "I didn't think I had done anything wrong." Innocence is never a defence, as I now know, to my cost. During my interview I explained that I had sent £250 to a friend of Jack's in Lebanon in the hope that this friend might be able to help him buy glasses. (Jack had said he'd helped buy glasses for friends of his in the past. He had also told me that this friend — a Shia, an affiliation which I knew would be anathema to Sunni-supporting ISIS — was broke and had a large family he needed to support. Whether his friend was Shia or Sunni, Jack had explained, he was "a brother, whom it was his duty to support in this life.") Since I hadn't already made any donations to charities supporting refugees stuck in camps in Lebanon, I thought it would be a good way of directly supporting poor families there. Two hundred and fifty pounds wasn't a large sum, but would go a long way in a place like Lebanon: enough for a pair of glasses for Jack as well as food for his friend's family. I also thought that by sending money I might be creating some sort of social obligation, whereby, in return, his friend might be able to help Jack get to safety in Lebanon or elsewhere.

When the interview ended, the detective constable (whom we would get to know fairly well in the months to come) reassured me that I wouldn't be arrested as a result of my statement. He told me that I was protected by virtue of the fact that I was a parent: if I had been a friend, it might have been a different story. Although his concluding words were "you're not a criminal, Sally," he warned me that they might not be so nice next time.

That afternoon, police technical staff downloaded material from our computers (we had agreed to this procedure as an alternative to having the actual computers taken away). I decided to take advantage of their presence in our living room by asking them if they could possibly, while they were at it, correct the annoying pop-ups on my computer that were driving me crazy; they duly obliged. We also chatted to the police about a documentary that had recently come out, and which they recommended we watch. This documentary, *My Son the Jihadi*, had been made by Richard Kerbaj. Now whenever I hear this journalist's name I feel like brandishing a wooden stake and hissing through my teeth, but at the time we didn't know who Kerbaj was. This documentary prominently featured a case worker from a deradicalization charity based in London named the Active Change Foundation (ACF), and the police recommended that we contact this charity as well. Before they left, the detective constable told us that "there was no evidence Jack had done anything wrong," and that he was nothing like the brutal jihadi who was featured in the documentary — comments which made me wonder what extra information the police had about Jack that they weren't telling us.

That evening, John and I watched *My Son the Jihadi* on TV, and had tears streaming down our faces at the childhood footage of the English boy who had joined al-Shabaab and was killed in combat in Kenya in 2015. The police had told us that they might be able to arrange for us to meet his mother, also called Sally, and we told them that yes, we would like that, since so far, we hadn't managed to meet any other parents in a situation similar to ours. Although Sarah Khan, the director at the charity Inspire, had told us more than a year before that she would try to form a discussion group for parents of radicalized children after I had sent her a donation of £250, nothing had ever come of it. It was only later that we discovered that the police's helpful suggestion about putting us in contact with Sally Evans wasn't, in fact, motivated by altruistic concern for our welfare, but something much more sinister.

Prevent program

After my near-arrest, the police decided we needed more support. In our naïveté — reinforced by the fact I had been told I "wasn't a criminal" — we assumed this meant the police believed we need more social support to help us in our distressing situation. It was only later that we learned from a deradicalization charity that worked closely with the police that we were being offered support so that we ourselves "didn't slip into terrorism" (an odd phrase, I thought; no one inadvertently "slips into" murder).

In any event, two kindly seeming Prevent officers, not in uniform, turned up one afternoon to talk about any issues we might have. We already knew one of them and had found her to be genuinely concerned about helping us. The other was a senior officer who had many years of experience on the Prevent program. Over tea, we discussed issues such as what, exactly, was an extremist. Their answer for that came back immediately: an extremist was someone who opposes British values. Listening to the officer reel them off quickly, we discovered these values included democracy, rule of law, individual liberty, mutual respect, and tolerance for those with different faiths and beliefs. We then talked about the definition of a terrorist, which appeared to be someone opposed to British values who uses violence.

We did not get into the thorny territory of discussing whether someone was a terrorist if they were involved in another country's internal conflict where British values were not very much in evidence (e.g., was Britain breaking international law by bombing Syria, since — although we don't like it — Assad's government is, in legal terms, the UN-recognized, legitimate government of Syria?). To get into such territory seemed to go beyond the remit of a Prevent officer, although wasn't the whole discussion we were having beyond the Prevent remit? Surely it was more politics than policing. We had already been told by the police, in earlier discussions, that *if the political situation were to change, the definition of a terrorist could change, too* — i.e., today's terrorist could be tomorrow's ally. With arguments such as these, with the government and police being confused as to which definition applied when, it was no wonder that we as parents were confused. However, as I said, this was the discussion we *didn't* have.

During our conversation, the senior Prevent officer revealed that he was an evangelical Christian. He mentioned this as if it were a matter for disclosure, in the same way as a politician is obliged to declare company shares or party donations. Privately to me later, John expressed his shock at the revelation: he thought it was outrageous that an evangelical Christian could be a senior Prevent officer. I, on the other hand, thought that the officer's personal religion shouldn't matter: after all, wasn't that what our society should be aiming for, that people should be judged on their actions, as opposed to their creed? I argued that the officer should be able to separate his religious beliefs from his job, and Britain has a long tradition of the separation of church and state. I did concede, however, that the officer might not be so upfront about his disclosure to the Muslim families he met during the course of his job, and also that it would be unlikely that his Muslim equivalent — i.e., a fundamentalist Muslim — would ever hold his position of Prevent officer.

It is no secret that the Prevent program is hugely unpopular with Muslims, and it is not difficult to see why. Placing an entire community under suspicion, watching them closely for signs of "pre-criminal" behaviour, and then criminalizing anyone who does not report any suspected "thought crime," is the absolute worst strategy a government could come up with. Such a perfect climate for the fostering of resentment and victimhood is without a doubt going to create a breeding ground for radicals. In our case (as we saw later when the police statements against us were served), the police believed it was evidence of Jack's guilt that he didn't trust the police, and evidence of our guilt that we weren't at all surprised that Jack didn't trust the police. "If you don't have anything to hide, you don't have anything to fear," is clearly their motto. To us, the exact opposite occurred: we trusted the police (at least up to the point they arrested us) and were charged with one of the worst charges on the statute books as a consequence. It seems that, for us, a much more appropriate statement about privacy comes from Edward Snowden, who said, "Arguing that you don't care about the right to privacy because you have nothing to hide is no different from saying you don't care about free speech because you have nothing to say."

R, the more junior officer present that afternoon, was at pains to explain to us that the Prevent program wasn't aimed just at Muslims in the fight against extreme Islamic ideologies, it was also aimed at other extreme ideologies, such as the far right, Irish republicanism, and animal rights groups. She gave the example of a young person she had been working with who showed worrying anti-immigrant tendencies. During the course of her work with him, he was asked if he would like to receive a professional analysis of his DNA, which would reveal his genetic origins. When the test showed that his ancestors were from Eastern Europe, he realized he wasn't pure British after all. This realization, she said, had formed an important turning point in his deradicalization process.

This all seemed very well, but we couldn't help thinking that the other groups added into the Prevent program appeared to be mere "window dressing," designed to hide the fact that Islam was the true target. It seemed hard to believe that a young person showing Irish republican or far-right tendencies would be given a mentor and enrolled into a social care program of deradicalization in the same way as someone expressing an interest in Syria. Figures showed that, by 2013, 14 percent of referrals to Prevent were due to far-right extremism, while 57.4 percent were of Muslims. There is overwhelming evidence in the mainstream press and on Islamic fora that the Prevent program is bitterly resented by many Muslims, who believe that the resultant stigmatization of their community is a direct cause of increased hate attacks on Muslims in Britain.

Looking back on our discussions with the Prevent officers from the viewpoint of our arrest two months after their visit, John and I realized we were a perfect gift to counter-terrorism officers. We were living proof of their lack of discrimination in their targeting of extremist suspects. "Look," they could say to their Muslim detractors. "We're not just picking on you. We're picking on white people, who live in beautiful Oxford, who are middle class, not alienated or deprived, and even describe themselves as atheists." The feeling of being a scapegoat for all of society's ills and being a damned good public relations exercise for the police in the process, is something that daily fills us with anger, resentment, and despair.

One piece of evidence against me that the police unearthed from my computer was a paragraph I had written in April 2014 about my objections to the government's new policy of enlisting Muslim women in the "fight against terror." In mid-April 2014, the government had launched its new counter-terrorism strategy, asking Muslim wives and mothers to be the first line of defence against terrorism by reporting their menfolk for signs of radicalization. Events were held in London, Manchester, and Birmingham with teams of police, Prevent officers, and women from community groups enlisted to get the government's message across. Police officers were quoted as saying the Prevent program operated in the "pre-criminal" space, which seemed like a piece of nonsense. Isn't every person operating in the pre-criminal space if they haven't committed a crime?

My response to this news — like every middle-class leftie person's response to something that perturbs them — had been to write a letter to the *Guardian*. In it, I expressed the opinion that this strategy would backfire by turning a whole community against the police. To me, the comparison to Nazi Germany, where the populace was urged to inform against the Jews, and imprisoned if they didn't, or the comparison to Mao's China, where children were urged to denounce their counterrevolutionary parents, was very apposite. This last point I didn't make in my letter, but I did (anonymously) say that as the mother of a convert, I believed that dealing with idealistic young men who talked about going to Syria was a matter best dealt with in the home; after all, in Islam, "paradise lies at the feet of the mother." In addition, many of these young men talked about fighting against tyranny in Syria in the same way young British men had talked about defeating Franco in the Spanish Civil War. George Monbiot, for example, wrote an article for the *Guardian* in February 2014 to this effect, hypothesizing that if the Terrorism Act 2006 (which forbids fighting abroad for a "political, ideological, religious or racial motive") had been in existence in the 1930s, George Orwell and Laurie Lee would have been arrested as terrorists, rather than hailed as heroes, on their return from the Spanish Civil War. That Orwell and Lee were "fighting to defend an elected government against a fascist rebellion," Monbiot adds, "would have no bearing on the case." It is difficult to believe that the *Guardian* would print Monbiot's article in today's political climate, in which even raising a comparison between Orwell and a jihadi would risk being labelled a "terrorist sympathizer" — the term given to those MPs who voted against air strikes in Syria in December 2015. And George Monbiot, despite being someone we know in Oxford and who is in a position to write articles about the ethics of our dilemma, has never dared go near the topic of ISIS again.

In light of subsequent events that showed I was, in fact, unable to deter my son from leaving to follow what he thought of as his Muslim duty, my letter looks naive and misguided. The *Guardian* certainly didn't bother printing it, perhaps to protect me and my "pre-criminal" view from reaching the public eye. Even so, having it on my computer now stood as evidence of my collusion with radical Islam, and in our subsequent trial, I ended up having to defend myself against it in court. However, I still believe that Prevent would not have deterred Jack from leaving, since the program would have concluded, like us, that he was off to visit a friend in Jordan. And I also believe that the Prevent program has damaged community relations in Britain to a huge extent, while making the population as a whole no safer from the threat of terrorism.

Chapter 12

Anti-radicalization

Active Change Foundation (ACF), November–December 2015

Walthamstow Central is a bustling, multi-ethnic neighbourhood in northeast London, not far from Tottenham Hotspur's home stadium. Its hodgepodge of winding residential streets, with their neat Georgian terraces; numerous small, independent shops offering TV repairs, sewing, money transfers, and payday loans; and busy cafés and restaurants with the cuisine of multitudinous ethnic groups on offer, combine to give the appearance of a thriving and hustling community, getting by on its diverse wits and resourcefulness. To my mind, it couldn't be less like Oxford, where human diversity is segregated into distinct areas: leafy North Oxford, with its wide streets and wealthy academic and professional populace; East Oxford, with its trust-fund hippies and organic tofu; and the council estate areas of Blackbird Leys and Rose Hill, which became famous in the early 1990s for their riots, joy riding, and burned-out cars. Only one area in Oxford came close to my first impression of Walthamstow, and that is the area in East Oxford around Cowley Road, the student and racially mixed neighbourhood, where Jack used to hang out with his Sudanese, Afghan, and Turkish friends when he was bunking off college.

John and I visited Walthamstow in November and December 2015 because this was the location of the Active Change Foundation (ACF), the charity the police recommended to us to help us in our communications with Jack. ACF had agreed to take us on as a "de-radicalization project." We already felt we knew one of the project staff because he had appeared in the Richard Kerbaj documentary *My Son the Jihadi*: he had taken Sally Evans, the jihadi's mother, through the various steps that tend to characterize the radicalization process and the methods used to counteract each step. Since many of these methods were too late for us, since Jack was already in Syria, we were going to concentrate on how best to communicate with him, given that all his messages to us were couched in religious terms and that we didn't have much of a clue about Islamic theology, apart from how it was portrayed in the media. This fact was later reinforced by Shiraz Maher from King's College London, who told the police that it was obvious to him we did not know even the basics about Islam.

The first thing that struck us about the centre was its friendly, busy, and professional atmosphere. The shabby, nondescript entrance from the street opened up into a very different, more inviting world: first, a big, open space with numerous pool tables and table tennis tables, where groups of young people of various ages were making themselves at home.

In an area of urban deprivation like Walthamstow (rates of homelessness in Waltham Forest are the highest in London), the risk of radicalization is seen to be high. One of ACF's programs involves providing a safe space for young people as an alternative venue to the streets, offering a well-resourced contrast to the poverty of their surroundings. Indeed, one of the sources of interest to the media after the story about Jack broke, was why a youth from a comfortable background, who fitted none of the usual stereotypes about poverty, alienation, and radicalization, would choose to go to Syria. The answer is still elusive.

Next to the youth recreation space was a classroom-type area where very small children were being taught by an imam ("They are learning about the meaning of the words of the Qu'ran, not just reciting them," explained Hanif Qadir, the director.) Upstairs were the open-plan offices, where young women in hijab alongside women in jeans gathered in animated discussion groups, and young men with long beards sat at desks next to clean-shaven youths with trendy haircuts. "We are very mixed here," said Hanif. "There are Christians, Muslims, and everything in between." John and I immediately felt at ease and began to explain why we were there.

At the end of what was to be the first of several meetings at the charity's headquarters, it was agreed that we would start an "intervention" with Jack, supported by Hanif. Hampered as we were by our lack of Islamic knowledge, we would receive help in the form of phrases from the Qu'ran that would support our arguments. John would take the lead in this and would ask Jack to explain his notion of the religion to him. This would be counter to the approach we had taken to date, which had been to confront him head-on about what we assumed to be his beliefs. One of the things that we were hoping for at this stage was that Jack himself might eventually be a useful asset to ACF's deradicalization program, teaching alienated young Muslims that taking jihad to Syria was not a practical or useful way of solving oppression in the Middle East. We explained to Hanif and his colleague M that Jack was charismatic, with the gift of the gab, and kids seemed to gravitate toward him.

ACF had a "young leaders" program, whereby young people went out to schools and community centres to speak to their peers about radicalism. During our first meeting, one such young leader, nineteen years old and dressed in a smart suit, turned up at the offices after one of his speaking sessions and gravely shook hands with us all. I was struck by his poise and maturity; it seemed that this charity, which was running such impressive programs, with clearly dedicated staff (whose working day often didn't end until 9:00 p.m.), would finally be able to provide us with the help we needed.

And so it seemed, at least until a disastrous introduction was made to the journalist, Richard Kerbaj himself, who was to change our lives, and Jack's life, forever. In the early stages of our relationship with ACF, we believed that the intervention with Jack was indeed working. Jack had been able to explain himself to Hanif in the religious language the director understood, and we didn't; and he was able to explain the "creedal differences" between his views and those of the jihadi group everyone assumed he was part of.

Certainly, at the time of our meetings with ACF, we never could have imagined that the kindly, avuncular director would completely betray us and become a chief prosecution witness against us. His later witness statement explained that he had purposefully been duplicitous in telling us one thing and his handler at the Metropolitan Police another, because he hadn't wanted us to disengage from the intervention he was conducting. Although he had told us in our sessions that he was using his "high-level contacts in government" to help us send money legally to Jack to escape Syria — including a mysterious figure he called "M" in the Lake District whom he wanted us to meet — he later maintained in court that John and I had made this story up and were trying to present him as a Walter Mitty–type character. And although we had spent much time poring over maps of the region in order to plot Jack's escape route, his court-room denial of such assistance was pure theatre: "I had to twist my head back into my neck when I heard the police had given permission for the parents to send the money," Hanif said, as John and I stared at him in shocked disbelief from our position in the dock.

When our contact with him ceased after our arrest, we heard a few of his alarmist radio appearances, in which he warned about the threat of blood-thirsty, returning jihadis. Finally, everything made sense to us. Clearly, Hanif had hoped that he would be appointed the governmental expert in assessing each of these returnees and receive generous Home Office funds to do so. Unfortunately for him, the government didn't reward him for his co-operation with the police, and after using him, merely spat him out, withdrawing all their funding as they did. Since then, we understand, the charity has been evicted from its three-storey Walthamstow premises, and of its estimated twenty or so employees, only three remain.

Syria update, October–December 2015

After Russia's military entry into the Syrian crisis in support of Assad in September 2015, the whole power balance shifted significantly. The Syrian army, backed up by Russian air strikes, began to regain territory in the western part of the country, near Assad's power base in Damascus. Russia, a long-standing ally of Syria, had a particular interest in protecting its own military base, Tartus, which was located on the Mediterranean and strategically important as its only warm-water port south of the Black Sea. The base was also symbolic evidence of the friendship between Syria and Russia: Russia had been allowed to maintain access to the port after the fall of the U.S.S.R. as part of a deal that wrote off Syria's debts to the Soviet Union.

In November 2015, Putin increased his attacks on ISIS territory in retaliation for the bombing of a Russian airliner in Egypt
the month before that had killed all 224 people on board. On
November 20, 2015, Russia killed six hundred fighters in Deir
Ezzor province alone, in a series of eighteen cruise missile attacks
launched from the Caspian and the Mediterranean seas.

Although Russia insisted that it was targeting the economic base of ISIS and the rebel forces, such as oil refineries,
training camps, and ammunition depots, the U.S.-led coalition maintained that the Russian air strikes were also hitting
Western-backed rebel groups and civilian targets. In the proxy
war between Russia and its allies and the U.S.-led coalition that
followed Russia's entry into the crisis, issues surrounding the
numbers of civilians killed in each nation's air strikes were vigorously contested. The same attacks would be reported very differently in the Russian-owned *Russia Today* press and the Western
media: the latter would often report that when its own air strikes
killed civilians, it was because ISIS fighters were mixed in with
the civilian population and were deliberately using civilians as
"human shields."

The U.S.-led coalition was stepping up its own air strikes after
the ISIS-claimed attacks in several different locations in Paris,
including the Bataclan theatre, where 130 people were killed on
November 13, 2015. The U.K. government added its voice to the
increasing outrage by voting on December 2, 2015, to join the air
strikes on Syria. The country's antiwar protestors, who argued that
increased air strikes would not make Britain any safer, were defeated 397 to 223 in the House of Commons vote.

With the ratcheting-up of the war by Western and Russian
forces, ISIS began to lose territory. By December 2015, it was estimated that ISIS had lost 14 percent of its territory since January
2015. Much of its territory in northern Syria, including the crucial

Syrian border-crossing town of Tal Abyad, was lost to Kurdish fighters. In Iraq, it lost Tikrit and the Baiji oil refinery.

The ancient Syrian city of Palmyra is a potent symbol of the violent struggle between the war's opposing powers, and the cultural devastation that occurred during ISIS's rampage through Iraq and Syria. Capturing the city in May 2015, ISIS destroyed tombs, temples, and antiquities, including the two-thousand-year-old Temple of Bel and the Temple of Baalshamin, a World Heritage Site. Acts of destruction included the lopping off of the heads of statues as a demonstration of ISIS's victory over the site's pagan heritage. Echoing the public outrage that greeted the destruction of the Mostar Bridge in the Yugoslavia War twenty years earlier (arguably exceeding the outrage over the destruction of the populace), UNESCO described the blowing up of the Temple of Baalshamin as a "war crime." It was later, in March 2016, that Russia and the Syrian forces gained an equally symbolic victory by recapturing Palmyra, with Russia marking its success by staging a concert by Saint Peterburg's symphony orchestra in the ruins of Palmyra's Roman amphitheatre.

With many foreign ISIS fighters becoming more aware of the group's brutality and realizing that much of the fighting was against other Muslims and not Assad, there were increased reports of defections. By September 2015, the Syrian Observatory for Human Rights reported that 185 ISIS defectors had been killed by ISIS; and by October 2015, Aljazeera America reported that all men between the ages of fifteen and twenty-five were required to register with the police in Raqqa, prompting fears of imminent military conscription. Defectors who had managed to escape spoke about brutal punishments meted out to those caught attempting to flee the city, including stoning, shooting, beheading, and crucifixion in the public square. At the beginning of January 2017, it was reported by the activist group Raqqa Is Being Slaughtered Silently that one

ISIS militant was even ordered to kill his own mother in front of hundreds of people after she urged him to leave the city. In response to the tide of defections in Raqqa, ISIS was putting up barriers and checkpoints around the city, trapping those who remained inside.

Jack's messages, December 2015

It was against this backdrop of defections and brutal ISIS reprisals that we received Jack's messages in early December 2015. He was asking us to send him money so that he could leave the hell that was Raqqa, and his messages were urgent. The situation was every parent's nightmare: their child was in danger and they were powerless to do anything about it. Aware of the fact that we had been warned by the police against sending money, we asked our Prevent officer what we could do. She promised she would speak to her superiors.

The events that followed, in the month of December 2015, constituted the set of circumstances that led to our arrest in January 2016. We liaised with ACF, the police, and our Prevent officer to try to obtain the necessary permission to send the money. Finally, on December 27, 2015, after another desperate message from Jack, our Prevent officer phoned to say we could go ahead. She had sought permission from her senior officer, who had said, "No court in the land would convict a parent for trying to save their child."

John phoned me in a state of high elation in order to give me the good news as I was walking back from a trip into town. At his words, the feeling I experienced was like a physical release of a huge burden; the relief rose in my chest, and I realized I was feeling happy for the first time in two years. This feeling was to last for two days. I plummeted back down to earth when the police investigator phoned me at the hospital where I was working to say the advice had been "premature," and we were to hold off sending the money.

A meeting had been arranged for officers to visit us at our house the following day in order to explain.

Communicating with Jack

People have said they don't know how we are able to cope with our son's being in a constant situation of extreme danger. Although I know they are just expressing their sympathy, the only response possible is that when you have no choice, you just have to get on with it: the alternative to coping on a day-to-day basis is curling up into a little ball and not getting out of bed.

I had experienced such a state of being with postpartum depression, and that deadening despair and feeling of utter worthlessness I would not wish on my worst enemy. But by the end of 2015, I was not depressed — I was angry. Anger motivates action, whereas depression has the effect of preventing any action at all. I didn't want antidepressants or sleeping pills from the doctor; I wanted strategies and help from official channels, and I wanted Jack to wake up from the mad, self-righteous state he was in.

Because he didn't fear death, believing that Allah had an appointed time of death for everyone, I could not appeal to his sense of self-preservation. His only concession was that, according to his religion, it was incumbent upon him not to throw himself into the path of danger (hence, I suppose, his statement that martyrdom operations were "un-Islamic"). This meant, he explained, that if the coalition or Russian planes were overhead, then he was obliged to take shelter. I knew I had to take comfort from small mercies such as this.

Of course, I was not always rational and brave and concentrating on action, rather than giving in to despair. Since Jack was always in the forefront of my mind, every little thing that happened in daily life could trigger panic-inducing thoughts. When I had a bad toothache, for example, and was treated on the National Health Service, I thought of what would happen if Jack had the same excruciating pain: his chances of receiving proper medical attention were slim because there were so few doctors or dentists, and those medical staff who hadn't fled to safety were busy treating severe battlefield injuries and victims of bomb attacks. When we were tucking into our Sunday lunch, I thought of him not having enough to eat or clean water, or being cold in the Syrian winter because of a lack of kerosene or electricity. These thoughts would become even more pressing three years on, when Jack was held in Kurdish detention in what we knew were squalid and life-threatening conditions. Constantly, I had to push my imaginings away, as there was absolutely nothing I could do, particularly after the police took away our passports after our arrests.

We were arrested on January 5, 2016, after we'd tried to send the money a day after the police had told us they had withdrawn their permission. Jack had needed the money for people smugglers in order to escape Raqqa, and had broken his cover in the city. We knew he had put himself in sudden, terrible danger and had told the police we wouldn't have been able to live with ourselves if we didn't do all we could to save his life. From our reading of press reports, we knew exactly what happened to people trying to leave ISIS territory and weren't prepared to entertain the idea that our son could be beheaded or crucified at any moment as a suspected potential defector.

Until our arrest, I had harboured ideas of camping on the Turkish border, trying to make contact with people who might cross into Syria and might somehow, miraculously, be able to get help to Jack. I knew that the parents of the Sudanese medical students who had gone to Syria from Khartoum were doing just that, and I'd thought I might be able to join them somehow. Now that the police had put paid to any rescue attempts, our anxiety had fewer, practical ways in which it could be usefully channelled in the search for solutions. I had to remind myself that there are many other families in my position: people whose relatives were soldiers, or fire fighters, or racing car drivers, who also live in constant fear that their loved ones will not return to them.

There have been occasions when I lost control of my rational self completely. Numerous times I had to leave work because I couldn't stop crying (on the last occasion, the NHS decided that perhaps it was better if I didn't try to work there anymore). In one instance, John handed me a piece of black plastic he'd found on the living-room floor, saying, "I believe this is yours." It was a piece of the phone that I'd hurled at the wall a few weeks before in a fury, in reaction to the legal bill for two thousand pounds, payable immediately, that I'd just received in the post. My desperation had been due to the fact that I knew we couldn't pay it. We didn't even have the funds for that month's rent.

My secret source of support was that I believed I would know telepathically if anything happened to Jack. Although I knew this was superstitious and without scientific foundation, I held on to it like a life raft. My basis for maintaining such a stance was three-fold. One was that Jack and I occasionally came out with the same words (mere coincidence, I knew). The second was that I had been told since I was a child that psychic ability runs through the female line of my family: my maternal grandmother was supposedly the seventh child of a seventh child (although I found out later she was actually the first child [out of seven] of a fifth child [out of eleven]), and she had known the moment of her daughter's death. The story went that she had stopped dead when out on a walk one day and had said, "Something's happened to R." It turned out that R, who had been a very large baby and had been damaged by forceps at birth, and who was away at a special school, had died at that exact moment. The third was that I had experienced several predictive dreams in which I learned of the birth dates of my and my friends' children. In the case of Jack, I had dreamed he would be four days late, which he was. In an example of one friend, who only discovered she was pregnant when she was about eight months along, and was therefore very unsure of her conception date, I dreamed that her baby would be born eleven days from the date of my dream, "within school hours." Her son was born on the predicted date, at 2:40 p.m.

While my rational self knows that this is mumbo-jumbo, I still find it consoling, and have a residual belief that there may be phenomena of psychic closeness to people in our lives that we don't yet understand. It seems no weirder to me to believe this than to believe that the hopes and wishes that we project into the sky are somehow looked upon favourably by a divine being. This doesn't mean that I don't appreciate the sentiment when friends and family say they are praying for us; it just means that, like homeopathy, I can't see how it works.

Although it feels as if I haven't slept properly for several years, and most nights I have horrible dreams about drownings, suffocation, missing limbs, and bombings, I convince myself these have nothing to do with Jack. My only accurate predictive dreams to date have been connected to births, so these violent dreams I can dismiss as just being the products of anxiety. When I lie awake for hours after being woken by such a dream, I use the time to devise my overall strategies to get my family's life back in order, or just to make plans for the next day.

With regard to the technical aspects of communicating with Jack, the complications were many. First, we knew that every word was read by MI5. We knew the phones were bugged and our Facebook conversations monitored in real time. We also suspected that bugs had been placed in our house, particularly when a couple of electricians turned up to "check all of our electrical sockets and smoke alarms," ostensibly to "confirm that we were receiving adequate electricity supply and fire protection." No one had bothered in the past ten years to check that we were receiving adequate electrical power or fire protection, but apparently the landlady had been convinced she needed to comply with the terms of the "electrical certificate," so we were not able to object. (Although when I questioned one of the electricians as to whether he was planting bugs, he stormed out of the house saying he "hadn't wanted to do this job in the first place." Which seemed an odd thing to say.) Now whenever John and I want to convey the fact that someone is listening to us, instead of casting our eyes heavenward to indicate the presence of God, we cast our eyes ceiling-ward at the smoke alarm to indicate the presence of MI5.

Second, we knew that there was a danger of Jack's messages being read at his end. Newspaper reports revealed that ISIS officials could demand to see personal phones at any time and that people were being imprisoned or worse for suspect messages. We also knew that a number of foreigners had been killed for being "spies." It seemed to us that there was a danger of Jack being seen as a likely spy suspect since he kept in fairly regular contact with us, unlike, we believed, many other young people who had gone out to Syria. These factors meant that we were much more careful about saying things that might put him in danger than we were about things that might alert the authorities at our end. We also told him that he should say whatever he needed to say in order to stay alive; we strongly believed that, despite his protestations that Allah alone had control over his life and death, he clearly wanted to live.

Chapter 13

Arrest

Police advice sheet, December 30, 2015

On December 30, 2015, I was summoned to a meeting at our house to meet the detective constable and the civilian investigating officer so that they could explain why we couldn't send the money after all. As I had to leave work early, I ended up having to explain to my NHS manager that Jack was in Syria. Up until then, during my five months of employment, I had managed to keep this quiet. Although (or perhaps because), she was a reservist sergeant in the territorial army and still undertook occasional tours in Afghanistan, she was very understanding of my situation, if shocked, and did her best to be supportive in the months ahead.

That afternoon, the conversation between us and the police and our friend *K*, who had arrived to provide us with moral support, raged back and forth. I discovered there was a document that had "extra information" on Jack's activities that the police would reveal to us, but not until ten days from then, as it "still needed to be redacted." (In actual fact, a document revealing information we didn't already know was never forthcoming, so for a very long time we were in the dark as to what extra "secret intelligence" information the police held on Jack, if any. It would be almost three years later that the police finally responded to our lawyer's disclosure request by saying that, actually, they had no such information at all.) The DC gave us an advice sheet, which stipulated that if we did send the money to Jack, we would be "liable to prosecution," but that they could not prevent us from doing so.

As he was leaving, DC *N* said he would return in five days' time to take a statement from me as to why I believed Jack had left the "group he was with." He said he would bring coffee and asked me what coffee I liked to drink. Resenting the fact that he was turning a life and death situation into a picnic, I snapped, "Whatever we terrorists drink." Later on, when his witness statement was served to us, I saw that he had included my retort in capital letters, presenting it as evidence of my self-confession.

With regard to the police's inability to prevent us from sending money to Jack, this turned out to be untrue. When I tried to send a payment the next day to provide Jack with the means to escape, it was blocked by Western Union, who held it until after the completion of our trial. And when we were both arrested five days after this for sending money, "having reasonable cause to suspect that it would or might be used for purposes of terrorism," it turned out that we hadn't been just "liable to prosecution": the police were determined to press hard for a prosecution. All they needed was for the Crown Prosecution Service to agree.

Sally Lane

Richard Kerbaj, January 2016

The circumstances of our arrest were well known, having been splashed all over the papers. What made everything infinitely worse and provided a point of no return for us in terms of prosecution, was the involvement of a *Sunday Times* journalist, Richard Kerbaj, whose unscrupulous behaviour may have cost us our freedom, and much more importantly, put Jack's life in greatly increased danger. Our first mistake in agreeing to meet Kerbaj in January 2016 was not to do any research into his previous articles. Even a cursory glance at his nearly three hundred article titles — stretching over eight years — would have given a large clue as to his political agenda: titles such as "Met Ignored Extremism Among My Fellow Muslim Officers" (September 2016); "Jailed Islamists May Murder Warden and Post Video Online, Government Fears" (March 2016); "Charities Bully on Doorstep for 'Terrorist Funds'" (February 2015); and perhaps most sinister of all, "Muslim Population in Britain Rising 10 Times Faster Than Rest of Society" (January 2009). Clearly, Kerbaj didn't believe that Muslims were part of society, like the rest of us. This last article was given extra spin by the former U.K. Independence Party leader, Lord Pearson, when he quoted it to support his claim that since Muslims "are breeding ... faster than the rest of us" it was hard to know "at what point they reach such a number we are no longer able to resist the rest of their demands."

If we had dug a little deeper, we would have found out that Richard Kerbaj had been personally chosen by Rupert Murdoch to work alongside Mazheer Mahmood, the fake sheik, in writing unsubstantiated stories about prominent Palestinian supporters being accused of "terrorist" sympathies. One such case is cited by Dr. Robert Lambert, co-director of the European Muslim Research Centre at the University of Exeter, in which Mahmood attempted to cast aspersions on the integrity of Mohamed Ali, CEO of Islam Channel TV in London, in a sting operation for the *News of the World*. This operation was followed up by a smear article on Ali in the *Times* by Richard Kerbaj, entitled "Nothing Criminal About Trying to Establish an Islamic State." As Lambert makes clear, Mahmood and Kerbaj's accounts were wholly discredited, and had been instigated as part of Murdoch's agenda of creating "suspect communities" through reporting that "fails to distinguish between terrorists and the communities in which they live." In a poignant case of poetic justice, Mahmood is now serving jail time for his part in perverting the course of justice in another case, that of the singer Tulisa Contostavlos, also a victim of one of his sting operations. No doubt, Tulisa is now feeling vindicated that the man who attempted to ruin her life is now receiving a dose of his own medicine.

When Kerbaj visited John and me on a Saturday at our house in Oxford in mid-January 2016, he told us that he had been "hand-picked by Murdoch" while still a young journalist in Australia. An Arabic speaker and a Druze, Kerbaj had certain advantages in infiltrating the Muslim communities he was reporting on, and Murdoch was keen to transfer him to London to work as his security correspondent for the *Sunday Times*. It was to become apparent with his article on us that Kerbaj was still using the same tactics he was well versed in using within the Murdoch empire in Australia: i.e., a scurrilous article in a rag such as the *News of the World*, followed up with a more educated-sounding article on the same topic in a "reputable" newspaper like the *Times*. In this way, Murdoch is able to target multiple audiences with the same message by pressing each audience's appropriate buttons. And each day, we, the obedient sheep, nosh on our Murdoch-served fodder before mindlessly discarding it the following day as so much waste product. So it is that journalists like Kerbaj laugh at our stupidity and media empires are made.

It was only much later that we discovered that there might have been another reason why Murdoch sent Kerbaj to London so expeditiously in 2008. In April of that year, the *Australian*, the newspaper for which Kerbaj then worked, had got into trouble over one of Kerbaj's articles that suggested Dr. Mohammad Abdalla, director at the Islamic Research Unit at Griffith University, had begged Saudi Arabia for $1.3 million to fund Islamic extremism. Only after two members of the Australian parliament intervened in support of the respected director was this claim shown to be fictitious. It is understood that the *Australian* chose to settle the matter quietly, rather than allow the case to appear in court. Shockingly, this case followed hot on the heels of a similar defamation case that also involved a false article by Kerbaj. In 2007, Sheik Abdul Salam Mohammed Zoud had successfully sued Kerbaj and Nationwide News Pty Ltd for claiming in a 2005 article that he had delivered a hate speech in Sydney urging insurgents to wage war against Australian soldiers. Zoud was able to prove he wasn't even in Australia at the time.

The reason for our carelessness in researching Kerbaj's background was that Active Change Foundation had recommended him as a sympathetic journalist who had agreed to help us in our predicament, which after our arrest had become much more clearly defined. We were parents who had been criminalized for attempting to help their son. Surely what was needed was the media on our side to highlight the societal implications of our situation, at the same time raising the important issue of the lack of government policy to deal with the hundreds of young British people who had gone to Syria only to suffer immense disillusionment. We had seen Kerbaj's documentary and knew that ACF trusted him to deal sensitively with their deradicalization work. We arranged with Kerbaj that all our dealings with him would remain confidential because of the risks to Jack's life, and that all resultant material would remain anonymous. We were also assured that our conversations with Kerbaj would be part of a long-term project that would gather information with the aim of helping other families in our situation.

It was clear on our first (and only) encounter with Kerbaj that he was admirably accomplished in the art of journalistic seduction. He was unexpectedly youthful, good-looking, and wore very expensive clothing. I felt flattered that he had taken the time to dress in a suit on a Saturday morning, when we were in our casual weekend garb. As I hung up his very heavy overcoat, which he removed carefully as if it were a piece of military equipment, I marvelled at the fineness of the cloth and the silkiness of its lining. As the day wore on, John and I relaxed in his company. His Australian accent, his articulate volubility, and his repeated use of the phrase, "I'm on your side, mate," combined to make us lower any residual guard we might have had, and we began to speak freely.

Looking back, I can see how Sally Evans, the mother of Thomas, the boy who had joined al-Shebab in Somalia, must have trusted him completely to tell her story, allowing a film crew into her home repeatedly, even when friends and family arrived to console her on the death of her son. When you are lonely and frightened, and don't know where to turn because all the official channels are closed to you as your son is a suspected criminal, it is very easy to be persuaded by a clever, handsome, silver-tongued journalist who continually assures you he is "on your side," while seeming to provide a sympathetic and understanding ear.

As a single parent, Sally Evans must, I imagine, have been even more susceptible to Kerbaj's sympathy; at least John and I had each other to talk to. In May 2016, *My Son the Jihadi* won a BAFTA award for best single documentary, and I am not in the least surprised that the judges were won over by the emotional power of the film. It is only when one thinks a little deeper about its messages that other, more disturbing, issues start to surface.

Issues, such as: Where are the Muslim voices in the film? I put this question to Kerbaj as he sat at our living-room table, telling us stories about his encounters with unusual foods at Iraqi banquets. "Other people have mentioned that," he said. "And my response is that the Muslim voice in the film is the mother of Thomas's wife, who was shot in the face by jihadis in Somalia."

This to me wasn't a very adequate response: the mother hadn't actually spoken at all in the film, and given that Thomas had converted to Islam in the U.K., surely it would have been helpful to explore issues surrounding the British Muslim response to radicalization. As it stood, although the documentary shows the devastating impact of radicalization on the family left behind, one is not left with any further understanding or the how, why, and what-should-be-done issues that the personal story raises. Now, knowing more about Kerbaj's work, and the audience he is aiming at, I can see that his documentary merely reinforces the prevailing narrative of "Muslims bad; they do terrible things; nice English families are destroyed by their actions." I have no doubt that, by taking on John and me — another white family — as his next project, Kerbaj was expecting to formulate an identical narrative out of our particular situation. It was clearly a stance that proved appealing to the BAFTA judges.

Alarm bells should have rung much more loudly in our ears than they did on two instances during our day with Kerbaj.

The first was when he told me he liked to employ creative writing techniques in his news articles; he had studied creative writing at college and was clearly interested in the emotional effects of language that engages the senses as well as the rational part of the brain. There is nothing wrong with this, of course, unless the creative writing of a news reporter ends up including the element of making things up — i.e., fiction.

The second occurred after John told him a traumatic account of his time on an archaeological dig in the Arctic when an Inuit boy, who, together with his brother, had been employed to protect their party of academics against polar bears, died from hypothermia in a boating accident when not wearing a life jacket. His brother, who had spent some time in the freezing water after the boat overturned, had lost the use of his legs. As John finished his account, Kerbaj said, "What a great story!" He then recovered himself, realizing that what he had just said might seem somewhat callous, and added that, of course, it was a very sad story. You could almost see him itching to film the story himself, milking it for all its emotional worth.

Much later, I was to think of this conversation about Kerbaj's creative tendencies when we learned that the journalist behind the most high-profile contemporary "Muslim scandal" — i.e., the "Trojan Horse affair" — was, surprise, surprise, none other than Richard Kerbaj.

This story — about alleged efforts by Islamists to take over secular schools in Birmingham — turned out to be based on a fake, anonymous letter sent to the Department of Education and then leaked to the *Sunday Times*. The letter purportedly outlined a five-step strategy, called "Operation Trojan Horse," to "parachute" fundamentalist Muslim governors into secular schools, which were in the process of becoming academies. After forcing the secular headteachers to resign by "wearing them down and weakening their resolve," these academies would then be taken over by Islamist head teachers and run on hard-line Salafist principles.

It didn't take long for this letter to be exposed as a hoax. Only nine days after Richard Kerbaj's story appeared on March 2, 2014, the *Times* revealed that the anonymous letter contained a major inaccuracy: one of the headteachers whom the conspirators were allegedly trying to remove had actually been dismissed twenty years before. Any decent journalist or editor would have checked such basic facts before running the story in the first place. As it was, the whole country had been whipped into a frenzy of unwarranted fear for nothing.

The whole blown-up Trojan Horse affair had the effect of wasting a considerable amount of time among the police, the West Midlands council, the Department of Education, school governors, teachers, parents, and the Muslim community. I could just imagine Richard Kerbaj chuckling at the furor he had instigated and wondered if the anonymous letter-writer had actually been Kerbaj himself in one of his creative periods.

The sealed knot that clasps together an unscrupulous and ambitious journalist, high-level government contacts, and anonymous sources means, of course, that suspicions as to the origins of the story cannot be proven. Therein lies the genius of Richard Kerbaj's particular modus operandi. Not only does he gain the credit for breaking the story, his paper also gains the kudos for exposing the story as a fake. All that lingers in the public's mind afterward is a general feeling that dirty dealings are going on in the Muslim community and that the "rest of us" should be vigilant against the many possible insidious Islamic plots that will inevitably have the effect of destroying our secular, civilized way of life, and end up with bombs on the Underground. A tiny whiff of (fake) suspicion is all that is required.

Kerbaj promised to send us what he had written so we could check it for accuracy. When he phoned a few days later, however, he read out only small excerpts from his piece, and even then it was clear that Jack would be identifiable from the context. And although his brief had been to write about the predicament of all those young people trapped in a war zone, he had focused on Jack alone. In response to our objections, he made a few token changes, but it was still clear that he had not stuck to our agreement at all. What's more, his deadline was the end of the week so that the piece could be published that Sunday. This definitely contradicted our arrangement that the piece would be part of a long-term project. If Jack were identified in Raqqa, and if it became known he was trying to leave ISIS territory, ISIS would kill him. I asked Kerbaj not to go ahead given the circumstances. Kerbaj, however, lost his temper, saying, "I've already spent ten hours on this piece; I'm going ahead."

What happened next was what set our lives and Jack's life into a trajectory of official sanction and punishment from which they have never recovered. Kerbaj was deaf to my entreaties that I didn't care in the least about his ten hours; I only cared about the life of my son. He also didn't listen to the pleas of ACF, who supposedly tried to negotiate. A day after we asked him not to go ahead, a young, scruffy "journalist" knocked on our neighbours' doors, asking about Jack. A couple of days after this, a shockingly amateur piece appeared on the Oxford University student gossip website *Hackox*, which, judging from the date of its first-ever post, was set up only four days after Kerbaj's visit to our house. The final line of this laughable piece was: "ISIS could not be reached for comment." (Is that really the best that undergraduates from one of the most prestigious universities in the world could come up with?) It seemed very strange to us that the story about Jack had remained a secret for a year and a half and that suddenly Oxford University had become aware of it a few days after a *Sunday Times* journalist had become involved. We then remembered that Kerbaj had mentioned he had contacts at the university through a close friend.

Distraught, we again phoned ACF to ask them to remonstrate with Kerbaj on our behalf but were informed that the latter had categorically stated that "since the story had now appeared in a public forum" (i.e., *Hackox*), it was now in the "public interest," thereby entitling him to go ahead with his piece.

The opening line of Richard Kerbaj's resultant article in the *Sunday Times* on January 24, 2016, informed the world that Jack had admitted to his parents in September 2014 that he had joined

ISIS. This is a blatant lie, as Kerbaj well knew, as he taped our entire conversation with him. Who would know about our private conversations with Jack, us or Richard Kerbaj? In addition, any agreement about anonymity had gone straight out the window, and Jack was not only named, but also shown in a half-page photograph. Clearly, Kerbaj's penchant for using creative writing techniques in his articles had overridden any concern for the truth or for the impact of his actions on the life or death of his article's subjects. Thanks to him, the nickname "Jihadi Jack" is now burned into the minds of millions of people around the world. And despite any supporting evidence, and as a result of a journalist's lie, Jack himself is believed by millions to be a raping, murdering monster who chops off heads. Anything John and I said to the contrary — based on our own evidence — was dismissed as the feeble protestations of parents in denial.

Later on, when the gag order implicit in the contempt-of-court rule kicked in after we were charged and briefly put in prison, we were unable to say anything relevant at all. To sue the *Sunday Times* for libel, we would likely need at least £5 million in lawyers' fees (this was the amount Murdoch had to pay his lawyers to keep Rebekah Brooks, former editor of the now-defunct *News of the World*, out of prison during the hacking scandal). Libel cases, apparently, are never funded by legal aid. As the adage goes, "A lie can go halfway round the world before the truth can get its pants on."

An additional insight that John and I gained from our encounter with an unscrupulous journalist is how close the links are between the security services, newspaper defence correspondents, and deradicalization organizations that work closely with the police. When I asked Kerbaj how he knew about Jack, he told me that ACF had told him about him. When I asked ACF the same question, they said that Kerbaj had known about Jack *before* they broached the subject. Confronted with this piece of information,

Kerbaj changed his story and said he "had known about him from his Facebook site" and it was "his job as defence correspondent to know about these things." He had no answer when I asked him how he knew to look at Jack's Facebook site in particular. Perhaps it was because someone somewhere — who was already monitoring Jack for other reasons — had pointed him in the right direction.

I had never been much of a conspiracy theorist, generally believing more in the "cock-up rather than cover-up" explanation of coincidental happenings, but now I'm much more willing to consider the "right-wing conspiracy" version of events that John referred to in January 2016 in an exasperated comment to the press. It would seem naive not to.

Jack interviews with the *Independent*, January 2016

After our arrest, Jack was much less communicative with us, and certainly no longer told us where he was, or anything about his day-to-day life. We believed he was having to keep his head down, and that communication with us was now probably much more risky. For our part, we had to explain to him that it was now very difficult to help him: our bail conditions stipulated that we were not to send him any money or arrange for anyone else to do so. If we did, we would be put straight into prison.

Somehow, Jack managed to do two interviews of his own toward the end of January 2016, both with the *Independent* newspaper. In the first, on January 25, 2016, Jack was quoted as saying, "Its sort of awkward when the media thinks you're ISIS and you're not. Thinks you have a son and you don't. Maybe they got bored worrying about what colour socks certain celebrities wear and took out the frustration on me?" Later, he explained what we had always suspected: "It doesn't help, admittedly, that bare [lots of] different people have used my fb account (some of whom are extreme etc. and only got my password through one guy I stupidly trusted)."

A follow-up article on January 30, 2016, carried his denial of reports he had joined ISIS, and quoted him as saying he had travelled to the so-called Islamic State to spread the word of Allah and help "take down" the government of Bashar al-Assad.

"I can speak Arabic and English," he said. "That's like my only skill." He added, "I'm not ISIS, but I believe in the Sharia. I believe we should follow Islam how the first Muslims did." When asked what he thought about ISIS's recently released video saying they would attack the U.K., he replied, "I'm doing my own thing. I don't focus that much on what ISIS does. Also, this may sound strange but this is genuinely the first time someone's told me they threatened to attack the U.K., which is probably a bit embarrassing, seeing as I'm in Syria and you'd expect I'd hear these things. If Britain stopped bombing Muslims in Syria, the Muslims in Syria would stop attacking them. Is that hard to understand?"

Jack's naïveté and defiant immaturity are painfully apparent in these interviews. While he clearly expects his words to be received in the spirit in which they are offered — "I'm not ISIS, I don't focus on what they do, I'm doing my own thing, and I'm trying to follow my chosen faith" — he evidently has no concept of how these comments would be viewed in the U.K. It was as if he were a lamb leading himself to slaughter, and all we could do to save him from himself was to point out that yes, he was young, stupid, and opinionated, but there was no evidence he had been involved in any violence or had hurt anyone at all.

Our consolation in the face of his public exposure was that he must be in a place where ISIS didn't know where he was, or he wouldn't dare denounce them in such a way. Indeed, sixteen months later, when he was captured by the Kurds, his jailers expressed surprise and admiration that he had dared to tackle ISIS publicly in such a manner. Whether he was brave or crazy, they didn't know. Perhaps he was both.

Intervention by Reprieve, January–February 2016

One welcome and unsolicited source of support that turned up for our side was the human rights charity Reprieve. Reprieve phoned during the time we were being besieged by the media after the story broke, and initially John was skeptical, believing the caller to be yet another pesky journalist trying to get a story. Once we had been assured of the charity contact's legal credentials (and their legal director had thoroughly scared us with the notion that now that Jack had been "outed" he was in as much danger from a British government drone as he was from any Syrian threat), we arranged to meet.

I knew a little about Reprieve from my time at Oxfam, and also recollected the TV appearances twenty years beforehand of Clive Stafford Smith, who had been one of the few lawyers fighting for justice for the detainees in Guantanamo Bay. I remembered him as being very lean, as if he were too busy taking on the world's most powerful government to waste time eating. When I looked at his profile on the Reprieve website, I discovered that he had represented three hundred prisoners on death row in the southern United States and that he had prevented the death penalty in all but six cases (a 98 percent "victory" rate). Surely, I thought, if this was his success rate in the most difficult cases, it would be a small matter for him to get a jury to realize that John's and my arrests were ludicrous, and also, that he was the person who could rescue Jack.

Chapter 14

Photosynthesis in a capitalist society

Asset freeze, January 2016

Another chilling outcome of our arrest was a police threat to ruin us financially. The instrument of this threat was a one-page document, which we were required to sign and which detailed the sanctions that could be levied against us, *whether we were eventually charged or not* with fundraising for terrorism. The financial officer in charge of explaining this (surely illegal) method of punitive action against as-yet-unproven-guilty persons, shook his head sorrowfully and sucked his teeth repeatedly when expressing his concern at the "difficult position" we were in.

The threat of freezing all our assets ("all bank accounts and credit facilities, property and vehicles held in our control") was part of the government's counter-terrorism strategy, we were told, and was a "*preventative* tool to stop the *potential* funding of terrorism." It appeared that this freeze was currently under consideration and could be imposed at any time — i.e., even before the CPS had made the decision to press charges or not. Although an asset freeze could be legally challenged once imposed, there was nothing we could do in the meantime if the Treasury agreed with the police that our names should indeed be included on a "list that can be viewed by all financial institutions globally." A further warning in the document stated, "Please be aware, for an individual on the financial sanctions target list in the U.K., upon being delisted there is the potential for customer relationships with existing banks to be closed and affect any future applications for credit." The document concluded with: "The asset freeze is proportionate to manage the risk of terrorist financing with exemptions that will allow for everyday living expenses."

"So, if I want to buy something, I have to ask Her Majesty's Treasury first?" I asked.

"Yes," came the reply, accompanied by regretful teeth sucking. "Purchases will be at the discretion of the Treasury."

When John and I discussed it later, I found myself wondering if I would have to ask the Treasury if it was permissible to buy Heinz baked beans, say, instead of Tesco's cheaper house brand, or if there was just a list of government-approved items to choose from. Whatever the case, it seemed that even if we were found innocent, sanctions could still be maintained; it would then be a matter for the wary institutions themselves to decide what brand of beans we could afford.

As it turned out, Tesco-value baked beans were the least of my worries. Two months after our arrest, NatWest bank, where I had held my personal account for twenty-five years, suddenly decided it could "no longer provide [me] with banking facilities." There was no explanation, and when I asked for one under the Data Protection Act, none was forthcoming. This followed several frustrating weeks of trying to understand why my PayPal account wouldn't work — the "reason" being that PayPal had also decided that my account was now terminated, and no, they couldn't tell me why. My credit cards at Halifax and RBS followed suit. Realizing that in a capitalist society a person with no bank account cannot actually exist as a human being, I was desperate. How could I collect my salary in cash? Where would I put my cash once I had collected it? Why was the world treating me as an outcast when all I had done was try to help my child? Why had the world gone bonkers? And what had happened to innocent until proven guilty? It so happened that one thing I didn't have to worry about was the destination of my pay cheque, since a couple of months after I was declared *persona non-existent*, I lost my job as an administrator at the NHS for being a suspected funder of terrorism, and as a consequence no longer had a pay cheque to put anywhere.

Perhaps I would need to become a Zen Buddhist, I thought, since when you have nothing, you have nothing to lose. And perhaps my new Buddhist friends would feed me and my family, too, since unfortunately, although the police and British government seemed to believe otherwise, we were not actually capable of supporting ourselves via photosynthesis.

To date, my one remaining bank account has proved loyal, so I have not yet had to call on imaginary Buddhist friends. And, instead of employing me, the British government decided in the end to give me a sum from Employment Support Allowance to live on — for three months, at least — so I didn't have to wait for scientific breakthroughs in plant-based survival techniques. Nevertheless, I still felt as if I was somehow in semi-human suspension, waiting for my real life to reassume its normal sane and predictable path, where strange men do not shake their heads sorrowfully at me while casually ruining my life and where I suddenly find myself unable to buy a £2.28 ebook because the British government believes it needs to keep the world safe from my online purchases.

Chapter 15

Lack of joined-up thinking

Syria news, February–March 2016

On February 27, 2016, the UN Security Council adopted a resolution to impose a partial ceasefire in Syria. The U.S. and Russia agreed to halt the air strikes on "those parties to the Syrian conflict that have indicated their commitment to and acceptance of its terms." The High Negotiations Committee (HND), representing most of the anti–Syrian government rebels at the UN, made clear that its commitment to the ceasefire was "conditional on the lifting of sieges, release of prisoners, a halt to bombardment of civilians and the delivery of humanitarian aid." It was agreed by all parties that the truce did not extend to ISIS, al-Nusra, and "other terrorist organisations designated by the UN."

This ceasefire was considered largely successful until July 2016, when fighting again broke out in areas around Damascus and Aleppo, and intensified thereafter. During the time of the truce, Assad's troops made several gains with Russian support, and notably recaptured Palmyra from ISIS in March 2016, reported by the Syrian Observatory for Human Rights as the "biggest single defeat for the group" in two years, with four hundred ISIS fighters killed in the battle. As of March 2016, official reports confirmed that 4.8 million Syrians had fled the country, and 6.6 million were displaced internally.

Again, during the temporary truce, the difficult issue of what constituted a moderate rebel raised itself. On several occasions, Russia stated its belief that the extremist forces were disguising themselves as members of the moderate opposition, whereas the U.S. maintained that Russia was using this claim as an excuse in order to bomb U.S.-backed rebel forces. Amid multiple violations of the agreed ceasefire, and numerous compensatory attempts to establish temporary, short ceasefires (with the request of only a few days' peace to allow humanitarian supplies in), it is somewhat surprising that the truce was considered successful for as long as it was.

For John and me, the ceasefire had little bearing on Jack's chances of safety. We knew he was still in ISIS-controlled territory, and the truce did not apply there. Now that the police were hampering our efforts to help him at every turn, we needed to find friends, supporters, and contacts who might be able to help him instead.

Search for official help, March 2016

In March 2016, John and I contacted everyone we could think of who might be able to help. We met with our local MP and his assistant at his constituency office in the local leisure centre, but he unfortunately appeared rather stunned by the whole business and merely commented that "there has been a lot of negative publicity about your son." He seemed to imply that we had been foolish in contacting the media in the first place, not understanding that we had been forced into the limelight against our will and then had to defend ourselves, and Jack, about the allegations.

John, a proud Canadian, wrote to the Canadian embassy, explaining that we were all (including Jack) Canadian citizens, and could they help in any way? The consular official wrote back to say that Canadian officials would intervene in a case only when a Canadian is being oppressed "because he is a Canadian." Since Canadians are generally viewed as being the nicest people on earth (if a little earnest), and no doubt most people think it would be impolite to oppress them, this seemed an unlikely avenue to pursue.

Only slightly less fruitless were John's conversations with the Canadian consulate. In one conversation, a desk officer admitted to him that there was a "lack of joined-up thinking" and no policy on how to deal with U.K. citizens currently in Syria. She referred John to the travel advice of the Foreign and Commonwealth Office (FCO), which advises people to "leave the country by any practical means," and said that she was trying to "join up the Foreign Office, Home Office, and Police teams with regard to Jack's case." Nothing more was heard of her efforts in this regard.

I wrote to David Cameron, who was still prime minister at the time, with a plea for him to intervene. The hand-signed letter I received in response stated that, as a parent himself, he appreciated how difficult this situation was for John and me. "The situation in Syria is clearly incredibly dangerous," the letter continued (helpful of him to point that out); "Whilst I appreciate your concerns, the Government has been clear for some time that we advise strongly against all travel to Syria" (again, such wise words in the circumstances). Cameron ended by urging us to "continue to engage with the police and the Government Legal Department on the issues referred to in your email." In other words, business as usual: government by insincere positioning, patronizing sentiments, and zero action.

We also arranged to meet with my former Oxfam contacts and Green Party contacts, and started to research prominent Muslims in Oxford. Oxfam told us they themselves were feeling the force of strict surveillance in Syria, with every single link in their supply chain having to be tested for terrorism before any humanitarian aid was allowed into the country. Meanwhile, Syrian civilians were starving. The Green Party was sympathetic and said they wanted justice for us and Jack, and also cited the absurdity of the British government's sending of billions of pounds' worth of arms and finance to Saudi Arabia, which then used them to bomb civilians in Yemen. With regard to approaching Muslims in Oxford, we got only so far with this when we were overtaken by events, and were then forced to curtail publicity for our case until it was safe to do so again.

"Foxes" and "chickens": coded messages from ISIS territory, February–March 2016

On February 29, 2016, after not hearing from Jack for almost a month, I received some strange messages on Telegram, which took me a while to figure out:

> Jan once dreamed the chickens were in the shed.
>
> Mrs Big died in my arms.
>
> …
>
> I'm going to send u my mums cousins name
>
> You help him give Mrs Big a sum to bribe the fox

Suddenly, this latter message made the rest make sense. Mrs. Big was a chicken that Jack had had when he was young, which was savaged by a fox. John had driven to the vet, while Jack held Mrs. Big in the back of the car. On the way, Mrs. Big died in Jack's arms, and he had been distraught. I realized that in these coded messages he was sending me, Jack was the beleaguered chicken, ISIS guards were the foxes, and the mum's cousin's name was the name of the people smuggler we should send money to.

Here we were again, being placed in the excruciating position of Jack being in hiding and being desperate for money to escape.

Me:

> Is the fox keeping Mrs Big in a cell now?

Jack:

> Nope. But on the way to the vet. Foxes love money.

Me:

> On way to vet sounds serious.

Jack:

> No, no. Mrs Big is fine. She does a convincing fox impression. Language etc. But she looks very chicken like. Although so do a lot of the foxes here. But we don't know the future. Maybe they realise. So it's like back up.... Only seed is needed. Everything else is sorted. Even a fox suit.

Me:

> You know what happened last time.

Jack:

Think how to use intelligence. Make a good
helpful move.

Me:

We have explored all intelligent options possible
and the best one is just you being completely
honest about the danger you are in. It's difficult to
explain everything — you just have to trust me.

Jack:

Danger

Real

I don't want to scare you.

But there's real danger

I don't want to go into too much detail

But there's people here who want to kill me

They don't know where I am

But it's not exactly a small place.

Me:

Are you in hiding at the moment?

Jack:

Yes

Me:

Did the publicity in this country make things
worse?

Jack:

> Yes
>
> The path already opened and shut twice.
>
> ...
>
> I can't waste time.
>
> My contacts probs just gonna leave without me.

Me:

> You just need to hold on for couple more days
> and we can send you what u need.

Jack:

> Two days is good inshaa Allaah. A week is too
> long.
>
> Don't flop.
>
> Speak tomorrow in shaa Allaah.

Reprieve, judicial review, March 2016

On March 22, 2016, Reprieve lodged an emergency judicial review at the High Court, appealing the decision of Thames Valley Police not to allow us to send money to Jack, citing Jack's coded messages as proof that his life was in imminent danger. Jack was in hiding from ISIS, explained the appeal summary, and had a narrow opportunity to escape his situation. On March 16, 2016, he had advised his parents that "a week [to send the money] is too long."

The legal justification for our case was a section within counterterrorism legislation that allows for the sending of money "with the permission of a constable," i.e., Section 21 of the Terrorism Act

2000. Sending funds in this case, argued Reprieve, would have the effect of avoiding risk to a U.K. citizen. The right to life under article 2 of the European Convention of Human Rights was also invoked.

Our case was to be heard by the Queen's Bench Division of the High Court, an administrative court where challenges to official bodies, such as the police or the government, can be made. A single High Court judge is able to adjudicate on all such cases.

The timing of our case could not have been less propitious. The day before our hearing on March 23, 2016, there were three co-ordinated suicide bombings in Brussels: two at Brussels airport and one at a metro station. Thirty-two people were killed, and three hundred people were injured. In such a climate of fear, there could not be a worse time to hear a terrorism case such as ours, whether or not there was any evidence to suggest the case should even be heard under the terms of terrorism legislation. We commented as much to our lawyer, Tayab, as we walked toward the court. "But the values of the judiciary are supposed to be above politics," I argued. My naïveté at this stage was based on the fact that we had not yet been charged, let alone sent to prison. The judiciary, I felt, was our last hope. We were being prosecuted by the police, blacklisted by financial institutions, had our benefits suspended by the government, and shunned by society. Our human rights lawyers and the courts were all we had left.

Halfway through the hearing, events became mired in confusion. The judge mooted the opinion that we were seeking his permission to send money only in order to absolve ourselves from prosecution — which, he said, considering there was a criminal case pending against us, was an inappropriate reason to call upon his judgment. "Why don't you just send the money and then accept the consequences?" was the gist of his comments. When he was informed that this was indeed what we'd tried to do, but that the money had been blocked, it became clear that the circumstances surrounding the blocking needed to be established. We learned from the evidence of the police prosecutor that it was the securities and fraud division of Western Union that had blocked the transfer; this action had been taken after they contacted the National Crime Agency (NCA), and the NCA action had been made after they had contacted Thames Valley Police. In other words, it was the "local constabulary," in the words of the judge, that was the ultimate decision-making body. As I'd mentioned in my letter to David Cameron, it surely wasn't right that the power of life and death should rest in the hands of Thames Valley Police.

Proceedings were stopped to allow the judge to hear evidence directly from the National Crime Agency. "Although, my lord," said the police prosecutor, "I don't know if there will be someone at the NCA at present to answer the phone." At this comment, the red mist that had been rising in my head throughout the whole process suddenly erupted through my mouth. "Perhaps they would if their son was in danger," I called out from my position on the back benches, feeling myself boiling with absolute fury. I was instantly hushed by John, the lawyers, and our Reprieve representatives, but the judge brushed off the interruption as if he hadn't heard.

The hearing concluded with the agreement that further evidence would be sought from the NCA, and court would be resumed after the judge's two-week holiday. The police's position remained unchanged in the face of our challenge under Section 21. This section didn't apply, they said, as it was designed only to be used if the permission sought from a constable was to allow payments to get through "for the purposes of terrorism" in specific circumstances agreed upon by the police. Generally, it was explained, this section was only used for situations allowing for informers to be protected — e.g., the payment would assist in maintaining their cover. For the consent provision to apply to Jack, we would have to say that he was involved in terrorist activity and we were seeking permission in order to send money despite that fact. Their logic was unassailable and boiled down to "damned if you do, damned if you don't." It seemed highly ironic, and completely unjust, to us that the only way Jack could receive any money from us was if we agreed he was a terrorist.

Why the police were setting up such a farcical situation, when they had revealed no evidence that Jack was involved in terrorist activity, and when a young British citizen's life was at stake, we had no clue. We assumed, because of inflammatory newspaper articles, that it was because of the fear that Jack might come back to commit a violent act on British soil. But anyone with religious views "might" do that, and Jack had declared that he never wanted to come back to Britain as he had no affection or respect for the country (we were rapidly feeling the same way). I thought about other "guilt by association" examples that might be analogous to the situation being applied to him: for instance, a computer whiz kid who manages to hack into his friend's account "might" hack into the Pentagon to steal military secrets; or a Muslim farmer who buys fertilizer at a hardware shop "might" be using it to build a bomb (or might be using it on his potatoes).

Terrorism is the only crime on the statute books that is a "thought crime" — i.e., the only crime of which you can be convicted on circumstantial evidence and on the suspicion of an observer. The wording has been designed to prevent violent acts at the planning stages, which is, of course, in the interests of public safety. However, potential injustice lies in the fact that innocent people can be convicted of a crime that has not yet been committed and which they had no intention of committing. Guilt by association is flimsy at the best of times. When the stakes of being wrong about your suspicions are so high (e.g., an innocent person could be imprisoned or even killed), it becomes downright dangerous. We knew that Jack wanted to live in a country where he could lead an Islamic life, speak Arabic, and raise a family. In order to do those things, he needed to remain alive. The British police seemed to be determined to do everything they could to prevent that from happening.

✳   ✳   ✳

As it happened, after its suspension, the judicial review was never resumed. John and I were charged with fundraising for terrorism on June 1, 2016, and were obliged to attend a bail hearing on June 9, 2016. All our efforts to help Jack were put on hold. He now had no option other to rely on his wits, resources, and luck. Although he had told me that "luck" is un-Islamic because it denotes a lack of faith in Allah, I knew he would now need the luck of an entire lifetime if he was to survive.

Chapter 16

Westminster Magistrates Court

Westminster Magistrates Court, bail hearing, June 9, 2016

Emma Arbuthnot, Deputy Chief Magistrate at Westminster Magistrates Court, a.k.a. Lady Arbuthnot of Edrom, could not possess more impeccable establishment credentials if she tried. The daughter of Michael Broadbent, wine director of Christie's, she entered the Arbuthnot clan when she married James Arbuthnot, a direct descendant of James V. The Arbuthnots have owned their lands in Kincardineshire since Anglo-Saxon times, when they married into the Swinton family, which had gained a reputation for bravery by clearing Scotland of wild boar. The Swintons are one of only three families that can trace their unbroken land ownership to before the Norman Conquest, making them one of the oldest landed families in the British Isles. It is clear that power, authority, and privilege have an extremely long pedigree in this country.

REASONABLE CAUSE TO SUSPECT

John and I did not know any of this when Emma Arbuthnot walked into the court. Along with the rest of the assembled lawyers, barristers, journalists, court officials, and our group of friends, we, from behind our Perspex dock, merely obeyed the "All rise" command, and then waited until she was seated before we settled ourselves down again. At first glance, she looked like any other middle-aged, perhaps kindly, bespectacled woman with the rather haughty bearing that comes from acknowledged authority. Appearances, of course, can be deceiving.

The police barrister stood up to summarize the case. By now, the charges against us were so familiar I almost didn't listen properly to their presentation. Included in the prosecution's evidence was an email I'd sent to a friend in May 2014 (where I'd exaggerated for effect as I'd needed a good excuse for not having contacted her in a long time), in which I stated that Jack had been talking about fighting in Syria. What the police barrister deliberately omitted was the following line of the email, which went on to say that Jack had decided *not* to fight in Syria.

After court reporting restrictions were agreed (since publicity of the fact that Jack was trying to leave Syria could have fatal consequences for him), Tayab presented our case for bail. Absurdly, I felt as if I was a proud parent watching a school play (I was having problems believing that any of this was real and imagined that any moment now a theatre director would shout "Cut!"). Tayab was at his dazzling best. His quicksilver mind, his verbal brilliance, and his compelling way of presenting lines of reasoning all combined to present an evocative argument that any reasonable person could not possibly resist.

The press were scribbling down his words as fast as they could. Most of the journalists were fresh-faced young people. It had been my dream to be a journalist when I was younger, and I surveyed them with a twinge of envy, not just because they happened to be on the side of the dock that represented freedom.

As Tayab was finishing off his final flourishes for the bail application, I started to sense that something wasn't quite right. Tayab himself seemed to sense this as well, and even stumbled slightly over one of his words. I realized what it was. Lady Arbuthnot had her head down and didn't even seem to be listening.

Part of our application for bail was based on the fact that we both had responsible jobs to uphold. This assertion was easier to justify in John's case, since he had a farm to run. I, in contrast, didn't really have a career, since the Oxford hospital where I'd been employed wasn't keen on my working there after my arrest and my freelance editing work had also taken a nosedive: my main client, Oxford University Press, had strangely stopped returning my calls and then had blocked me from contacting their HR department. Having my computer confiscated twice by the police had posed problems, too, since I couldn't work without the main tool of my trade.

Lady A. was unmoved by the validity and importance of our respective jobs. When Tayab explained that John needed to be at the farm to take care of his farm business, she snorted and declared, "Crops just grow in the ground; they don't need looking after." I could feel John's outrage as he stared incredulously at her. Clearly, we were meant to believe, Lady A. was an expert agronomist as well as a top-level magistrate. Our need to take care of E, our eighteen-year-old son who was in the middle of his A-levels, and our fears he would lose his home if we weren't able to pay the rent, were dismissed by Lady A.'s confident retort, "They're not going to lose the house in the next few weeks."

Her concluding comments explained everything. She stressed the fact that we had defied the police in sending money to Syria, despite repeated warnings not to. She said that I had even paid for his ticket out there (failing to mention that I paid for his ticket to Jordan, not to engage in terrorism in Syria). The police had been most helpful, she maintained, in suggesting ways that Jack could be assisted once he crossed the border into Turkey, and had even obligingly provided the addresses of the British embassy in Ankara. Looking straight at me, Lady A. said, "She knew exactly what he was up to."

I thought, *Well, I'm glad you know exactly what he is up to, as I have spent two years of my life trying to find out.* Lady Arbuthnot's conclusion was that she had no doubt we, as parents whose hearts ruled their heads, would commit further offences by sending more money as soon as we received the next desperate message from our son. She therefore had no choice but to order that we should be refused bail and remanded immediately at Her Majesty's pleasure.

Shock and bewilderment reigned in the court room as Lady A. swept out, her mission accomplished. Her decision not to grant bail ran counter to the recommendations of the police and the prosecutor; even Detective Inspector *T* looked stunned. Standing next to us, the West Indian court official uttered "Shocking!" under his breath.

John and I were allowed to meet with Tayab and Itpal Dhillon, his firm's Head of Special Cases, before being taken off to our respective prisons. Their expressions were bleak; as, I'm sure, were ours. They reassured us that there was another bail hearing in two weeks' time at the Crown Court, and there was a good chance that the magistrate's decision would be overturned. I remarked to Tayab that he could have turned cartwheels and juggled with his feet during the hearing and Lady A. still wouldn't have been impressed. What was most frustrating was that we still had nothing to show for our efforts: i.e., Jack was still in danger. Then, with the gallows humour I imagine is common to people who have just been condemned, we started joking that the court-room scene would make a great short film, and discussed which actor would play each of us. I suggested Sanjeev Bhaskar for Tayab, for likeability and lack of pretension, and then suggested the glamorous Amal Clooney for Itpal, forgetting that Amal wasn't in fact an actor, just married to one. No one sprang to mind for John, as none of us could think of a middle-aged Canadian actor who could play an idealistic, Green, anarcho-communist farmer with an ability to expound on any topic with fervour and at great length — from global politics to how long it was acceptable to keep rice in the fridge. When Tayab asked me who I thought would play me, I remembered that people used to say I looked like Felicity Kendall because of my plump cheeks. That, however, was in my youth before my face started to collapse like a melting candle, so I supposed it would now have to be Dot Cotton from *Eastenders*. I would need to check she wasn't already dead.

Chapter 17

Prison

On my way to HMP Bronzefield

"My life was not supposed to turn out like this," I said as I held out my wrist to be handcuffed to the warden who was escorting me to the police van. She was West Indian like the first warden, with a friendly, wide smile and a gap between her front teeth. "You'll get bail," she said comfortingly, referring to our next application in two weeks' time at the Old Bailey. I chose to believe her, since the prospect of spending the next seven months in prison while we awaited trial was too awful to contemplate.

The police van had been held up in traffic on "the other side of London," so I'd been in a police cell for a couple of hours before it arrived around 7:00 p.m. to collect me and any other Westminster Magistrates Court prisoners waiting to be dispatched to various prisons in the southeast. I was going to "Bron," it seemed, whatever that was. All I could glean was that it was a women's prison somewhere near Heathrow. John was going to Wandsworth, which

I later discovered was "the worst prison in Europe." John's experiences in Wandsworth — including three days in solitary — indeed are testimony to the sort of hellhole it was. But all that I was to find out later. For now, I was simply required to be locked into my allocated oblong box in the police van, while around me ricocheted the shouts and banter of my new prison mates. "We've got newbies," one of them yelled. I shrank farther into my box. I didn't want to have to introduce myself or explain why I was there.

Infused with the pathos of the knowledge that I might not see the outside world again for a very long time, London had never looked lovelier. As we travelled west into the setting sun, packed in like veal calves heading for slaughter, the streets were bathed in a rosy glow, and light reflected off the sparkling glass planes of the modern buildings as if the scene were a feature in a glossy prospectus advertising the city's investment potential.

As the buildings became sparser and the landscape flattened out into nondescript fields and wooden fences, I realized we were nearing our destination. By the time we reached the long, low sprawl of the prison, dusk was falling and the light was changing from pink to grey. *Welcome to HMP Bronzefield* read the sign at the end of the long paved driveway. Obviously, the "Bron" the warden had mentioned. I hoped I wouldn't stay long enough to start calling it by its cozy nickname, too.

The desolate scene that greeted me was like something out of *The Shawshank Redemption*: grey expanse of tarmac stretching to a high wire fence, and a two-storey brick building squatting a couple of hundred yards in front of us. A solitary wan face, indistinct in the gloom, gazed forlornly from behind one of the building's barred windows. Surprisingly, this window's outer frame was open to the night sky, and I thought, naively as it turned out, that maybe it wouldn't be so bad if you were still able to feel fresh air on your face. I found out later this window was within the staff quarters of the reception area, and I was never to discover another open window in any of the prison buildings I was allowed in.

What happened next seemed like a sick joke. While we were sitting in our seats for what seemed like an age waiting to be un-locked, the van's music system, which had been silent for the entire journey, suddenly broke out into a loud rendition of the plaintive ballad, "All by Myself." Was this airing of the extremely apposite lyrics some warden's idea of a cruel jibe, or was it simply the song that happened to come on the radio? Whatever the truth of it, the irony seemed to be lost on the prisoner who was singing along lusti-ly with a powerful, soulful voice that dipped and surged. In another life, she could have been a nightclub singer or an entrant on *The Voice*. The waste of human potential within my current surround-ings was just starting to sink in.

One more song followed the first — this time "I Believe I Can Fly" — which compounded the irony of our situation, particularly since during the chorus a pigeon flew across the tarmac yard as if it had been artistically captured to accompany the opening sound-track to an arthouse film. This feeling of being the wrong actor trapped in a surreal horror piece (*When would the zombies appear?*) did not leave me the entire time I spent at Bronzefield.

The bureaucratic detail of being processed as a "newbie" has now coalesced in my mind into a thick fog of official questions, surly responses (from me), fingerprinting, photo-taking, ID card, prisoner number, personal possession confiscation, and issuing of my new kit of grey sweatshirt and pants; five pairs of big prison knickers; five pairs of socks; plastic plate, fork, spoon, and knife; and toothpaste, toothbrush, and soap, all bound up together in a cotton net bag that would double as my laundry bag and suitcase for the duration of my stay. The staff were harassed, short-tempered, and shouty, and clearly desperate to go off shift. I resigned myself to my first night of dark-ness, physical and spiritual, in the cell that was to be my new home.

Prison life

My case worker was round like a small pumpkin, with a maternal air, although she was probably fifteen years younger than me. I believe I was probably fast-tracked into seeing her on my first afternoon because I was a suspected self-harm risk, mostly because I couldn't stop crying. I found out later that if you identified yourself as being at risk of self-harm, you would receive regular sight checks from the warden, including during the night when they would flash a torch through the door slit so you couldn't sleep.

By the time of my meeting with my case worker, I had worked out from my Bronzefield information sheet that I was in the "Remand and Early Arrivals to Custody" wing in House Block 2. The prison was a Category A prison, which houses "those whose escape would be highly dangerous to the public or national security." However, after meeting some of the other inmates, who had been arrested for minor misdemeanours such as pub brawls, and who didn't seem at all dangerous, I discovered that it was also a local prison and held people who came directly from the courts in the southeast area.

There were four house blocks, with number 1 being the Recovery Unit for those with drug or alcohol dependency; number 2 being my block for remand and early arrivals; 3 for those who had been sentenced; and 4 being the "Enhanced" block for those who were "collaborating constructively in the completion of the terms of their sentence," which I took to mean they had certain privileges as a result of good behaviour, but which I later learned was a euphemism for lifers. Block 4 was situated just behind ours. During my first night I'd heard blood-curdling screams issuing at regular intervals from that direction, which had sounded like someone being murdered, but which I supposed couldn't have been, since surely no one got murdered in such a regular-sounding fashion.

At my case worker meeting, I poured out my tale of despair in between sobs. I was worried about my son *E* being on his own and in the middle of his A-level exams. I was also convinced that I was being treated more harshly than the other prisoners because of the nature of my charge. My legal advice from Tayab had been not to mention the charge itself to the other prisoners; rather, to say I was in for "financial reasons," which was true, in a way. I wondered, however, who the other prisoners would hate more: a banker or a terrorist.

The case worker informed me that other prisoners would only know what I told them, and that any articles that referred to any of the prisoners were removed by officers before the newspapers reached the house blocks. I was also worried that I was talking too much, having remembered Tayab's warning that prison officials could be called up as prosecution witnesses during the trial itself. My case worker reassured me that she had nothing to do with the courts process and that I could speak freely.

When I asked why I wasn't given a double room, she explained it wasn't that no one would want to share with me, it was a precaution designed for my protection so that I wouldn't feel pressured into talking about my charge. There were three other people who were in on the same charge, she told me, and they didn't want the substance of that information "leaking out to the wrong people." I wondered who she meant by "wrong people" — perhaps the anti-Muslim English Defence League would target the prison with violent action, knowing there were suspected terrorists inside? Whatever she meant, I was soon able to identify the other three people she mentioned through a process of deduction (suffice it to say, it seemed unusual for three females of the same Somali family to be imprisoned together, one of whom was elderly and immobile). In the end I never did discuss my charge with the three of them, believing increased surveillance of communications between us could actually make things worse.

After my case worker meeting, I stopped crying and started planning how I would survive prison life. Making friends, I had already decided, was crucial to this process. The first time I spoke to someone who wasn't a prison official was during my first outing in the exercise yard, where women were strolling around in their already-established friendship groups. I was surveying the fence, scaling it in my imagination, when a small woman with bleached blond hair and a missing tooth approached on her own walk around the perimeter.

"I don't suppose anyone's ever escaped from here," I remarked, conversationally. "Apparently, someone tried," she replied. "They used a paper-mâché balloon, but didn't get very far." "Good idea, though," I said. It was clearly a very stupid idea, but I didn't want our dialogue to end and said the first thing that came into my head. The small woman and I then continued our stroll together. She told me that she was in for eight weeks for being drunk and disorderly and for having bitten a police officer, which was how, she explained, she had lost the tooth. Secretly, I thought of the police officers I would like to bite, too, and then thought of how in the circumstances this would be interpreted as a terrorist threat. "Rabid Mother Savages Officer in Terror Plot" was my imagined *Daily Mail* headline. I didn't say any of this to my new friend, *J*.

When she asked what I was in for, I dutifully followed my legal advice and said, "Finance stuff." *J* became my first prison friend, and it was she who saved my skin the next day when a guard threatened to lock me up all day for what he clearly classified as insubordination, but what was actually a minor disagreement that got out of control.

That incident kicked off when I came down to breakfast wearing sweatpants and my prison nightshirt, the regulation long blue T-shirt incongruously patterned with little red hearts, as if we were teenagers enjoying a sleepover rather than inmates in a top-security prison. The burly guard on duty confronted me and told me to go and change. I explained that I would love to change but I hadn't got anything to change into, as the regulation grey T-shirts hadn't been included in my kit. I had a regulation sweatshirt but it was much too hot for that. He repeated that nightshirts weren't allowed at breakfast, and I should go and change or I would miss it. I reiterated what I'd said earlier. When, bored with the argument, he tried to get past me, I instinctively blocked his path, and we continued our sidestepping dance for some time, he accusing me of being in his personal space — "No, you're in *my* personal space" — until he called over another guard, who would, I naively thought, adjudicate in my favour since I was clearly in the right, but who in actuality merely pronounced, "Just lock her up all day."

At that, my toothless new friend ran up to me and told me to just change into something dirty for breakfast to avoid being locked in my cell until breakfast the following day. I did as she said, realizing I'd been rescued, and the guard and I maintained an uneasy truce for the rest of the day.

Prison, I was starting to discover, was a state of constant of negotiation; instant and shifting friendships, mostly for survival; and learning how to interact with the guards in order to gain maximum advantage, or at least to incur minimum disadvantage.

Daily routine at Bronzefield meant being locked up for twenty-three hours out of twenty-four, with our cells unlocked at 8:00 a.m. for breakfast, locked again during the day except for an hour for all meals, exercise, and "association" with other prisoners, and locked for the night at 4:45 p.m. on weekends and 6:40 p.m. on weekdays. I managed to pass the time by reading a book that I had secreted from the landing into my cell (technically not allowed) and carrying out a variety of yoga routines that I tried hard to remember from my upmarket, £8-per-hour yoga classes in north Oxford, supplemented by jumping, stretching, and bending moves that I made up as I went along. Although there was a TV in my cell showing a limited selection of program (mostly endless reruns of *The Big Bang Theory*), I had no inclination to turn myself into a passive consumer of stupor-inducing drivel, so avoided it unless absolutely desperate for diversion.

Observing nature in the world outside my window became my saving grace. Liberty seemed to be such a simple thing that even a bird could possess. It occurred to me that humans are the only animals that oppress each other: other species will fight each other for survival or for food, but they do not lock each other up in a systematic display of dominance. Most species, I reckoned, would choose death over imprisonment, and I thought that perhaps when I got home, I should release my lone tropical fish into the murky waters of the Thames; maybe a challenging existence was preferable to swimming round on his own in pointless circles. (Before I get a visit from the RSPCA I should add that I didn't, in fact, do this.)

I wondered how John was spending his time at Wandsworth. Given his extroverted nature and his interest in other people's life stories, I guessed he had already gained a circle of eccentric mates whose odd and beguiling tales would achieve mythic status through their retelling to our close-knit group of friends. I couldn't have been more wrong.

My disguise as a fraudster was somewhat flimsy, particularly since there were four actual fraudsters on the wing, and one of them seemed rather confused by my answers to her questions.

"I can tell you what sort of sentence you're likely to get," she said, confidently. "Was it for more than five million?"

"Five million?" I spluttered. "No, much less than that."

"And they took your passport? But you wouldn't be a flight risk." She looked at me dubiously.

"I don't know," I shrugged, trying to look like a big-time fraudster who would be on the beach in Rio if it weren't for the slight inconvenience of being in a maximum security prison.

Another's response was, "Fraud if you're rich means you're a banker, and if you're poor means benefit fraud." I couldn't decide if it was worse to take the food out of the mouths of the children of single mothers or to destroy the entire world economy for my personal gain. I decided that another shrug was probably appropriate. Depending on how long I was going to be there, I might have to read up a bit on my supposed offence.

When John and I compared prison notes, I delayed for some time in telling him about the birds, the book, and the TV, as I had found out after my third day inside that my experience of incarceration was like being in the Hilton compared to the sensory deprivation he had been subject to. My friend Ingrid, who along with two other friends had been managing an appeal campaign to get our remand overturned, told me during my first allowed phone conversation that she'd managed to visit John, and he'd described to her the hell of his first three days. As soon as he'd arrived, he'd been put into solitary confinement, with nothing to do except stare at a wall for hours on end, and had been denied a phone call or access to a doctor, even though his old shoulder injury was flaring up making it impossible for him to sleep. His cell was filthy, with dust balls piled in the corners.

The only human John had spoken to during that whole time (not counting the guards during their five-second exchanges of information) was a Muslim imam who disappeared as soon as he found out John wasn't Muslim. When he'd complained about his treatment to one of the guards, saying it was against basic human rights, the guard had replied, "This is Wandsworth, mate. Get used to it." He was beginning to despair, Ingrid told me, having had only his negative thoughts to keep him company for the past seventy-two hours, and she feared he couldn't cope with much more of the same. She had told him that Tayab was mounting an appeal against our remand decision, but John hadn't wanted to get his hopes up and was resigning himself to spending seven more months in his inhuman conditions. I was more optimistic. I had great faith in Tayab's abilities, and I couldn't believe that the likes of Emma Arbuthnot could condemn us to a living death for a crime we hadn't committed.

A shortage of staff was the reason John was given to explain why he wasn't allowed out of his cell for three days for exercise or for meals. We later found out that there had been a stabbing and that the prison was on lockdown. I felt guilty at my comparatively manageable situation and wondered if the difference was due to the nature of men's and women's prisons. Bullying was clearly an issue at Bronzefield (my accent and the way I walked, for instance, were popular subjects for ridicule amongst a dominant and mouthy subgroup of my new prison mates), but I'd never felt physically threatened, even by the sidestepping guard, and I'd never thought I would be denied my half hour of fresh air once a day. I wasn't even that bothered by the mouthy subgroup, since they soon got bored if paid no attention.

Chapter 18

Bail appeal

Bail appeal, High Court, London, June 14, 2016

The next time I saw John after we'd gone our separate ways at Westminster Magistrates Court was via video link to the High Court. Tayab had indeed secured an appeal against our remand, which was scheduled to take place five days after the start of our imprisonment. With the help of our small team of friends, who had managed to put together thirty character references for us over a period of forty-eight hours, he had submitted 240 more pages to the judge to support our defence. John appeared on the video link wearing a shoulder sling that he'd fashioned from his jumper, his expression an ominous mixture of depression and anger. We were allowed to speak to each other for twenty minutes or so before the court proceedings, and then sat in on the hearing itself.

Both of us hung on every word from Justice Saunders as he gave his final verdict to the hushed courtroom. The judge began his preamble by giving a detailed explanation as to why his judgment was in no way a criticism of that of the previous district magistrate (which rather suggested that it was). Moving to the reasons for his judgment, he said, "The police have not opposed bail for the defendants who are of positive good character and devoted parents. They are clearly desperately concerned about their son." Then, concluding his decision by granting conditional bail, he added, "Two perfectly decent people have ended up in custody because of the love of their child."

John and I had never been so jubilant in all our lives. I instantly fell in love with the judge and felt as if my world was finally reassembling itself into its former sane and intelligible shape. John put his head down as he broke down in tears, and I gleefully high-fived the guard sitting at the table next to me. (The guard, realizing my high-five could be seen on the court video, discreetly decided to shake my hand under the table instead, and then, when the court session was over, gave me a hug.)

One piece of good news we received on our return had been that E, who had been staying at a friend's, had managed to do well on his exams, despite all the upheaval and upset. Possessing a good brain and a disposition that tended toward the logical and the pragmatic, he had kept calm and had focused on his studies. I teased him, telling him that he was our "Exhibit A" that proved we weren't dreadful parents after all.

And what of Jack's reaction to this latest episode? We hoped he might at least understand that it wasn't as easy as he thought for us to help him, and that it wasn't just that we weren't trying hard enough. We sent him a message letting him know we were out, and he sent back a typically flippant message about the insanity of the British justice system.

While inside, we had been prevented from keeping abreast of the situation in Syria, trying to gauge the pace of the advance of the Iraqi army and Shia militia northward and the Kurds and the

Free Syrian Army southward, both movements backed by American bombing from the air. For five days we had not been able to obsessively tune into Al Jazeera to find out how many deaths there had been in Syria and Iraq and where exactly the bombs had fallen. Both of us would feel guilt when we read the ticker tape at the bottom of the TV screen and reacted with relief when we realized that the deaths had been in Yemen, Somalia, or Egypt and not Syria or Iraq. The combination of war and loved ones makes deranged monsters of us all. All we wanted was for this unspeakable horror to end.

Chapter 19

No dogs, no Irish, no terrorists

Threatened eviction, June 2016

Settling back into normal life was easy, and within a couple of days prison seemed like a long-ago nightmare. What was most perplexing about the past two weeks was that two senior members of the judiciary had held such diametrically opposed views on our case — one who saw us as lying monsters and the other who saw us as devoted parents. This, with access to the same evidence. Strangely, near the end of this same month of June, a polarization of opinion came to be reflected in the country's population as a whole, when 48 percent voted for Remain and 52 percent voted for Brexit. Perhaps, we thought, a similar split might occur amongst the twelve jurors who would eventually decide our fate. We had long suspected that we lived in a bubble of liberal opinion in Oxford (the Remain vote, for instance, had gained the support of 73 percent of Oxford's voters). This meant that we would not be able to take the overwhelming support of our friends and neighbours, some of whom hugged us in the street as never before, as a reliable gauge of sympathy among the general population.

An official lack of understanding was apparent when an eviction notice was served on us six days after we had returned home. Our letting agency's letter informed us that they were giving us two months' notice to vacate the property. We were beside ourselves with the thought that, on top of everything else, we were about to lose our home of ten years and be forced onto the streets. It seemed that each time we thought there couldn't possibly be any more excrement to be thrown at us, another steaming pile arrived on our doorstep.

We naturally assumed that the landlords had decided they didn't want suspected terrorists living in their house. John immediately contacted our landlady, who was a human rights lawyer living abroad. Her speedy response was very telling. She told us that the letting agency had acted without her knowledge, and that, in addition, she hadn't been aware of our situation. As far as she was concerned, she said, there was no problem in renewing our tenancy and she believed "people are innocent until proven otherwise."

Another unwelcome discovery we made after returning home was the fact that the police were evidently still investigating us, even after the "alleged offence" of trying to rescue our son had taken place. The story was explained to me by my oldest friend, who was one of my character witnesses. (We'd been inseparable at school from the age of eleven, and as gym partners I had always performed the role of the sturdy pivot, while she — light as a fairy then, and even now, over forty years later — did the twirly things in the air.) While we were in prison, the police had visited her at her work and then her home in the Cotswolds to ask if she thought I "had changed" since Jack went to Syria. The question didn't seem to necessitate two detectives' making a 120-mile round trip, but

I recalled Detective *N* telling me in November 2015 that, since counter-terrorism was the "sexy" department, it had actually had its budget *increased* during austerity when other police budgets were cut.

John and I had a strong suspicion that the police were interviewing this friend in particular because she shared an unusual surname with one of our prosecution witnesses. Our bail conditions prohibited us from contacting any of the prosecution witnesses; if we did so, it would be seen as a serious offence, and we would be sent straight back to prison. I can only imagine the police's disappointment when they discovered that double appearance of the unusual surname really was just an unusual coincidence.

Bail hearing, Old Bailey, June 23, 2016

Our Old Bailey hearing took place on the day of the EU referendum. What had most concerned me about a possible Brexit was the loss of the European Court of Human Rights, which would have a catastrophic effect on British justice, particularly for people on charges such as ours.

It was a hot and muggy day, and we were all perspiring in our suits even though it wasn't yet ten o'clock in the morning. ("I blame all the immigrants breathing at once," joked Tayab.) Cameras were again fully in evidence outside the Old Bailey. I was surprised to see them, given the fact we were in the news only the week before, and there were more important political events going on. I suppose I was forgetting that we could, in fact, be put away for fourteen years for what we were accused of. And British justice wouldn't be served unless the public were informed as to whether I was wearing a floral shirt or a striped one, and whether John's tie was blue or some other colour.

There was a much more high-profile event than ours at the Old Bailey that morning, and that was the first Central Criminal Court appearance of Thomas Mair, who had murdered MP Jo Cox a week before, shouting "Britain First!" as he did so. The photojournalists were not there for Mair, however, as he was presented to the court only via video link. After much debate in the press, the Crown Prosecution Service had decided to try Mair under terrorist charges, although this information had not yet been revealed publicly.

As we walked toward the court, Tayab told us that he had written to David Cameron the previous day (who was still prime minister at the time), offering to facilitate the listing of Britain First as a terrorist organization. He said this somewhat wryly, since all of us knew that would never happen: homegrown political organizations that sometimes turned violent were not considered to be in the same category as foreign or religiously motivated organizations. The absurdity of our appearing on the same charges as an actual murderer occurred to both John and me.

Just as Itpal had predicted, our court appearance was brief — only ten minutes — and we weren't required to state our pleas. The High Court judge — Justice Saunders, as before — queried whether our trial would require a High Court judge since it didn't seem to be a case that was very complex in law; perhaps it could be tried by a circuit judge instead. This suggestion filled me with horror, since it would open up the possibility of having another Lady A. as trial judge, and I was mightily relieved when it was agreed that a High Court was indeed required because of the sensitivity of the case.

The trial date was set for January 9, 2017, and the trial was expected to last three to four weeks. We had lots of preparation to do between now and then. And Jack was still no closer to extracting himself from the desperate dilemma he was trapped in.

Back to the farm, June 2016

John returned to the farm, even though all he needed to do for the next three months, according to Lady A., was sit at home and twiddle his thumbs while his crops obligingly did their thing before offering themselves up for harvest. Perhaps Lady A. had staff on her own estates to carry out the daily tasks John needed to do: the plowing, harrowing, weeding, fence repair, equipment maintenance, roof fixing, supply purchasing, seed cleaning, milling, flour packing, pallet stacking, delivery organization, school visit hosting, and business accounting. All of which he managed with the support of the farmer who owned the land (the sixty acres he farmed were rented), and with the input of loyal commitment and technical expertise from two volunteers, one a retired engineer in his eighties and the other a retired squadron leader in his seventies.

John's business setup was a sort of agricultural-cottage industry not common in the U.K. since the nineteenth century, when family farms were much more prevalent, and before massive agribusiness tightened its control over British farming. Never one to follow a conventional path, John had started the business after his research at Reading University on ancient wheat grains, which he had bulked up by hand from seed banks around the world. The uniqueness of these grains lay in that they were landrace populations adapted to growing conditions not dependent on vast inputs of fertilizers or pesticides. His work had attracted the attention of Prince Charles, who had provided grants through the Prince's Countryside Fund to support his research plots, and to help finance school visits and milling and baking workshops held at the farm. Prince Charles had further demonstrated his enthusiasm for the project by planting eighty acres of his own land at Highgrove with John's heritage rye. The royal connection to "Jihadi Jack's father" had not gone unnoticed by the papers, although the flurry of press speculation had been brief.

The first weekend after our prison release, we returned to regular life in the company of one of John's young volunteer WOOFERs (Workers On Organic Farms) called Guillaume, of French background, who came to stay with us in Oxford. Polite and chatty, Guillaume took an interest in everything, readily joined in the French Canadian songs that John played on the guitar, even unselfconsciously doing the actions. It was so nice to have a normal young person in the house, doing normal things on his travels round Europe. As he helped cook a spicy chicken dinner based on one of his Martinique mother's recipes, we felt we had to apologize on behalf of the 52 percent of our countrymen who had voted a couple of days before to keep people like him out.

For the millionth time, I wished Jack had chosen similar normal activities on which to spend his time after he left school. The messages we'd received from him a few days after we'd returned home had been uncharacteristically resigned. Gone was the usual defiance and condemnation of everything he found hypocritical — from the British media to the Western governments that were bombing hospitals. Instead, he said he had "no plans" as he "had no money." He "didn't regret [his] travels and what [he'd] learnt and done, even if they end here." He said death was a "set appointment" and that we "should become Muslim before it caught [us] unaware." A Jack who was resigned to his fate was not one I could cope with; I would take his feistiness and intensity over this every time, even if that usually translated into unreasonableness. I knew that now he would need every ounce of fighting spirit he had in him to get out of his situation alive.

We needed to step up our efforts to help him. Now that sending money was no longer possible, and the judicial review had been stopped after we had been charged, we would need to think of other options. We hoped Tayab had plans up his sleeve that we could pursue, and had already tried to convince Jack to overcome his distrust of the British legal system and speak to Tayab directly. ISIS territory was under threat like never before. The liberation of Fallujah, near Baghdad, had been claimed by the Iraqi army toward the end of June, after the city had been under ISIS control for over two years. Over eighty thousand people were estimated to have fled Fallujah to live in internal displacement camps that had barely any supplies of food, clean water, or medicine. In Syria, various forces opposed to ISIS, including Kurdish and Arab fighters of the Syrian Democratic Forces, al-Qaeda, and "moderate" rebels, were starting to overrun the ISIS-controlled city of Manbij, which was about twenty-five miles from the Turkish border and a key transit point for ISIS fighters and funds. Two hundred U.S. Special Forces had been involved in this push for Manbij, which put paid to the American denial of "boots on the ground." Several ISIS-held towns in Deir ez-Zor province in eastern Syria had also come under heavy attack from Syrian and Russian air strikes. The latest talk was of retaking Mosul, ISIS's largest stronghold, with six hundred thousand people, with an attack that was believed to be only months away. With reports of civilians detained, tortured, and summarily executed by pro–Syrian government forces, it was hard to keep sane, rational, and optimistic when discussing with Jack what his options were.

Chapter 20

Imprisoned by ISIS

Jack on the run, July 2016 to April 2017

In the latter half of 2016, communication with Jack was sporadic, with only desultory Facebook messages letting us know he
was still alive. It was only at the beginning of 2017, after Jack
had finally managed to move out of ISIS territory, that we learned what had been happening to him during this time and why
his messages had been punctuated by long periods of absence.
Living on the run, he had been captured and imprisoned by ISIS.
Outside of Islamic State territory, and at last able to borrow the
phones of people who were anti-ISIS, Jack's tone and the content of his messages were reassuringly much more like his normal
self — although still clearly those of a committed Muslim — and
much less like the bizarre utterings of his Raqqa days, which we
had often doubted came from him.

Jack's messages, March 2, 2017

Jack:

They caught me 2 times

And promised me the third time they'll kill me lol

Me:

Is it easy for them to find you?

Jack:

No in Shaa Allaah I have friends

They only found me because I tried to leave.
They found me on the way. The great escape lol.
Me and my friend escaped. I might have to fight
them in the end.

Me:

I've heard in Turkey they arrest the people who
leave and send them back to Syria

Jack:

I want to see you both

And E.

From his position of relative safety, Jack also managed to fill us
in on an injury he sustained when his house was bombed.

Jack:

I look very different now

I have cool scars

I'm taller

Have a gingerish beard

Scars on my back

And a tiny line below my eye

And my foot

And hand

Do you want to see my arm?

Theres no lasting damage alhamdulillaah

I was standing up

I didn't hear any sound

And started flying

I flew like 5 feet

I'll skip gory details

This was like 2 years ago

One time a mortar exploded next to my head but
I was just below it by like 50 centimeters so it
exploded above me

Our conversation further revealed the aftermath of the explosion. Jack said he'd felt no pain, but when he looked at his hand, it was clear that it was badly damaged. His friends, however, seemed to be more concerned about his back, and they immediately began bandaging up what turned out to be a large hole in his back, before turning their attention to his hand. They bundled him into a car to take him to hospital, and he said it was then that the pain started. It turned out that the house had been hit by a howitzer shell, which was why there had been no noise, and that two minutes beforehand, he'd been standing, reading a book, right by the wall that was struck, but had moved over to the door. He had been, he said, "two minutes away from becoming flour." Miraculously, however, he had experienced no long-term damage. I told him I was very glad I hadn't heard about these things at the time. He'd been in a dangerous place, he said. Now his situation was much better.

He also told us details of his trial by an ISIS judge in Mosul:

Jack:

> I walked out of court in mosul when the judge annoyed me and got jumped by loads of different people

Me:

> Jumped?

Jack:

> Like arrested
>
> I almost had a fight with three prison guards
>
> I refused to go in my cell and they jumped me
>
> They forced me to go to court

Me:

> They released you? Or u escaped?

Jack:

> Escaped
>
> The court didn't finish because I walked out
>
> I had an argument with the judge

So they put me under surveillance in what they made a temporary prison in the court

And I escaped

And slept in a mosque

Then they found me in the mosque and arrested me again

Me:

Did they beat you?

Jack:

No

Me:

I am guessing not many people argue with a judge

Jack:

Kalb

The guy was an idiot

I wanted to slap him

got in a mini fight in prison because I thought they were bullying a little Syrian kid

So I attacked

But it got split up

Turned out the little Syrian kid was not a good kid

Me:

Did u argue with the judge about religion?

Jack:
> Yes
>
> He figured out that I don't believe that he's
> muslim

Me:
> Wasn't that a bit dangerous?

Jack:
> Yes
>
> But they can't hurt anyone except by the permis-
> sion of Allaah
>
> And as you can see I'm fine
>
> Alhamdulillaah
>
> And if anything happens then it's by Allah's will
>
> And its better then what any human could will
>
> Whether it's hard or easy

By the time we received these messages, there were already court reporting restrictions in place against us, which meant that we couldn't reveal them to the world to show that, not only was Jack not with ISIS, he had been imprisoned for opposing them. These court restrictions would not be removed, because, the prosecution argued, it was us who had requested them in the first place (when we had been afraid that any publicity that Jack was trying to leave ISIS territory would endanger him). Also, the prosecution pointed out, court restrictions were necessary in order to prevent the preju-dicing of a jury in our forthcoming trial (although the myth of "Jihadi Jack" had presumably done that quite well already).

Chapter 21

Chilcot inquiry and U.K. ISIS returnees

Chilcot inquiry report, July 6, 2016

The long-awaited report by Sir John Chilcot on the Iraq war — its prelude, conduction, and aftermath — was published on July 6, 2016. As expected, it damned the reckless and morally dubious behaviour of George Bush and Tony Blair in invading Iraq on the basis of flawed intelligence information. The threat posed to the West from Saddam Hussain's weapons of mass destruction had proved to be a figment of the U.S. and the U.K.'s wishful thinking, and the legal basis for invasion was highly questionable, since a majority vote on the UN Security Council had not been achieved. In addition, the objectives of "Operation Iraqi Freedom" had not been met.

Ever interested in the personalities behind the politics uncovered in the Chilcot report, I was most struck by the account by Sarah Helm, wife of Jonathan Powell, Blair's chief of staff, of the phone call between Blair and Bush a couple of weeks before the U.S. invasion on March 20, 2003. Sarah often overheard conversations between her husband and the prime minister on the "secure phone" at their home. According to her account, Bush was much keener to discuss Blair's "terrific" body language and his willingness to "kick ass" than he was to discuss the serious issue of obtaining a second resolution from the UN. With his flattery of Blair — telling him he was "really, really brave" — and bad jokes about the French (who were opposing the second resolution) — "What did the French ever do for anyone?" — Bush had clearly already decided on his course of action and merely needed our prime minister to go along with it. I definitely blamed the pair of them for creating a situation in which young people like Jack, who have a keen sense of the unjust balance of power in the world, feel they personally have to do something about it, however misguided and naive they may be in making the attempt.

In my Facebook message to Jack on the day the Chilcot report came out, I told him that many people were calling for Tony Blair to be tried for war crimes, but everyone knew this would never happen. I said I imagined that people where Jack was (i.e., the Middle East) were pretty angry about the content of the Chilcot report, but could he please not say anything too inflammatory in his reply to me since our trial was coming up. Jack made the flippant reply, "When don't I say something inflammatory?" but that was his only comment on the matter.

Crisis management company, July–August 2016

In the weeks after the publication of the Chilcot report, John and I struggled to make sense of our and Jack's situation in light of what we hoped would be a more enlightened political context. Typically, though, the calls for Tony Blair's appearance at the International Criminal Court at The Hague disappeared as soon as they'd arrived, and the nation settled itself to enjoy the Olympics in Rio instead.

Our plans for Jack began to centre on discussions with a private company that specialized in assisting people in dangerous places, whether through extraction, crisis management, tracking, or remote medical treatment. The work such companies do is perilous and extremely expensive. Although much of their work is necessarily "below the radar" because of security implications, it is perfectly legal and their public websites are impressive, bristling with pictures of satellites and helicopters, with the names of brigadiers and major generals in the "Who we are" section. However, in the course of negotiations, and while we were working out how we could possibly raise the required funds, the company decided after consultation with their legal team that they were unable to take on our case, while wishing us the best of luck in our endeavours. It seemed that even capitalism, which is generally believed in our society to have the answer to all situations, couldn't save us.

In any case, part of the problem in helping Jack was Jack himself. His refusal to compromise and his belligerence in maintaining his own religious world view meant that he saw many of our attempts at assistance as traps designed to put him in prison — we would rather he were in prison than dead, he believed (with some accuracy). He also believed that the U.K. government had already pinned him as a terrorist, despite their lack of evidence for this, and wanted to lock him up and throw away the key for a period of many years. There was, of course, a foundation for this, too, since many of the Syria returnees had indeed been put away on long sentences on not very substantial evidence.

Tareena Shakil

The case that I had come across earlier, and now looked into in more detail, was that of Tareena Shakil, from Burton-on-Trent, who had taken her toddler son to Syria because she wanted to "live an Islamic life," but who ended up back in her home country to become the first British woman convicted of membership in the Islamic State. In January 2016, Birmingham Crown Court sentenced her to six years: four years for ISIS membership and two years for encouraging acts of terror. (I noted with some alarm that her barrister, Tim Moloney, was also my barrister. I fervently hoped he was not going to get me six years as well.) In her defence, Tareena said that she had been coerced into posing with guns and allowing her son to be photographed with guns, and also how, once in Syria, she had realized she had made a mistake.

The journalists I spoke to who had covered her case said she had jeopardized her defence by lying about being kidnapped and taken to Syria, and also because her father had made money from selling his story to the newspapers. This latter point didn't seem fair at all, since presumably she was not responsible for her father's behaviour. Also, I speculated, perhaps he had been bankrupted, like us, by his daughter's defence and had seen some way of clawing back money from the system that had condemned her. Certainly, in the article I read on the case, he was quoted as saying that her trial had been a "farce."

There were obvious parallels between Tareena's story and Jack's, since Jack, once in Syria, had also expressed a desire to live in a state governed by Islamic law. Contrary to the belief of many people in the West, however, ISIS is not the only organization that represents a society living under sharia: the legal systems of Saudi Arabia, Iran, and Sudan are all based on sharia law. Moreover, an ICM Research poll, conducted by the *Sunday Telegraph* in 2006, revealed that 40 percent of British Muslims were in favour of sharia law being introduced into parts of the U.K. Unlike Tareena, however, Jack had never posed with a gun, had said publicly he had never had a gun, and had also publicly denied, while still in Syria, that he had anything to do with ISIS. We had been concerned that the fact he had openly made this last comment presented even more of a danger to his safety than a possible air strike, since, judging from everything everyone knew about ISIS, they did not take kindly to opposition to either their control or their ideology.

As his parents, we were just as confused by his public statements on the matter as the journalists, lawyers, and friends we discussed them with. The best explanations we could come up with were either that he wasn't, after all, in ISIS-controlled territory, but in another part of Syria or Iraq, or that the ruling ISIS faction had some sort of tolerance for the fact that he was a religious purist and had by now an extensive knowledge of the Qu'ran and accompanying hadiths, even if he didn't share their views on violent jihad. All we could do was trust that he knew what he was doing and had enough respect for his own life that he wasn't going to do or say anything deliberately stupid.

Jack's Channel 4 interview, July 25, 2016

On July 25, 2016, Jack's world view was broadcast to the world. We had received prior warning of this from the journalist who had interviewed him, so it didn't come as a total shock; nevertheless, having the whole world hear that he hated us, his parents, because we were *kuffar* (nonbelievers) and "rejected the religion of truth" was somewhat hard to bear. We hoped that he was saying such things to save his own skin, given the lunatics and fanatics that surrounded him, and because we had told him to do whatever he had to do to stay alive.

On the whole, Jack's comments in the interview — which was conducted via Facebook by Assed Baig, a freelancer, and broadcast by Channel 4 — broadly followed what we had come to expect of him, such as his defiance of the British government ("Am I a terrorist? Do you mean by the English Government's definition, that anyone that opposes a non-Islamic system and man-made laws? Then, of course, by that definition, I suppose they'd say I'm a terrorist."). Also explicit was his religious world view ("I came here searching for the truth, and people of the truth, and I don't regret that I came. I searched for the people of truth, and I found a lot of them here. I found people that act on what they learn and teach, and benefited a lot from them, *alhamdulillah* [praise be to God]. So it was an odd choice, but it was a very good choice, *alhamdulillah*, because if I didn't come here I wouldn't have met some very good, knowledgeable people.").

From our point of view, it was helpful for our trial and supportive of our public denial that he was with ISIS, that he stated he was "not currently a fighter" and said, "I oppose so-called Islamic State ... and do not agree with a lot of what they follow." However, it was less helpful when the broadcast included the follow-up statement attributed to him: "That doesn't mean I am with you, the dirty non-Muslims."

This latter comment was something Jack had supposedly posted on Facebook around the time of the interview. We didn't know how to explain the oddness of it. At first, I thought it might be a literal translation of something in the Qu'ran. It was often difficult to know with Jack how much of what he said was due to his interpretation of his new religion, how much was him being a argumentative teenager (although he was now twenty years old, it often seemed he was acting out a delayed teenage rebellion), how much was him having to fit in with the people around him, or whether it was even him making the Facebook postings at all. Until we could question him face-to-face about such things, most of the answers to these questions would remain unknown. Unfortunately for us, it would be the jurors who would decide whether it was possible for the phrase "dirty non-Muslim" to be uttered by someone other than a terrorist.

One particularly worrying bit of the interview was when Jack mentioned narrowly surviving the airstrike, albeit with just a "scratch," when the ISIS-controlled area he was in came under bombardment from British, American, French, and Russian forces. To us, it seemed that it was only a matter of time before the next airstrike wouldn't miss him by a whisker but would achieve a direct hit. The only way we could cope with such thoughts was to push them away as soon as they entered our heads. Jack himself had a fatalistic attitude about being targeted. His interview comment was: "I'm not worried. Everyone is going to die on their day. Whether it's by a drone strike, a Muslim understands that his life is between the hands of Allaah. So if they want to bomb me, they'll bomb me."

The attention that was being paid to a twenty-year-old's political and religious views was, in my opinion, way out of proportion to their actual importance to world events. All it was doing was increasing the likelihood that Jack would be killed — either by ISIS as revenge for publicly condemning them, or by the coalition forces, who could view him as an inconvenience. Jack's comments were confusing to a world that was used to seeing events in black and white ("ISIS very evil, kills all detractors" versus "Good coalition forces, ridding world of evil"). Someone who was in ISIS territory yet could condemn them; was very religious and didn't feel a need to apologize for it (unlike many British Muslims, who were often called upon to apologize for and explain their religion); and had gone to a war zone to "seek the truth" rather than fight, simply didn't fit the mould. It was easy enough for most people to dismiss him as a mentally ill aberration and assume that he wouldn't last long, one way or the other. For us, he was our son, and we just wanted the chance to talk to him like a normal person without the opposing forces of police, secret services, media, legal personnel, social commentators, and psychologists all distorting matters according to their own agendas. Even in China, one social commentator had thought fit to comment on our personal situation on a website John came across: "Foul parenting!" said the post. For some reason, given all the things that had been said about us and to us, there were days when this random insult from a complete stranger on the other side of the world upset me more than anything else.

Chapter 22

The terrorism of cheese

Police threaten to arrest cheese-makers, July 2016

In the weeks after Jack's declaration of hate toward us, and the collapse of our negotiations with the crisis management company, I started to slip into hopelessness and depression. I needed a plan to wrap my brain around, yet all potential avenues seemed to be being blocked, one by one. And our son was arrogant and ungrateful, hadn't been disciplined enough as a child, and had no appreciation of the fact that we were going to prison on his behalf.

The only positive development during the summer so far had been a fortunate encounter with David Rose, an investigative journalist who specialized in miscarriages of justice. Since we had been so badly betrayed by Richard Kerbaj at the *Sunday Times*, we were initially wary of David, but were quickly won over by his charm and intelligence, and his extensive experience in covering stories of the appalling treatment meted out to the Guantanamo detainees.

And he was a friend of Clive Stafford Smith from Reprieve, which was good enough for us.

In my opinion, the best thing that David Rose did in his *Mail on Sunday* article of July 9, 2016, was to highlight the unique role of cheese in terrorism. We can safely assume that approximately two million people (represented by the circulation figures for the *Mail on Sunday*) are now aware of what they can and can't do with cheese if they don't want to run foul of anti-terrorism legislation.

The story he recounted goes like this: John and I were worryingly short of money because of everything that had happened to us in the past year or so. Not only had I lost my job at the NHS, we also had legal bills to pay and our housing benefit payments had been stopped while Oxford City Council investigated us for benefit fraud over the previous five years. Their investigation had been at the instigation of the police, who seemed determined to crush us. As it turned out, the fraud allegation was eventually dropped, although the Council still instructed us to pay back thousands of pounds of alleged overpayments.

As David reported, our friends were aware of our dire financial situation and some of them offered to help. Both John and I are quite proud people and found it embarrassing to be so nakedly poverty-stricken. We had been portrayed by the *Daily Mail* as the middle-class couple, yet we couldn't even pay our rent. Pride, however, tends to take a back seat when you are desperate and need to keep a roof over the head of your second teenage son, so we gratefully accepted offers of assistance.

One such offer came from John's friends Gill and Simon, who run a farm in West Dorset. Simon was the high-profile editor of *Land* magazine, and Gill was well known as an artist for environmental causes. They'd been shocked at our personal and legal dilemma and, in an email to John, offered financial help.

The next thing they knew, two SECTU counter-terrorism officers appeared on their doorstep and questioned them for a number of hours about their relationship with us and their views on Islamic terrorism. Gill took one of them on a tour of the farm. "He said the problem was Muslims in the U.K. don't trust the police," she reported back to us.

The police told Simon and Gill they were forbidden to assist us with any money, including helping us with the rent. If they did, they could be arrested as accomplices to terrorism. "What if we pay the money directly to the landlord?" asked Gill. This was still unacceptable, came the reply, since this would free up funds that John and I could then use for terrorism. Gobsmacked by this logic, Simon and Gill asked if it would still be acceptable to give us cheese (John and they used to have an arrangement whereby he gave them his waste grain to feed their chickens in return for their handmade cheeses). The SECTU officer granted this exception, "as long as John and Sally don't sell the cheese," and allowed the concession to be inserted into the document the police asked them to sign.

When I had heard this story from John, I was shocked, bewildered, and angry at the absurdity of it all. It sounded like a comedy sketch — how could anti-terrorism police keep a straight face when writing documents about the potential dangers of unregulated cheese? A version of the Monty Python fish dance popped into my mind, in which instead of using flatfish to slap each other on the face, the dancers used slabs of fresh Mozzarella. Of all my emotions, it was anger that won out. All I wanted to do was get the hell out of this country as soon as I could, as how could I possibly live somewhere where police decided whether our friends were permitted to give us cheese?

David revealed other useful things in his article, such as the inaccuracy of previous *Daily Mail* comments that Jack had a son and was now known as Abu Mohammed. He even went so far as to report Jack's response to these inaccuracies: "The media make stuff up." Since David Rose *was* the media, and the *Daily Mail* was his sister paper, I thought it rather gallant of him to put this in.

Publicly disowned

Unfortunately, Jack's response to the *Mail on Sunday* article was not so favourable. In private Facebook messages to John and me, he accused us of not caring about what we said about him and said he hated us for rejecting the religion of truth. Publicly on his Facebook page, he denied having OCD or being reduced to begging for chips in cafés (as mentioned in David's article) or having been brainwashed or radicalized. To us, these comments seemed to have been prompted by a sense of wounded pride more than anything else. He also called upon us to become Muslim. Most hurtfully, he denied saying in his previous post that he loved us (that post had actually scared me more than anything else, as it had seemed valedictory, starting with the phrase "If I die tonight …").

Part of the shock of Jack's deciding to publicly disown us lay in the fact that he had never gone through a "being disrespectful to your parents" type of rebellion while he was still living at home. He had never been rude to me in the way that many teenagers are rude to their parents; we had always been close and had shared a similar sense of humour. I certainly was unprepared for his being personally rude to me in private messages, which was far more hurtful than his choosing to do so in a global arena. We could always try to explain away his openly posted, hostile announcements about us, in terms of the public positioning he might be being forced to adopt, i.e., even if he wasn't actually being coerced to say these things, he was still under pressure from his immediate surroundings to maintain a certain profile.

With the intricacies of our family crisis being splashed across the entire world, John and I felt exposed and in the grip of a media monster we had no control over. Even though we knew we were just entertainment for the masses, and we would be replaced by something far more interesting the next day, our situation was more serious than typical Jeremy Kyle fodder because of the perilous situation Jack was in and the dire legal situation we were in. Because of the power that the media had in influencing events, we had no choice but to enter into this unseemly public family rift in order to save all of us — i.e., to save Jack's life from both ISIS and a possible British government drone attack, and to save John and me from prison.

I tried to explain to Jack that we would have warned him in advance about the article, but that we didn't want the secret services scuppering our plans. We had a certain amount of evidence for believing this might happen, as in the days leading up to our meeting with David Rose our phones and computers had mysteriously started playing up. We couldn't get online, and I was not able to access one particular folder on my computer (other folders I had no problems with). The folder in question contained the name of the employer I had mentioned in my bail hearing — surely this was too much of a coincidence for us to be putting two and two together and making six? Our online difficulties were not due to problems with our Wi-Fi, as *E* wasn't experiencing any problems with his computer or phone, and British Telecom assured us that there was nothing wrong with our broadband connection or signal strength. Of course, we often experienced strange happenings with our phones and computers, and we just accepted them as an annoying but inevitable part of the ongoing monitoring we were subject to. We weren't particularly surprised that technology problems, after a period of relative quiet, were occurring just when we were in the process of speaking to a journalist and were absolutely certain that they weren't just the result of conspiracy imaginings.

The rollercoaster of emotions we felt about Jack and his situation seemed never-ending: fear, anger, desperation, helplessness, self-recrimination, anger again, disbelief, and incomprehension. Fear was always the final, dominant, and all-pervasive feeling. After Jack's latest Facebook outburst, I gave him a couple of weeks to cool off, and then contacted him with messages asking if he was still alive. I received no response. It was not until five weeks later that he finally sent another message, and by this time we were so relieved — the fear temporarily allayed — that we didn't want to mention the nasty public spat that had taken place between us.

Chapter 23

Evidence and the drone strike

Drone strikes against British citizens

Part of our difficulty in helping Jack was that we weren't entirely sure where he was. We thought he was probably still in Raqqa, as that was where he was when he had last been candid with us about his location. However, that was quite some months ago now, and at one point, when he had been silent for about a month, he told us he had "been in another country." After we'd briefly become optimistic about his ability to travel, we realized that he must have meant that he was still only travelling within ISIS-controlled territory and was still having to maintain a pretense of not being personally opposed to the ruling ISIS group. Lately, though, he had been coming out with statements, published in the press, where he disassociated himself from ISIS, which made us think that perhaps he wasn't in ISIS-controlled territory after all.

We had stopped asking him exactly where he was, as he was afraid that this information would allow the coalition forces to target him directly. The extrajudicial drone strikes that had already been carried out in August 2015 against British citizens in Raqqa and elsewhere had not occasioned the sort of public debate you might expect. David Cameron had been able to order the drone strike against Reyaad Khan and Ruhul Amin, who were both from Cardiff, without the authority of Parliament, saying that it was in "self-defence" as the pair had been plotting against the Queen and "other dignitaries" in London to mark Air Forces Day. *Wales Online* reported that MI5 had managed to pinpoint the location of Reyaad Khan from tracking a phone call he had made to British friends. MI6 officers on the ground had then passed on details of the vehicle he and Ruhul Amin were travelling in so that it could be targeted in a precision strike by an RAF drone.

When I first read about the event in the newspaper, I was struck by the casualness with which it was reported, and the relative lack of discussion that followed. The fact that the action was ordered on the sole authority of the prime minister, with Parliament only being informed after the event, and justified only on the basis on intelligence information, seemed to be a huge and shocking departure from normal democratic procedures. Since the mysterious non-appearance of weapons of mass destruction in Saddam Hussain's Iraq, one would expect that the general public would be more wary about the infallibility of intelligence information, yet we were being asked to take the prime minister's word on trust. Also, at the time that Cameron had ordered this drone strike, Parliament had not yet authorized air strikes against Syria, with the vote on that issue not taking place until four months later, in December 2015.

Some newspapers, of course, did raise questions about the legality and morality of this drone strike; it just seemed to me that the issue wasn't given its due prominence, given that it could be setting a terrifying precedent. The *Times* pointed out that "the specific event against which Khan is said to have plotted an attack had passed off peacefully by the time he was killed," and even the *Daily Mail* said, "Anyone who values ... liberal civilisation can be forgiven for feeling queasy about using drone strikes as an instrument of government policy."

From Jack's point of view, it meant two things: one, that he was very wary about revealing his location (although I wasn't sure how technically aware he really was, since although he didn't use a mobile phone that could be tracked, he still used internet cafés, which could be tracked by their IP addresses. However, if he was in a major city, perhaps this was secure enough). The other was that he knew that the government needed very little evidence to justify killing him, given that he had already been dubbed "Jihadi Jack" by the newspapers, and the authorities could not seem to countenance the idea that he could be something other than a jihadi while living in Raqqa. And if the comments in the *Sun* about him were anything to go by, a segment of the British public had already decided that Jack "was an extremely dangerous individual" who "should have his head evaporated by a sniper" and "who probably rapes kids and everything."

What I found interesting about these trolls was that they expressed the same violent sentiments they were condemning in the people they were writing about, even though the targets of their venom had not actually expressed any violent sentiments themselves. However, these were the people that Cameron assumed could be whipped into a frenzy about the imminent danger of jihadis, thereby justifying the use of pre-emptive force in self-defence.

We, too, had been sent to prison for five days and faced an Old Bailey trial for fundraising for terrorism on very little evidence. We were being called jihadi terrorist accomplices, even though we had absolutely no sympathy with the terrorist cause, were atheist (I should say agnostic, at least: I could never quite get rid of the fear of the retributive thunderbolt) and had worked for charitable or environmental causes all our lives. Perhaps David Cameron believed there was enough evidence to justify droning us, too. Jack himself had not been found to be a terrorist in a court of law, and the evidence against him was circumstantial at best, consisting mostly of fundamentalist religious stuff he had posted on Facebook. The few posts that appeared to express violent sentiments probably hadn't even come from him. (I noted that the *Sun* reader who thought that Jack should have his head evaporated by a sniper wasn't in danger of being considered a terrorist, or of being tried at the Old Bailey for violent provocation.)

It wasn't just Jack who believed there was a possibility that he might be targeted in a drone strike by the British government. We recalled that when Reprieve had phoned us amid the media storm following the first press story about him, they warned us that, as a result of all the publicity, Jack could be identified by the government as a threat to be eliminated. Not only was he being criminalized on no evidence, it seemed he could be executed on the basis of false newspaper "evidence," as well. Reprieve had run a campaign against extrajudicial killings, and it remained one of the charity's key concerns. As far as we could make out, few other organizations had taken up the issue, not even Liberty, the campaigning human rights and civil liberties organization, as headed by Shami Chakrabarti until she became a Labour peer in September 2016.

Planning for Jack's extrication from the dilemma he had got himself into involved a certain amount of guesswork. We assumed his closest border was still probably the Turkish but travelling in this area was fraught with great danger. Not only were there border guards everywhere, there were land mines, snipers, and spies. It was extremely difficult to know whom you could trust. The political situation changed every day. Manbij, the ISIS-controlled town in

Syria that was en route to the Turkish border, had been captured by the Syrian Democratic Forces (SDF) on August 19 after a ten-week offensive. The SDF was made up of U.S.-backed Kurdish and Arab fighters, and their victory dealt a blow to ISIS's ability to move fighters, weapons, and supplies in and out of Syria.

Many of the ISIS fighters had moved north to Jarablus after the fall of Manbij, but then Jarablus itself — the only town on the Syria-Turkey border that remained in ISIS control — was taken by Syrian rebels, backed by the Turkish military, on August 24. The U.S., however, was not completely comfortable with this, since, although it was a military victory to rid the town of ISIS, there remained the threat that the Kurdish fighters among the SDF would not want to leave the town after they had liberated it. "We have made it absolutely clear ... that they must go back across the [Euphrates] river," said U.S. Vice President Joe Biden. "They cannot, will not, and under no circumstances get American support if they do not keep that commitment."

Turkey, the U.S.'s ally in the conflict, was worried, as was no secret, about the growing influence and power of the Kurds in the northern part of Syria, fearing that they would try to establish an independent Kurdistan along Turkey's southern border. The game of global chess being played out in this volatile region still appeared to be ultimately controlled by the U.S., which was ensuring that, while certain groups could be used in achieving the U.S.'s objectives, these groups could not be allowed to gain too much power of their own in the process.

Negotiating Jack's deliverance from this mayhem seemed well-nigh impossible. All he wanted from us to help him was money, and money was the one thing we could not help him with. It angered me to think that our involvement with the crisis management company, which would have required us to raise unimaginable sums if plans had gone ahead, was perfectly legal; yet, when we attempted to send our own funds to Jack to perform the same function at a tiny fraction of the company's price, we had been banged up in high-security jails. The unfairness and insanity of the system never ceased to astound, infuriate, and depress me.

Living in a Raqqa basement, spring–summer 2016

Over a year later, we were able to glean more information about Jack's "quiet period" during the spring and summer of 2016 when a BBC journalist, Daniel Sandford, interviewed Jack by phone in 2017 about his time in ISIS-controlled territory (or "Dawlah," as Jack called it). Sandford had been able to interview Jack from the Kurdish prison he had been taken to after being captured by YPG forces in early May 2017. In the first few weeks of his incarceration, his Kurdish guards permitted Jack to speak to his parents for half an hour every other day, and it was during one of these phone calls that I was able to put Sandford in touch with Jack. It was in July 2017, when the British got involved, that all communication between Jack and the outside world was stopped.

During the quiet period in 2016, we had received only occasional, short Facebook messages from Jack, which, it turned out, was because he had been living in hiding from ISIS in a basement with "other brothers." Some of these brothers had helped him escape via a kitchen from one of ISIS's low-security prisons, which apparently constituted the last stage of their prison system.

We also found out how Jack came to be in Raqqa itself, and how his time in the city had opened his eyes to what ISIS were really about. For the first year or so, he had been living around Fallujah, and admitted that, at that time, he and his friends had been unaware of the extent of ISIS's carnage. "After I got injured," he said, "my friends took me to the hospital in Raqqa to recuperate. It was then that I had more time to read and learn Islam. I realised how many people ISIS had killed, including their former members who had turned against them. I realised people in Dawlah had been brainwashed into believing that Dawlah's path was clear, but when I asked, 'Where does it say what they believe?' they couldn't answer. I started trying to call them to the truth by having arguments about religion — I even refuted a Dawlah member in the street, right outside the police station. He wrote a report on me, which he sent to the emir." It was after this that Jack had embarked upon life on the run, sometimes walking around the streets in the daytime because he had nowhere to go, and then either spending the night in his basement or staying in the houses of friends, until a particular house became "known" and he would have to move on.

One thing that Jack said in this particular interview, which cheered me up, was that he wanted to "explain a few things to my mum." I guessed that this meant that the hurtful things he had said about us had been made under duress, and that, once he saw us in person, he would be able to tell us what the circumstances had been.

How much of this the U.K. police knew about Jack's situation through their MI6 contacts, I have no idea, but whatever they did know, they certainly didn't think to pass it on to us or believe we should be allowed to do anything except abandon him to the fate they said he had chosen.

Conversation with Jack, August 22, 2016

Five weeks after he stated to the world that he hated us, Jack sent a Facebook message to ask how we were, as if everything was perfectly normal. I didn't want to waste time on recriminations, as he was only ever on Facebook for brief periods, and I had to type as quickly as I could to impart and receive as much information as possible in the time available. He said he had been making good progress with his future planning, but he still needed money. He knew we had problems in that regard — I told him the police would love to put us back in prison if we broke our bail conditions and sent him money — and he said not to worry if we couldn't help with that. I asked him why someone else couldn't help, since he had lots of friends, acquaintances, and contacts, but he said he didn't know anyone else who could send him money. It seemed that even the Islamic *hawala* system of money transfer (where someone pays someone who pays someone, and somehow the original debt gets paid to everyone's satisfaction) didn't operate in ISIS-controlled territory.

I told him that I hated to think of the things he must have seen, and he said he had "seen things that he wasn't even able to generate in his imagination in England." I also said my biggest fear was that he would be captured and we wouldn't know. He asked about what sort of sentence the British would give him if he got arrested, and I answered as honestly and as optimistically as I could based on my own following of recent cases: I told him "a couple of years, probably."

Again, he asked me if I had thought about becoming Muslim, and I told him he would have to convince me in person, as I couldn't think about that at the moment as there was too much going on (to which he replied, "That's a terrible excuse"). All in all, we had a pleasant conversation, just like we used to, for almost a couple of hours, as if it were perfectly normal that he would be many miles away, chatting in the middle of a war zone, where people were being bombed, maimed, and starved, and I was sitting in the house he grew up in, surrounded by his football trophies and boxes of old toys.

Evidence, delivered August–September 2016

The police evidence on our case started to arrive and was delivered to us on CDs in "tranches." As we expected, the evidence was mostly copies of our Facebook messages to Jack, excerpted from discussions between him and us about the political situation in the U.K. and the Middle East. As well, there was some technical analysis of the photo that Jack had posted of himself on Facebook standing at Tabqa dam, twenty-five miles west of Raqqa. This was the photo that had been eagerly seized upon by the press as evidence of Jack's membership of ISIS. In addition to the evidence already mentioned that counters this claim, our own family photos cast doubt on this rash accusation: in July 2016, I had discovered an old photo of Jack doing the same gesture at the age of ten, posed similarly by water, but this time next to the harbour in Falmouth on a family holiday. After this Cornish holiday snap was used to illustrate a *Mail on Sunday* article about our family, published on July 9, 2016, Jack adopted it as his Facebook profile picture, posting an accompanying caption saying, "When I did this in Cornwall noone said ISIS lool?"

The exhaustive nature of the forensic analysis into our case was typified by a report by an IT expert who had analyzed the IP addresses of Jack's, John's, and my Facebook accounts. This expert had been able to analyze the locations where these accounts had been accessed between April 2014 and April 2016, and some unexpected countries had cropped up, including New Zealand, Germany, Switzerland, and the U.S., along with the more expected U.K. and Iraq. Since he assumed that Jack, John, and I had not visited all of these places, he concluded that all three of us must have set up proxy IP servers in order to hide our real IP addresses. While I was flattered to think that the police believed me technically capable of such a thing (what on earth was a proxy server, and how did it work?), the suggestion was clearly absurd.

He had also managed to discover that I had been accessing one of Jack's Facebook accounts, as he had found a mixture of U.K. and Middle East IP addresses on it, although he did admit that I had informed the police that I frequently accessed Jack's account from Oxford and read his messages (as Jack himself also knew).

When I saw the mountain of evidence served on us — the indexes alone for the statements and exhibits ran to thirteen pages — I thought of the immense cost of investigating us, and the hundreds of hours that had been expended. It was easy to see why our lawyers estimated the overall cost of the investigation to be in excess of £3 million. Amongst the evidence were Arabic translations; transcribed interviews; expert testimony from British Telecommunications staff; digital and IT experts; witness statements from tellers, shop assistants, friends, youth workers, detectives, civilian investigators, and civil servants; and downloaded emails, Facebook messages, phone app messages, and search histories. All of this information had been compiled, coded, tabulated, cross-referenced, and presented.

Chapter 24

Crusaders and infidels

Syrian ceasefire, September 12, 2016

The Syrian ceasefire deal struck between the U.S. and Russia was due to take effect from sunset on Monday, September 12, and was to apply throughout Syria for an initial period of seven days. There had already been so many unsuccessful attempts at peace — mostly centred round talks in Geneva that usually failed to get off the ground because opposing groups were unable even to agree on terms — it seemed to be foolish to be optimistic. Nevertheless, Ian Dury's song "Reasons to Be Cheerful" kept going ridiculously round and round in my head. I knew that the usual difficulties would no doubt rear their ugly heads, i.e., both sides believing that the other was using the ceasefire as an opportunity to build up its military strength; or one side would breach the ceasefire terms with an airstrike, resulting in retaliation from the other side; and so on, until we were back to square one. The war had already been going on for five years: war pundits seemed to be agreed that two-sided wars lasted an average of seven years, but multilateral wars with several opposing groups backed by different world powers could go on for decades. In the circumstances, Ian Dury's song definitely appeared to be mocking me.

The scariest thing for us about the ceasefire was that it was the first time that Russia and the U.S. had agreed to perform joint operations. The idea was that once Russia had used its influence to persuade Assad to stop his government's airstrikes, and the U.S. had worked with the rebels to do the same, both powers would join forces to pulverize ISIS, as well as Jabhat Fateh al-Sham, which had recently changed its name from al-Nusra in order to distance itself from al-Qaeda. (The name change had, strategically, come about when both Russia and the U.S. had declared that al-Nusra was working in concert with ISIS and was therefore a legitimate target.) And although both superpowers were in agreement on this, they had not been able to agree on who else al-Nusra was allied with; the Russians believed they were often allied with the Free Syrian Army (FSA, one of the U.S.'s "moderate rebels") and had used this belief as an excuse to bomb FSA areas. This new deal between the Russians and the U.S. scared John and me because, although we weren't sure where Jack was, we suspected that he was still in ISIS-controlled territory and would therefore come under the full, combined military force of two superpowers. All Jack had to rely on — since the British government had neutered any help we might have been able to give him — was his own intelligence and ingenuity. And luck. It had been over two years now that he had been in Syria, and we didn't know how long his luck was going to last.

On September 16, 2016, video footage emerged of an incident in the Syrian town of al-Rai, near the Turkish border, which the *Independent* described as "deeply embarrassing to the U.S." The "five or six U.S. special forces," which were there to support the Free Syrian Army, backed by Turkish artillery and jets, had been driven out of al-Rai by angry FSA fighters. The video showed the fighters chanting, "Dogs, agents of America," "They are crusaders and infidels," and "They are coming to Syria to occupy it." Since the FSA were considered America's allies and moderate rebels, it is clear why this incident would be seen as embarrassing. It also showed how deeply flawed was the system of deciding who was a moderate rebel and who wasn't, as well as the huge complexity of the situation on the ground in Syria, which seemed impossible for anyone to comprehend.

From a personal standpoint, it certainly made a mockery of Lady A.'s declaration that I "knew exactly what he [Jack] was up to." I had been trying to get a handle on the situation just like everyone else: if the government was having problems, with all its manpower, and security services, and commandos, and satellites, and "ears on the ground," and police, and counter-terrorism forces, then how could I be expected to be an expert? And where was the power of individual agency in this, anyway? I wasn't being allowed by the government to act as an individual (i.e., by acting upon my maternal impulse to protect my son), yet I was being accused of knowing, as an individual, the politics on the ground in Syria and my son's role within them.

All I could think of was, who was going to protect me from the state? John told me that Danton had said the same thing during the French Revolution, a century or so after Louis XIV had declared "L'état, c'est moi." For John and me, however, there was no great public uprising on the horizon. Unfortunately, we were living in an age where a grumpy cat picture could generate millions of "likes," but a sympathetic *Mail on Sunday* article on our case barely raised a flicker of interest on Twitter. During this period in the run-up to the trial, we felt impotent and in limbo. We dreaded the sound of the phone — particularly late at night or early in the morning — in case the call contained the news we feared. When we'd asked Jack how we would know if anything had happened to him, he'd said

someone would inform us, as "many of the brothers spoke English."
I knew other parents had found out about their children's deaths by
seeing their images on Facebook, which seemed to be the ultimate
cruelty.

In the absence of popular, institutional, or social support (apart
from our small group of friends), we were increasingly grateful for
random acts of kindness from individuals: the police officer who
one day leaned across the desk as we were signing the bail sheet,
to say, "For what it's worth, I feel sympathy for your situation"; the
farmer whose land John was renting, who, knowing we were skint,
gave us a gift of a large leg of lamb; my friend and former publishing boss, Esther Whitby, from nearly thirty years ago, who both
encouraged my short story writing, and at the age of eighty-two,
lobbied numerous high-level and influential people from her "old
girls' network" on our and Jack's behalf. I wanted to say to the police officer that his words were actually worth a great deal: it made
us think that even an institution like the police, which was actively
trying to prove our guilt and was doing its best to drive us into the
ground, morally and financially, was composed of individuals who
might have their own opinions about things.

One of the few moments of comic relief in this limbo period came via one of the few journalists with whom we'd become
friends. She had covered a couple of terrorism stories in which she
had criticized the Midlands police's treatment of suspects' families,
and as a consequence was no longer invited to this police force's
press briefings. This might seem like merely petty behaviour but is
another example of how the police can control civil society if they
so choose.

In our case, the comic (in retrospect) relief occurred when the
journalist phoned to ask if she could come up to see us to get an update on our situation. When I agreed, she added that she had some
feedback "about my face" from the other journalists who'd attended

our bail hearing. I was somewhat hurt by her comment but was aware of the fact that my face doesn't look particularly friendly when it's not doing anything. (I have regularly been told, ever since I was a child, to "cheer up, it might never happen.") I thought that her advice, whatever it might be, was probably well-intentioned and would be designed to improve my appeal to the jury.

However, during the two weeks until her visit, I started to feel resentful about the implications. Everyone knew the media was all about image, but why should this be to the exclusion of justice? Why should I be judged more harshly because I had a saggy, fifty-four-year-old face and wasn't attractive like, say, Madeleine McCann's mother? Also, since our situation was hardly cheery, surely I couldn't be expected to grin like a loon. Things weren't helped by my friend's twenty-one-year-old son, who said, "Ah, yes, I can see why she would say that," and then after much prodding revealed that I had "resting bitch face." *E* confirmed that *resting bitch face* was a social media thing. I now felt worse, knowing that our chances of being sent down were compounded by my unfortunate face, and it was no wonder that Jack had condemned everything about our shallow, looks-obsessed, Western society, and had claimed that the media were only interested in him because Kim Kardashian's backside was having a day off. I was also having feelings of *Et tu, Brute?* about my friend-journalist.

When she eventually turned up at our house, and we were some way into our conversation, I gently brought up the issue of my face and asked her what the advice was she'd promised me. She looked at me blankly. "You know," I prompted her. "You mentioned it on the phone." After a few moments, I saw comprehension dawning on her (very pretty, not saggy) face. "Not your face!" she exclaimed. "Your case!" We agreed that the next time she hurt my feelings, I would ring her straightaway.

✖   ✖   ✖

Meanwhile, I discovered that Ian Dury and his song had definitely been lying to me. There were absolutely no reasons to be cheerful. The initial seven days of the ceasefire were barely up before one of the most cynical blows of the war was dealt: a convoy of thirty-one UN aid trucks that had been held up outside Aleppo waiting for permission to enter rebel-held areas of the besieged city was blown up just as it started to deliver its supplies. At least twenty people were killed in the attack, including Omar Barakat, the local director of the Syrian Arab Red Crescent. Eighteen trucks and a warehouse full of food and medical supplies were also destroyed. The subsequent bombardment of Aleppo lasted for three hours.

America blamed Russia and Syria for the attack, saying two Russian bombers were tracked in the vicinity of the convoy within one minute of the attack, and that the tail section of a Russian-made bomb was found among the warehouse debris. Russia denied the allegation, saying the attack had come from rebel militants' mortars on the ground. Whatever the truth, it was clear that the ceasefire was well and truly over, despite John Kerry's insisting otherwise at the UN General Assembly in New York, with his claim that the original Russian-American agreement should still be a basis for further talks.

Chapter 25

The return of Lady A.

Then things took a turn for the worse, most particularly for John. On Monday, September 26, he ended up back in the dock at Westminster district magistrate's court, the same court that had sent us down to Wandsworth and Bronzefield. This time, however, I was not in the dock with him; rather, I was in the public gallery observing the proceedings from the enviable point of view of freedom, as if I were a ticket-paying theatre-goer.

What was most heart-stopping about being back at Westminster magistrate's court was that we'd received the news that John's judge was going to be none other than Lady A. herself, she of the aristocratic lineage and the "send them to the gallows" mentality. Once again, she had the power to condemn John to three and a half months at Wandsworth before our trial had even started. Our legal team told us she must have specifically requested to hear the case, as it could be heard by any of the court judges, and the original papers had in fact been served on another judge. This did not bode well.

The reason for this alarming turn of events was that John had breached one of his bail conditions. Given the heavy-handed reaction to this event — two nights in a police cell in High Wycombe,

Sally Lane

being "blue-lighted" from the police cell to the court, his court appearance attended by a counter-terrorism detective inspector, a detective sergeant, and a special prosecutor — one could be forgiven for thinking he had tried to skip the country, or worse. In fact, all he had done was forget to sign in at the police station on the day we'd had friends — a family with young children visiting from Ireland — staying with us overnight.

Usually, in such a circumstance, our lawyers told us, the police would let the culprit off with a stern warning and not rearrest them. However, SECTU took a dim view of the "I'm really sorry, I forgot" excuse and questioned John at the police station as to the real reason he had failed to appear.

John had looked a sorry figure when *E* and I went to visit him at the police station on the Sunday of his incarceration: his hair was wildly askew, and he was holding up his several-sizes-too-large prison track pants in front of him like a potato sack. Apparently, he hadn't been permitted to wear his own trousers as strips of metal had been detected in the lining of the pockets, and he wasn't allowed a belt for the voluminous track pants in case he hanged himself with it.

When Lady A. entered the court room, she was smiling. This was instantly suspicious: surely the eerie smile — which I could hardly believe she was capable of — could only be the smile on the face of a tiger. Her opening comments that "Mr. Letts is clearly under a great deal of stress" didn't give any clue of her intentions. In the end, she kept up her strange smile throughout the whole hearing, delivering the verdict that Mr. Letts had clearly suffered from spending a couple of nights in a police cell (perhaps she thought that Wandsworth, where she had sent him before, had just been a jolly picnic in the park) and that the signing-in conditions should be made easier for him to remember by being restricted to one police station only.

John and I and our legal team were utterly baffled by her complete transformation: it was as if a magical pixie had spirited away her evil personality in the night and replaced it with that of a kindly fairy godmother. This feeling was compounded when she encountered John and me about an hour later as we sheltered from the rain outside the court eating our sandwich lunch. "Good luck!" she said to us brightly, as she made her way back into court, as if John and I were about to compete in some sort of horse gymkhana.

We wondered if her change of personality had anything to do with the fact that MI5 had no doubt been eavesdropping on John's recent phone discussions with Prince Charles's farm manager about his wheat-planting regimes at Highgrove the following season. All aristocrats' power derives from the Crown, after all. Of course, if this were indeed the case, we would never know.

Corn picking, October 9, 2016, South Downs

On Sunday, October 9, 2016 (only three months to go until the trial), John and I went corn picking in the South Downs. I had taken the opportunity to get out of Oxford and get some fresh air, as I was still feeling bruised by the row I'd had with the job centre the previous Friday. My "work coach" — whose expression was as wooden as the desk she sat behind — had told me the "job centre's business is not to support you when you have a downturn in your freelancing," and that I should be making more of an effort to find work where my status as a suspected terrorist wasn't a barrier to employment. She was also unimpressed that I hadn't had to make use of the job centre's services since Thatcher's Britain some thirty years before, when the legions of unemployed had resembled Soviet Union bread queues as they stretched around the block. After all, she had boxes to tick and, what was more, in her governmental role as scrounger-seeking missile, she had people like us to root out and destroy. When I started spluttering in my anger ("Do you have any idea what sort of strain we are under at present?" and "Do you realize I was fired because people are scared to work with me?"), she told me off for shouting. (This was somewhat embarrassing as it was an open-plan office, and I hadn't even realized I'd raised my voice.) All in all, it hadn't been a good day.

The South Downs, therefore, was a welcome antidote to airless government offices and heartless officials. The rolling hills around us were capped in fresh, green grass, and the views were both liberating and tantalizing in their promise of limitless and open-ended travel. When this was all over, I said, I would walk the whole of the South Downs Way (one hundred miles from Winchester to Eastbourne). (My pledge recalled the words of John's former flatmate in London, who'd done time in Dartmoor prison for drug dealing, and who told us he'd done lots of walking on Dartmoor, "although never many steps in any one direction.")

The reason for our visit was that John had been growing unusual varieties of maize at a farm near Lewes as part of his seed selection project. In an experiment that was the antithesis of artificial genetic modification, he was growing different populations of corn varieties from all over the world and then picking for replanting the cobs that were already ripe. In this way, he was selecting strains that were naturally early ripening, and would, over time, be able to develop an entire population that ripens earlier than its cousins. This sort of seed selection has been carried out by our ancestors over millennia; now, it is usually only well-funded research centres like the John Innis Centre in Norwich that carry out such painstaking work, and not maverick and slightly bonkers farmers who are making their own attempts to maintain biological diversity.

For me, as a non-scientist and a romantic, the appeal of John's corn-growing project on that Sunday's blustery afternoon lay in the beauty of the corn crop itself. I had never seen such a stunning variety of colours in one field. The cobs had kernels that were lilac, pink, buttery yellow, pale yellow, light blue, red-purple, and blue-black, sometimes with all of these colours side-by-side in the same row. The varieties had been sourced from a number of different seed banks in Japan, America, Canada, and Holland, and possessed such evocative names as Abernacki Red and Hooker's Blue. The dense rows of six-foot-tall corn plants that swayed in the breeze above our heads represented a strange and lovely experiment in which corn varieties that had probably never encountered one another before were now joined together in a beautiful display of hybrid vigour. As we harvested the cobs, and the crimson field poppies nodded their heads, and the coastal mist, which blew in from just a few miles away, created an ever-shifting cloudscape of gold, grey, white, and pink, I felt almost happy. I wished that Jack was there with us to share in the happiness. He would have thrown himself into the activity with his usual enthusiasm — or at least, the boy that I remembered would have. In the place he was now, we had no way of knowing what he was seeing, eating, or thinking; who he was meeting, talking to, or hiding from; what he was scared of; or what he was planning. All we could hope for was that he was planning something, and that whatever that was would get him somewhere safe.

Chapter 26

Heading for the border

Messages from Jack, October 2016 to March 2017

On October 12, 2016, we received a message from Jack that we hoped meant that all might be about to change. He said he was close to the border, and would we now be able to help him? Although we knew that our bail conditions prevented us from sending him money, we became hopeful that someone else — official or otherwise — might be able to help him now that he was no longer in a terrorist area. Since he had also managed to reactivate his Facebook account that I was still able to monitor, I could see that he was also contacting friends asking for financial help. It was difficult to make out the Arabic messages with the notoriously gobbledygook "Google Translate," but it was clear that money was being discussed when figures in Roman numerals appeared amid the Arabic script. Unfortunately, it seemed that Facebook was also being alerted to this financial discussion, since the day after these messages were posted, the correspondent's Facebook account was shut down with the explanation, "This message has been temporarily removed because the sender's account requires verification." Even Facebook was determined to ensure that Jack starved to death through lack of funds, whether he was in a terrorist area or not.

Although we felt cheered that Jack was finally close to the border, we were chilled that he told us that he had escaped from an ISIS prison. Apparently, although he had been put in solitary confinement, he had "argued a lot" with the guards, I assumed over theological issues. This to us seemed typical, i.e., that Jack, with his defiant nature, love of debate, and insistence on establishing "the truth," would argue with people who had the power to harm him. It bolstered our earlier view that the argumentative messages that Jack had posted when he'd originally asked for money in December 2015 did not disprove the fact that he was in danger: the police's view that no one would have a theological argument when their life was at risk did not take into account Jack's contrary personality. It certainly wasn't a reason for them to prevent the sending of money designed to save his life, because "he might be lying" about what the money was for. As I had tried to explain to David Cameron in my plea to him, Thames Valley Police should not have the power over life and death, simply because of an unfounded and unevidenced doubt on their part about what might be true, based on nothing but a hunch. Surely you should save someone's life first, I argued, and only afterward establish their guilt or innocence when they are still alive to defend themselves.

For six weeks after receiving the optimistic messages that Jack was finally moving in the right direction, out of where he was, we were suddenly plunged into despair again, as suddenly all contact from his end ceased. We assumed the worst, and at the beginning of December sent him a desperate message asking if he was still alive. The answer came back in the middle of December that yes, he was still alive, but he had been imprisoned by ISIS again, had managed to escape again, and was now in hiding. I asked him if he had argued with the guards this time, and he replied that no, if you do that in Syria, they kill you; apparently, his earlier imprisonment had been in Iraq, where it seemed that things were different.

After his incarceration in Syria, from which he'd managed to escape via the kitchen, his friends had taken him to a Syrian city where he was able to rent a house, but where he needed to keep his head down so as not to break his cover. It turned out that some of his other friends had either been imprisoned or killed, and that he had received a threatening message from the "men in the black masks" that if he tried to escape again, he would be killed. Most of these details he told me himself, but the details of his actual escape I had gleaned from the English-language messages he had sent to a U.K.-based freelance journalist, who was newly on board and clearly trying to help him.

As far as our own ability to help him was concerned, we were no further forward. This became even more of a concern when Jack revealed that his wife, A, was pregnant, the baby was due in a few months, and A was in Mosul, which was many miles away from where he was, and was currently being heavily bombed by the Iraqi government and coalition forces in an attempt to force ISIS from the city. This was the sustained attack that been planned for many months, and now that the Iraqi government had routed ISIS from nearly all other areas of Iraq, was designed to defeat the terror group in its last urban stronghold.

At the end of January 2017, Iraqi Prime Minister Haider al-Abadi declared on state TV that Iraqi forces had liberated eastern Mosul from ISIS and was now preparing to retake territory on the western side of the Tigris River, which divided the city into two. It was reported that ISIS were using civilians as human shields as they fought to entrench their position in the densely packed, narrow streets of the old city in the west. By the beginning of March 2017,

Jack told us that he hadn't heard from his wife in several weeks and feared the worst, adding that she could have died from starvation. Then, briefly, he was elated when he managed to access his old Facebook account and found messages from the middle of March indicating that she was still alive. When I pointed out to him that it was still only March 4, not March 11, he realized the messages were from a year ago and slumped back into a depressed-sounding state. I knew that the Western narrative that local women in Iraq were being forced to marry foreigners certainly wasn't true in Jack's case: he clearly cared deeply about his wife, was proud that she was educated, and "not naive" in worldly matters, having grown up during the Iraq War, and had often told me that women were separate from but equal to men.

During some chats in January 2017, Jack sent us a couple of his Qu'ranic recitations, in which his voice was strong and melodious and the words were beautifully phrased. He seemed more like the old Jack, who confided in us the way he used to. After he told us about his injury and asked if I wanted to see a picture of his arm, I declined, saying my dreams were bad enough already. I told him that I thought I'd noticed scars on his arm in the famous Tabqa dam photo of him in the newspaper, and also that he had been holding it rather oddly. He said he was surprised that no one else had noticed that, since the photo had been reproduced around the world.

Old Bailey trial, January 9, 2017

Our trial was due to start on January 9, 2017, and we reassured Jack that court restrictions were still in place, so we wouldn't talk about anything publicly that might endanger him. Since he was in hiding, it was obviously important that the terror group didn't find him, as had happened to other people he knew. One particular friend, with whom he had been staying while in hiding, had been arrested at his house — the door being kicked in during the arrest — although we learned that he was released a couple of months later. Luckily, Jack hadn't been home at the time. When I asked him how he himself had been treated during his own previous period of imprisonment, he said he had been kept in solitary confinement and had been given very little food but hadn't been beaten.

Outside the Old Bailey on the first day of the trial, a small demonstration of our friends and supporters gathered, holding placards bearing messages such as, "For the love of their child": the words of the appeal High Court judge who had overturned Lady A.'s remand decision. Friends who were also giving character statements or were "witnesses of fact" were not allowed to attend the demo to avoid accusations of bias.

Entering our plea on the first day was a surreal experience. We were in the oldest court room at the Old Bailey, a stately, wood-panelled chamber, rebuilt in 1902 on the same site as an ancient court that had operated there since at least 1585. For much of its existence, the Old Bailey had been located next to the even older Newgate Gaol, for ease of transporting prisoners to and from court. I read that hangings had been a spectacle in the street outside the court until 1868, by which time wealthier observers were travelling to the executions by London underground trains. There was even a "dead man's walk," where prisoners were pelted with rotten fruit on their way to court, and where many executed prisoners were buried.

As we sat in a wooden dock, with Perspex separating us from the benches below, as well as from the raised dais, where the judge and attendants sat straight ahead of us, a court official told us we were in the notorious Court 1, which had hosted some of the country's worst criminals. Apparently, I was sitting in the same space as Peter Sutcliffe, the Yorkshire Ripper, who had murdered thirteen women;

Dr. Crippen, who had poisoned and dismembered his wife; the Kray twins, who had terrorized the East End of London and murdered two men; and Ruth Ellis, convicted for murdering her lover, who in 1955 became the last woman to be hanged in the U.K. It seemed inconceivable that I, a suburban charity worker, whose only previous brushes with the law consisted of one parking ticket and a summons for nonpayment of the poll tax in the 1980s, should be breathing the same air molecules as the Yorkshire Ripper, let alone be charged with an equally heinous crime. Our chatty court official also explained the origin of the term "sent down": apparently, the cells were located directly beneath the dock, so that, as soon as they were convicted, defendants could be taken below ground via a trap door to begin their sentence. I had an eerie feeling that this trap door could open at any minute in the floor of the dock, creating a convenient "long drop" for a body to be hanged in, although our new court friend assured us this wouldn't happen.

The first day of the trial was the "admin day" to establish court procedure. Lord Hilliard, the trial judge, seemed to be taking a long time to decide on the admissibility of expert testimony. Our defence was not proffering a defence expert witness who would, I imagine, have tackled such questions as the difficulty of establishing the definition of a terrorist during a civil war overseas; or, perhaps, might have introduced academic issues such as those raised by Olivier Roy, author of *Jihad and Death: The Global Appeal of Islamic State* (2017), which found that jihadis were more likely to be violent criminals who had converted to Islam, rather than converts who later turned to violence. The rationale for not offering such a defence expert was that such issues would widen the scope of a trial that should be about parents trying to rescue their child. The prosecution, however, was putting forward as a witness Shiraz Maher, the radicalization "expert" at King's College, whom we had gone to earlier for advice.

Justice Hilliard seemed to be thinking aloud as he pondered the merits and demerits of accepting or rejecting expert advice, and how this expert advice might affect the state of mind of a defendant. In his discursive statements on the matter during the court session, he likened the situation to that of a patient receiving the opinion of a brain surgeon: "If a brain surgeon informs a patient they have a brain tumour," he opined, "then they probably have a brain tumour." Although I certainly agreed with him on this one, my next thought was that Shiraz Maher could hardly be compared to a brain surgeon, and that the nature of Shiraz's analysis of our situation was in no way similar to the technical analysis of an X-ray printout. In fact, during our time in Shiraz's office, he had mistakenly identified a Twitter account as belonging to Jack, when, according to dates, times, photos, and phraseology, it was clearly no such thing.

The judge's desire to clarify this issue, and to establish the legal argument on which the trial would be based, set in motion a whole chain of events. The first was that the prosecution and defence were sent away to find case law that had a bearing on the admissibility of expert testimony in our case and were instructed to return to court the following week to present their arguments. Our team quickly got to work, with the junior barrister soon unearthing a money-laundering case that appeared relevant, in which the defendant was judged according to whether he knew the property that he had laundered was "hot," or not. If he did not know it was hot, argued the defence in this case, how could he possibly be accused of laundering it? The answer lay in a subjective or objective reading of the relevant words in the legislation, "reasonable grounds to suspect." Our defence team argued that "reasonable grounds to suspect" should be equal to "reasonable suspicion"; i.e., the defendant needed to have a subjective notion that they were doing something wrong. This, after all, is the basis of *mens rea*, the "guilty mind," which is at the heart of criminal law. The prosecution, however, argued that an objective reading of the legislation was sufficient, i.e., even if the defendant did not think they were doing anything wrong, they "ought to have known," since there was external evidence available to them that indicated the wrongness of their action.

I discovered some months later why a money-laundering case was so pertinent to ours, in the absence of any other terrorism cases that could provide relevant examples for comparison. The head of public law at our firm, an expert on financial blacklisting, told us that terrorism legislation had been lifted wholesale from money-laundering legislation. This was because after 9/11 the terrorism legislation had been revised with much haste — in only three weeks — and with such little deliberation that money-laundering legislation had simply been used as a template. "Reasonable cause to suspect" that a property was hot had therefore been translated to "reasonable cause to suspect" that a terrorist was going to commit a crime. While the intention of this legislation was clearly to prevent people from carrying out a terrorist atrocity, such as an attack in a public place, it certainly didn't seem to apply to people like us, who had been caught in a police trawl that trapped anyone who might be trying to assist someone the police suspected might be involved in suspicious activity. It seemed to us more akin to the "stop and search" police policies that had been so discredited years earlier, when the only reason required for someone to be regarded as suspicious by the police was that they were Black.

As Tayab pointed out, when you consider the case of murder, which, like terrorism, carries the highest penalties in the statute book, the burden of proof required for a conviction is very high, encompassing evidence such as a murder weapon, a motive, and forensic evidence, as well as circumstantial evidence. In the case of terrorism, all that is required is suspicion in the mind of a police officer.

Having to sit in court motionless and silent, while dry academic arguments ramble back-and-forth for hours in complete detachment from the real world, is a peculiarly excruciating experience. At any moment, we knew, Jack could be killed, and these theoretical arguments would cease to have any relevance at all. But sit we had to, for this was British justice.

Trapped in this unbearable situation, I had a sudden memory of an incident from over fifty years before, when I was four years old. A shy and obedient child, I'd been taken next door to visit an elderly "auntie" for tea and had received a strict warning from my mother to be on my best behaviour. As soon as we arrived, I was installed on a very high bar stool and was told to keep quiet and not move while the adults — my mother and auntie — conducted their conversation. Marooned on my high stool for what seemed like an eternity, and physically incapable of doing anything about it — I silently began to cry. And here I was again, a grown-up, incapacitated by people more powerful than me, and again, the only thing I could do was sit still and cry.

When our defence team and the prosecution put forward their cases on the subjective versus objective legal interpretations at the Old Bailey a week later, Justice Hilliard took three days to make his decision. His final conclusion — not unexpected, according to our barrister — was that the objective interpretation, i.e., the existing version, should be upheld. Disappointed that Justice Hilliard had not proved to be a radical reformer after all, we returned to Oxford from London, informing our band of supporters and placard-holders that our legal team would appeal this decision at the Court of Appeal — the Royal Courts of Justice on the Strand — the following month.

Police evidence and betrayal, January 2017

John and I discovered that it is perfectly legal for the police to disclose additional evidence that has a bearing on a case right up until the time that the case goes to trial. This means, of course, that defence lawyers have little time to prepare their response to such evidence, and that the prosecution deliberately uses this practice as a technique to control the trial process.

Via documents finally disclosed by the police, John and I learned we had been badly betrayed by a number of people we had trusted. The extent of the betrayal was, in our eyes, breath-taking, and we felt stupider, more naive, and more gullible as more "expert" witness statements were served and more handwritten notes of telephone conversations and private meetings were revealed. It was clear that we had been strung along by a series of people who had purportedly been helping us assist Jack, but in fact had been reporting back our every word, thought, and facial gesture to the police from every "private" conversation we'd ever had with them.

Chief among these betrayers was the charity worker, Hanif, who had been enlisted by our Prevent officer to help us communicate with Jack by using Arabic phrases and Qu'ranic verses that he was familiar with and we weren't. All of a sudden, after reading the handwritten notes from a telephone conversation Hanif had had with our Prevent officer, we realized that at the same time he was saying to us, "You're part of our family now, we will help you get your son back, Jack could be a great asset in our anti-radicalization work," he was saying to the police, "Jack is very argumentative and disrespectful to his parents, he has Salafi views, he could be a danger to the state." (It is interesting to note, however, that Hanif, in his police statement, maintained that he did not believe Jack was a fighter. This opinion of his ran directly counter to the statement of Shiraz Maher, who contended that it was unlikely that anyone who went to Syria would be anything *other than* a fighter. Even the prosecution's two chief witnesses could not agree on such a crucial point.)

John and I were gutted. We had treated Hanif as a favourite uncle, believing he was our saviour as we trekked down to London to see him on trips we couldn't afford, all the while believing that he would, as he had promised, use his "high-level contacts" to cut through the bureaucracy preventing us from assisting our son. We had been gulled by our desperation, our trust in the humanitarian nature of charity work, and our personal liking for an articulate, friendly, "fixer" figure, who professed to distrust the police and their methods as much as we did. We felt like the Disney cartoon character who suddenly grows a large pair of donkey ears when he realizes he had been made a complete ass of. John commented that it suddenly made sense why Hanif would place his phone directly in front of him during our cozy, around-the-table chats, and would merely chuckle when John asked him if he wasn't concerned that "they" could be listening to us. "They know everything already," had been his breezy response.

Another part of the puzzle that fell into place when we read the police's notes concerning "Operation Kilojoule," the investigation into John and me, was the suggested role of Sally Evans, the mother whose son had become a jihadi in Kenya. Being the trusting, blinkered idiots we were, we had believed the police were acting out of concern for our welfare when they suggested they could put us in touch with Sally Evans as she had been through a similar traumatic experience. I had been initially keen on the idea, but then thought that the experience might be upsetting for her, as our son was still alive and hers wasn't. John was less keen, as he believed our situations weren't that similar: her son was a jihadi and ours wasn't. We therefore didn't pursue the proposal. Disclosed Thames Valley Police strategy documents revealed that in fact, Sally Evans had been briefed to report back on all our proposed meetings with her, in regular feedback to the police. Hanif, similarly, had been instructed to give weekly reports on his supposedly "confidential" sessions with us.

Again, we realized what imbeciles we were to believe that the police could have been acting out of a sense of social welfare. In another situation, their behaviour could be seen as entrapment — i.e., they were trying to get us to behave in a certain way so that we would incriminate ourselves. However, in our case, since we were trying to get police permission for a particular action — i.e., to send money to Jack — the police could not be accused of trying to entrap us into doing something we wanted to do. That said, and our gullibility aside, their behaviour in the whole process still strikes me as shabby, underhanded, undemocratic, and immoral, given that a life is at stake.

Chapter 27

Raqqa, a city under siege

Jack's messages, March 29, 2017

Jack:

What's new

If anything happens to me this is a letter I wrote today

It's for the general people

I'll write one for you guys

As well

Me:

What do u mean, if anything happens to you?
Are u in immediate danger?

Jack:

In Shaa Allaah

I'm in immediate danger from like 6 months

Haven't I told you that I'm on the run

I don't even have a house

The pkk are attacking

Me:

I thought u said u were in a better position

Jack:

I'm in hiding from isis and you guys can't send me money because I'm isis supposedly lol

I am but it's still not good

Me:

Can't u flee with all the other people who are fleeing?

Jack:

No because I'm british

It's obvious that I'm not Syrian

We only have one or two ways to get out and there both closed

And if isis catch me leaving they will kill me

They promised me that

Me:

Are ISIS people leaving?

Jack:

Money's not important because there's currently

no path anyway but I hope you understand how stupid the government is and how they probably caused my death. If Allaah wishes me to die

John:

Jacko, dad here. I love you my son and I will do everything to take care if your wife and child. We will tell the world of how stupid and evil the government here is. And how they refused to help. Please don't give up. We will meet again, here or in heaven my boy. I promise.

Me:

Jacko mum here let's not think about the next world, let's concentrate on this one. I know u will get through this. You just need to be strong and smart as you have been these past 3 years. We love you.

It is difficult to describe the terror of knowing that your child is in the most dangerous place on earth and there is nothing you can do about it. Knowing, also, that there is a powerful range of forces lining up to *ensure* you can do nothing about it. Knowing while you are sending the messages that they could be the last you will ever send.

In hiding in Raqqa, Jack was surrounded on all sides by regime forces, Turkish forces, and Kurdish forces. Also, under the new presidency of Donald Trump, a column of armed personnel carriers, plus five hundred troops, were deployed in Manbij, northwest of Raqqa. Although this U.S. show of force was greater than anything that had been employed by Barack Obama during the six years of war, the American government reassured the public that these troops with their back-up vehicles were stationed in a purely "advisory capacity." The attack on Raqqa from the north by the SDF (Syrian Democratic Forces), which was composed mainly of Kurdish forces, was imminent, although estimates of the timing of the attack ranged from a couple of weeks to a couple of months.

Not only was Jack in one of the most dangerous places possible, he was also prevented from escaping by the tight grip that ISIS held over the city and the checkpoints stationed around it. Reading one Syrian website that had been set up by group of citizen journalists and activists from Daraya, a Syrian town in Damascus suburbs, I was initially heartened by the news that civilians were being allowed to leave the city. However, on a closer reading, I learned that they were only allowed to leave if they obtained a travel permit bearing an ISIS stamp and gave a "convincing reason" for their reason to leave.

Me:

> I read that Is is letting is fighters leave but not civilians

Jack:

> Who said this

Me:

> Internet, but many sites are saying it

Jack:

> I'm stuck
>
> I don't know where to go

Me:

> What are other people doing in your position?

Jack:

>If he's civilian or can pretend to be civilian

>He goes

>As for me

>I'm wanted

>And obvious that I'm not syrian

>I have no money

Me:

>How are you living?

Jack:

>I have enough money to eat

Me:

>The website I just read said that is evacuated raqqa after worry about dam collapse

Jack:

>There's many people who left

>But I don't think the dam collapsed

>My friends are leaving because they look syrian

>I don't know any smugglers

>The guy we thought we knew

>Isn't around it seems

We knew that at the time of these messages that ISIS had ordered the evacuation of Raqqa residents to the hills surrounding the city, for fear that the Tabqa dam, weakened by U.S.-coalition airstrikes, would collapse. This news had been smuggled out by the activist group Raqqa Is Being Slaughtered Silently. We had also read that coalition forces were behind an airstrike that killed at least thirty civilians who had been sheltering in a school outside Raqqa a week beforehand. The U.S. was apparently providing substantial air and ground support to the Kurdish-led SDF forces closing in on Raqqa and the dam.

Raqqa itself seemed to be like the Berlin of 1945 — i.e., all the international forces were converging on the city with a view to dividing up the spoils. No one quite knew how this was going to play out. Turkey had apparently given up its claim, but how the Americans and Russians would assert their interests was anybody's guess. Being preoccupied with the war itself, the media didn't seem to be forecasting what would happen once ISIS had been driven out. The case of Mosul was much clearer: once territory had been liberated by Mosul, Iraqi government forces were in control, with both the direct support of the American government, and with the indirect support of Russia, through the Iran-backed Shiite militias. Although it was predicted that, in Mosul, a vicious sectarian war between the victorious Shiites and defeated Sunnis would continue after the defeat of ISIS, the situation did not seem to contain the complex international jostling that was taking place over the border in Syria.

The territories captured and run by the different military forces in Syria changed rapidly. Territories even changed hands in a cynical exercise of power politics, as forces jostled for position as if they were in a giant chess game, no doubt preparing for a carve-up of the country into international areas of influence after ISIS forces had been defeated. The most obvious of these manoeuvres was the "handing over" of eight villages by the American-controlled Manbij Military Council to Assad's regime forces, in order to create a buffer between the Kurdish-controlled areas to the east of the country, and the Turkish or rebel-controlled areas to the west. It was Russia that brokered this agreement, which was carried out in order to placate Turkey, whose overriding concern was that Kurdish areas in the west and east of the country should not "join up," thus creating one contiguous Kurdish territory that would present a threat to Turkey's southern border.

How one young, naive, English convert came to be in the position where absolutely everyone was against him — his own government, the coalition, the Syrian regime, the Russians, the Kurds, and ISIS — was beyond us. Finding people to help us, or to help him get out of the infernal mess he had got himself into, seemed to be akin to climbing Everest blindfolded, with your hands tied behind your back. During our anguished message-conversations with Jack, he told us that the regime or SDF forces had blocked all routes out of the city. Our only potential sources of help seemed to rest with journalists. We contacted people we knew, and a few offers of possible on-the-ground contacts were given to us to check out.

One by one, the journalistic contacts failed for one reason or another — mostly because no news agency would risk its staff or its own on-the-ground contacts by operating in one of the most dangerous regions on earth — and my coping strategy of concentrating on a coherent plan started to fail me. Once, on my way to court on the train between Oxford and London, I broke down completely. The trigger had been a polite, chatty little boy, no more than three years old, who got on the train at Reading with his grandparents and sat opposite me. "I'm going to the zoo," he informed me, matter-of-factly. "That's where I live," he said, indicating Reading's urban sprawl beyond the window. His manner and his precociousness reminded me so much of Jack at the same age that I started to cry.

And then I couldn't stop. Between Reading and London, the passengers around me quietly handed me tissues, one by one, as those I held in my hand grew sodden.

"Why are you sad?" asked the little boy as we drew into Paddington station. I didn't have any words for him, and I hope he wasn't disturbed by being presented with so much grown-up despair. The incident did make me believe in the kindness of strangers, however. As well as my tissue-givers, the toilet attendant at Paddington station also demonstrated everyday human compassion, by taking one look at my wrecked face and waving me through the barrier without charge.

Just as we were becoming desperate and beginning to try to take the step of suing the government over its refusal to help Jack (somewhat difficult, when the U.K. doesn't possess a bill of rights, and U.K. citizens have no actual citizenship rights when abroad), we received a message from Jack saying he had managed to leave the city and was in a safer place.

There was a marked change of tone to his communications — gone was the harsh, bitter cynicism with which he told us that he hoped we knew that our government had signed his death warrant — instead, he seemed overwhelmingly relieved and optimistic. Although he would not give us details of where he was, or how he had managed to escape, he told us that he was still working on his plan to leave the country, locate his wife, and enable her to join him once he was out. I knew there was no point badgering him to give us a clue as to where he was. At least the certainty of a horrible death, which was linked to his continued presence in Raqqa, now appeared to be allayed, and we felt a temporary sense of reprieve.

Court of Appeal, March 8, 2017

Also at the beginning of March was our appeal at the Court of Appeal — the Royal Courts of Justice — against the judgment of Justice Hilliard, which held that the phrase "reasonable grounds to suspect" should not be given a subjective interpretation.

The three High Court judges in their robes walked in solemnly and took their places at the high table ahead of us. I searched their faces, looking for signs of compassion or engagement. The one in the middle, whose name I've forgotten, seemed to have a benign smile on his face, which appeared kindly and encouraging. When I compared notes later with Esther, my eighty-two-year-old friend, who faithfully attended all our court sessions, I found that she and I agreed that when the legal arguments became too abstruse to understand, we resorted to trying to decipher the judges' body language. Unfortunately, however, High Court judges appeared to be practised in the art of remaining poker-faced.

As it turned out, some of the judges' thoughtful questions surprised us and raised our hopes that they might even rule in our favour.

"What about fake news?" asked one of them, when the argument turned to the issue of whether a defendant could be convicted of acting on a belief that was false, but which had been given the authority of emanating from an official media channel. I was greatly surprised by the pertinence and topicality of the question, believing, like most people, that judges do not really live in the real world of the twenty-first century.

"What if the defendant is stupid?" asked another, elucidating the point that even if the grounds for objective suspicion are as clear as day, a stupid person would not be capable of grasping them. I myself had previously asked our lawyer the same question, and she had informed me that, unfortunately, I would have to be legally classified as a cretin not to be held mentally responsible for my actions.

All in all, we felt cheered and hopeful after the Court of Appeal session, which had lasted more than two and a half hours. So it was with some disappointment that we received the announcement three weeks later that we had lost. The Court, however, did concede that there was a public interest in appealing this judgment, ruling that the question of appeal "had merit." This meant that we were given permission to appeal to the Supreme Court, the highest court in the land, which had promisingly defied the government with their recent ruling that Brexit negotiations should only go ahead after a parliamentary debate. In the meantime, our trial date was reset to September 2017. We had the summer to intensify our efforts to help Jack.

Limbo, May–September 2017

In the limbo period, trying to extract Jack from the pit of hell while waiting for the Supreme Court appeal and our trial, I decided to knit Jack and his wife's baby a blanket. We had been told the baby was due that month (May), and that it was believed to be a boy (we weren't sure why), so I chose to make the blanket a blue one. Since I am a novice knitter (unlike my late mother, who could knit, watch TV, and carry on a conversation all at the same time), my blanket was far from perfect, with misaligned sections and lumpy bits. However, I rationalized to myself that a mother in war-torn Iraq wouldn't care about a few dropped stitches. I wasn't completely foolish: I knew that the chances of my lumpy blanket actually reaching Iraq were about as remote as peace in Syria within the next three years. I also knew that the chances of babies surviving in Mosul were greatly reduced: as well as the dangers of the conflict, food was scarce, with newborns having to survive on boiled grains and water. Breastfeeding was often impossible because the babies' mothers were themselves undernourished and couldn't produce much milk. My knitting contribution arose out of a desire to feel that I was doing something, both as a future grandmother and as an otherwise powerless human being. I wondered if there was some atavistic urge for womenfolk to create things with their own hands as soon as new, vulnerable life was on its way. Perhaps handicrafts are also something women do during war-time when confined to the house: all those knitters during the Second World War who created complete outfits for strangers in occupied Greece, laying the foundation for Oxfam's current legions of knitters who can rustle up garments for Somalian orphans and displaced Yemenis at a moment's notice. Knitters of the world unite, as Marx sort of said.

Chapter 28

Escape from ISIS territory

Escape, May 3, 2017

On May 3, 2017, we received the extraordinary news that we'd been awaiting for three years: Jack was out of ISIS territory. The relief was overwhelming: it felt as if our nightmare was finally over and we might now be able to breathe, laugh, and socialize again like normal people.

The conversation, which seemed like a miracle, went like this:

Jack:

> It's me. When u get this message send me something to make sure it's me.

Me:

> Finally Ive been so worried. OK. Ill test you.
> What was the name of the head of discipline at your school who gave you C3s [detentions]?

Jack:

Mr Davis? So many people used to give me C3s.

I'm out by the way.

Me:

Weve been worried sick. Out of the country???

Jack:

Out of what they call isis territories.

Me:

OK, that's fantastic news. Are u safe and unharmed?

Jack:

I'm fine. They gave us a house. And internet.

As the conversation went on, we learned that Jack had escaped from Raqqa with a group of refugees and had been offered a place of safety by a Kurdish group in northern Syria. He was on a working farm with a swimming pool — which he sent a photo of — and his newfound friends kept offering him cigarettes. He gave us details of how he had escaped from Raqqa:

> It took a long time to organise. It involved walking for like 30km, a lot of walking in thorns, annoying prickly stuff. At first we went on motorbikes; afterwards it was just walking. We had to walk straight behind the guide because there were landmines.

He'd found out that the Kurds already had a dossier on him consisting of British newspaper cuttings and reports from Kurdish spies in Raqqa. "Apparently, my file is very, very good," Jack told us. "The [Kurdish] spies confirmed I was one of the good guys. It was very clear I was not a member of said group. I was within their territories openly saying they're not upon the truth. People genuinely thought I was crazy for the doing that; people inside their territories are too scared to even speak. It was amazing that they didn't kill me, they said they would, they were just trying to scare me. The important thing to them is hierarchy." The rest of the dossier, apparently, was made up of British media articles.

Later on in the conversation, he explained that people detained by ISIS would be questioned for a month and tortured, and that some of his friends had been treated in this way. It seemed that he had been spared this: the only explanation I could think of for this was that by this time Jack knew the Qu'ran inside and out and was able to provide Qu'ranic verses to back up his understanding of Islam.

I was reminded of an incident related by a Syrian journalist living in Raqqa, who used the pseudonym "Tim Ramadan" in his series of pieces for the *Guardian* about life under ISIS. In this particular incident, Ramadan had been stopped at an ISIS checkpoint and had been asked religious questions, being warned he would be "sent to a sharia education camp if he didn't know the answers." After he'd related what he said were "Islamic stories and legends of early Muslims," the guard let him go. Part of the absurdity of this incident, as Ramadan reported later, lay in the fact that he had conjured up the stories on the spot from his own imagination.

Jack's plan now was to get a phone so that he could search for his wife and plan his escape across the border. Because the Kurds had adverse relations with the Turks, this would not be the border we might expect. The Turkish border, he explained, had a big cement wall, cameras, and border guards who shot people. He had lots of questions about how he would be treated in England and what sort of court process he could expect. The Kurds, he said, had given him a choice of either being returned to Britain or living in a Kurdish city. Since he would know no one in Kurdish territory and wouldn't be able to leave the house as he didn't look Kurdish, he said he'd opted for the British option; the Kurds had assured him they would negotiate favourable terms with Britain for his release, including the condition that he wouldn't be imprisoned. On May 11, 2017, he told us the whole process of handing him over was starting, and he would keep us informed, "in shaa Allaah."

In retrospect, our joy at Jack's escape from ISIS territory and our eager anticipation that he would now be returned to us seem absurdly naive, childish, and fantastically misjudged. We'd been told by the police, on the advice of the Foreign Office, in December 2015 that they would be able to help us once Jack left ISIS territory. Now the Foreign and Commonwealth Office (the FCO) was denying they had ever said this, and what they had actually meant was that they would only be able to help once Jack made it across the Syrian border. What we didn't know in those heady and foolish days of early May 2017 was that one of the most protracted, anguished, frustrating, inexplicable, and seemingly unreal periods of our entire battle to extricate Jack from Syria was about to begin — and that once the impregnable, immoveable, illogical, and implacable portcullis of the British state slams shut against you, there is absolutely nothing you can do about it.

✳   ✳   ✳

One of the first ways we tried to raise awareness of the government's promise to assist in Jack's return was via an interview in mid-June 2017 with Daniel Sandford, BBC Home Affairs Correspondent.

After two weeks in solitary confinement — that he'd been told was for his own protection because the other cells "were full of

REASONABLE CAUSE TO SUSPECT

terrorists" — Jack had given an interview to three supposed BBC journalists, although he suspected they were actually just "random Kurdish people" as their English was poor. It now turned out that these "journalists" were shopping out the video of the interview, asking £10,000 — which no British broadcaster or newspaper was prepared to pay. We started to suspect that Jack was being treated by the Kurds more as a high-value hostage from whom money could be made than as a British citizen about to be returned to his country.

Daniel Sandford convinced John and me that we should do our own interview to help put pressure on the British government to negotiate with Jack's detainers. He promised that nothing would come out in the broadcast about Jack's wife, as Jack was extremely worried that any publicity would endanger her safety in Iraq. This promise was not adhered to. In fact, the whole interview ended up making Jack's situation worse, with his being put into harsher solitary confinement with no phone privileges or adequate food and accused of "leaking information" to the British press.

Jack's messages to us after this period of solitary were harsh, bitter, and despairing, unlike those jubilant messages after he first escaped from ISIS territory. On July 1, he wrote:

> I now only have 30 mins [on the net] every week.
> If I'm not out in 2 days I'm going to do some-
> thing crazy. I don't want to go crazy so I might
> have to solve this in another way.
>
> Ive had enough
>
> Where are the Canadians?
>
> I lost my wife. I still haven't seen my son. I've
> had enough.

I used to think going crazy would be nice and much easier. But I don't want to go crazy any more. But I don't know if it's too late.

Even though I hate dowlah [ISIS], I met good people. I had real friends, not dowlah members. Rather we were against dowlah from the inside. Not that anyone cares. People who were ready to die for me. In the outside world. Out of dowlah.

The pen is lifted. Whatever I do without intention is not written down

It's obligatory under Islam to have patience but if there's something someone physically can't do, then he's not responsible.

A week beforehand, Jack had told us that he was occasionally being allowed out of his cell:

Sometimes in the morning they let me go out to a patch of sand, sometimes there are lizards there, the lizards are quite interesting. I watch the ants, ants are actually quite interesting.... [It would be good to be] where I can see the sun, see trees, birds, and walk around for more than 10 minutes a day.

Now, it seemed that even that was not allowed:

The whole 23½ hour thing is no longer 23½ hours, it's now 24 hours. There's no such thing as going out any more.

John and I were in a quandary. Having believed that publicity was key in extricating Jack from his situation, we now found ourselves blackmailed into keeping quiet by whoever was controlling Jack's capture. We guessed that this must be the British authorities, since the Kurds had allowed Jack to communicate with the outside world before details of his situation appeared in the British press.

Realizing Jack was being punished for our going public, we began to panic about an interview we'd pre-recorded with the *Victoria Derbyshire* show, a BBC current affairs program, and tried to prevent its release. It had already been substantially delayed by emergency coverage of the tragic fire at Grenfell Tower, but the program refused to pull it completely, assuring us they wouldn't put Jack in danger by saying anything negative about the Kurds' treatment of him. In this respect, they were true to their word, but the interview on the whole was very hostile, with its theme of "Why should we let him back in this country?" and no mention of the fact that, as Jack said, he "hadn't actually done anything."

One of the major problems of our engagement with the media, which continued for the entire period leading up to our trial, was that there was a contempt-of-court order in place against us. According to the terms of this order, John and I were not allowed to talk about our knowledge of Jack's activities between the time he left the U.K. and the time of our alleged offence in sending money to him. This was supposedly to prevent the prejudicing of a future jury in our criminal trial; however, what it amounted to was a gag order preventing us from defending Jack with information we knew to be true. It meant, for example, that the *Victoria Derbyshire* interview did not broadcast Jack's statement, which we had quoted, that he'd "never had a gun in his life" (hardly something a hardened ISIS fighter would say), on the grounds that airing this would reveal our knowledge of his activities. Similarly, since there was already a considerable amount of disinformation in the press about him, it also prevented us from correcting mistruths that had come to be accepted as fact. This didn't matter so much for our own sakes, since we knew we could address these issues at trial. But for Jack, it meant that he was being held indefinitely on false charges with no opportunity to put his side of the story. He had been convicted by the British newspapers and was now unable to defend himself via the same route.

David Rose, who had championed our cause from the start, was the only journalist who attempted to reveal what he could about Jack's escape and his life in hiding from the terror group, without breaching the contempt-of-court order (although apparently, he was told by a judge his article had "sailed close to the wind"). But now that we were aware that Jack's treatment was linked to media involvement, we knew that we had to be extremely careful, and for the next five months — until we realized that the Kurds were, in fact, manipulating the media via their own strategy — we tried to work below the public radar and exert influence in other ways.

British government response, May 2017 onward

The British government, as represented by the Foreign and Commonwealth Office, came up with a range of excuses as to why they couldn't help us, none of which revealed the real reason: they simply didn't want to. The first excuse on May 26 was that it was "difficult for them to establish the whereabouts of British nationals in Syria." We pointed out to them that Jack had already given us a description of the prison he was in ("a terrorism prison with guard towers that used to be a school"), and its location ("on the outskirts of Qamishli"), a town in northeastern Syria about five minutes' walk from the Turkish border. Jack had even given us the name of the prison governor, in the expectation that a British consular official could simply ring him up.

In another display of creative excuse-making, the British government informed our lawyer on June 6 that Jack was unfortunately being held by the "wrong" Kurds — the Syrian Kurds, rather than the Iraqi Kurds. Apparently, if the latter had been detaining him, the government would have been in a position to help, since there was a consulate in Erbil, Iraqi Kurdistan, but regrettably no staff a few miles away in Syrian Kurdish territory. The only way that the British government could speak to the Syrian Kurds was via their Iraqi Kurd intermediaries. However, they helpfully added, if Jack were able to make his way to Iraqi Kurdistan, they would be happy to assist him there. After — with some difficulty — managing to secure a face-to-face meeting with the FCO, I pointed out to Jim Collins, Head of Special Cases, that since Jack was being held under armed guard twenty-four hours a day, he was unlikely to be able to jaunt eastward across the border. To this, I received the diplomatic equivalent of a shrug — i.e., a blank expression and no comment.

John then, adopting Jeremy Paxman's forthright and vigorous interviewing technique on the BBC, asked Jim Collins's assistant at least ten times whether the FCO's Iraqi intermediaries had actually *asked* their Syrian Kurdish contacts about Jack. After valiantly fending off each of John's questions, the assistant finally caved in and admitted that, no, they had not; any contact by British government officials with the Syrian Kurds was theoretical only.

The recurring refrain — repeated ad nauseam in every letter we ever received from the Foreign Office — was that "FCO advises against all travel to Syria, and has done so since 2012. The government has no consular presence in Syria, therefore we are unable to assist." Some of these nine or ten identically worded letters went further, to say there was nothing in either domestic or international law that obliged the government to do anything at all.

Unfortunately, according to our lawyers, it appeared that the government was technically correct in saying that any possible action was at the discretion of the Foreign Office — i.e., if a British citizen got into trouble abroad, they did not have any *right* to assistance. There also appeared to be a complicating clause that meant that the Foreign Office could not do anything that might influence foreign policy. This meant that if Boris Johnson's policy as Foreign Secretary was to do nothing about Syria, there was nothing anyone could do to challenge it. Any appeal to justice, morality, natural law, decency, British values, common sense, or mercy fell on extremely deaf ears. You could bash yourself senseless against the brick wall of the British establishment — the brick wall doesn't care, and you just end up bloodied and bruised from your efforts.

It seemed to me inconceivable that this could be the case. The government's saying it "advises against all travel to Syria" when Jack was already in Syria seemed akin to saying, "We advise against getting raped and murdered when abroad," even though when such things did happen to British citizens, consular officials were generally expected to help. Certainly, their cheerful leaflet *In Prison Abroad* listed the ways in which the FCO could help if a British National was arrested or detained overseas, including contacting them in prison and visiting them "if that is what they wanted," giving them information about the local legal system and providing lists of local lawyers, and putting them or their families in touch with a prisoners' welfare charity, "Prisoners Abroad." Importantly, it emphasized that, if detained, the prisoner should insist that the British Consulate be notified: "this," stated the leaflet in bold letters, "is your right." It seemed that all these forms of assistance were available to you — unless your name happened to be Jack Letts.

In their more general guide, *Support for British Nationals Abroad*, the FCO pledges that its most vulnerable customers ("customers"?) would be contacted "within 24 hours of being notified of their situation." To us, it was clear that Jack should be assessed as a priority case. His conditions were appalling, and he was being held on no charge. All we were asking for was for him to have a fair trial in his country of citizenship. John, in particular, had stated loudly and firmly in several interviews that if Jack had done anything wrong, he wanted nothing to do with him, and that Jack should be allowed to defend himself. I could never bring myself to say the first part of this, since I couldn't imagine my gentle, intellectual, and idealistic son being involved in violence and believed him when he said he hadn't been. But we both thought it wasn't too much to expect the British government to assist in his being brought back to England so that he could tell his side of the story. Didn't we as a country believe in the rule of law and not in the rule of the mob?

We also couldn't understand why the government wasn't at least interested in questioning Jack about what he knew about ISIS in Syria. Surely, he could be of use in supplying intelligence information about other British citizens who had travelled there, and perhaps even provide answers to families desperately seeking information about their loved ones — the three teenage London girls who had vanished, probably into Syria, for example, or John Cantlie, the captured journalist? Jack had told us that he had seen things in Syria and Iraq that he "couldn't even generate in his imagination in England." Perhaps it was his story that the British government didn't want to get out, for fear that it wouldn't fit neatly into their simple "evil jihadi" narrative that fuelled their counter-terrorism strategy.

Kurdish officials had apparently questioned Jack about well-known ISIS members who had been stationed in Raqqa, some of whom he had seen in that city, or knew had been killed. He had also been asked identification questions that he was told had come from the British government (such as "What is the colour of your dad's car?"). Beyond that, however, it appeared that the British government hadn't the slightest interest in either Jack's welfare or in any useful regional knowledge he might possess.

Meeting at Foreign Office, June 28, 2017

The Foreign and Commonwealth Office on King Charles Street, SW1, sandwiched between Horse Guards Road and Parliament Street, and a stone's throw from Downing Street, was designed by its Victorian architects to showcase the riches and glories of the mighty British Empire. On our visit, it was difficult not to be impressed by the grand columns, richly decorated ceilings, sweeping central staircase, and fabulous murals. I didn't know what the effects would be on the psyche of those who spent their working lives amid such splendour, although I could hazard a guess that those effects might include a sense of personal importance. Indeed, some months later at a second FCO meeting, which I'd refused to attend, a sense of regret at loss of empire was expressed by Jim Collins, Head of Special Cases, Consular Affairs, and related to me afterward by John. Just before the meeting, Collins had opened the room's window blinds, which overlooked a magnificently portico'ed courtyard. This ornate and spectacular chamber below, he grandly explained, was the famous Durbar Court, "from where we ruled India."

In this, the first meeting, John and I were not there to admire the architecture; we were there to ask consular officials why they couldn't help us. I had warned John that if they said, "We advise against all travel to Syria" one more time, I wouldn't be responsible for my actions.

As the consular assistant poured the tea into the finest bone china cups and offered us expensive chocolate biscuits, it occurred to me we might as well still be living in the days of the Raj, where four o'clock teatime was unfailingly maintained even while the horrors of the Indian Mutiny raged on. Certainly, in that moment, Syria seemed another world away, and I had the absurd thought that it would be considered rude to even bring the subject up.

John had no such qualms, of course, and launched into a series of heated questions about the government's failure to act: Did they know that Jack currently feared he was losing his mind and believed he had experienced what he said was "universally considered a mental breakdown"?

I knew that Jim Collins indeed did know about it, as it had prompted our meeting here in the first place. When I'd received Jack's message on June 25 that he was being kept in a dungeon in solitary confinement, he'd been shouting at himself like a crazy person, and had punched the wall of his cell until his hand bled, I'd phoned the emergency line of the FCO in a screaming and sobbing panic. This had achieved the effect of this instantly arranged face-to-face meeting, unlike our previous polite letters, which had produced no response whatsoever.

John asked what the Foreign Office intended to do about the situation.

Both Jim and his assistant were regretful that there was nothing they could do. They hadn't even had confirmation about Jack's whereabouts.

Had they asked their Iraqi contacts for information about him?

Yes, said the FCO, they had.

And had this produced a response?

Unfortunately, not.

(Then followed John's previously mentioned episode of repeating the same question, where the assistant admitted that, although British consular officials had asked their Iraqi colleagues about Jack, the latter had not actually passed on the query to their Syrian contacts.)

John:
> What is the position of the Ministers on Jack's situation?

FCO:
> We cannot comment on this, since our role is to produce recommendations which the Ministers will or will not take up as appropriate.

John:
> Is there any will on the part of the Ministers to assist anyone in returning from Syria?

FCO:
> At this stage, there is no policy in place to address the issue of Syrian returnees. As you know, we advise against all travel to Syria and have done so since 2012.

There it was: the dreaded trigger phrase uttered — seriously, how could Boris Johnson, then foreign minister, get paid thousands of pounds a year to produce only one paragraph on Syria in five years? — I was starting to feel violently angry, and butted into the conversation:

Me:
> How would you feel if it was your son?

FCO:
> Yes, I can see that it would be very distressing.

Me:

>And how would you feel if it was your son and you were faced with someone like you?

FCO:

>In that situation, I would at least know that I had done everything I could to assist him.

At that point, my boiling rage would not allow me to stay in the room without doing something violent — flinging the tray of bone china cups to the floor, perhaps. I stormed out, leaving John to deal with the regretful Jim Collins, who, it turned out, had managed to secure himself an OBE — no doubt for his admirable stonewalling abilities in the face of tricky political situations the government would rather ignore. I realized after a few moments that the assistant was trotting behind me, presumably to make sure I left the building without hitting someone. As she and I took the lift down together, I broke my furious silence by asking her how she could possibly do her job, given that her job was to do absolutely nothing. She didn't reply.

A year and a half later, when we received disclosure from the FCO after our Freedom of Information request, we learned that Jim Collins had judged this on-elevator comment of mine to his assistant to be "unkind." Just as well she wasn't being locked in a dungeon with no food, company, or hope, since Jim Collins's Foreign Office vocabulary would never have been able to rise to the occasion.

Chapter 29

"Disappeared" in Rojava

NGO/MP response, July–August 2017

Having been failed spectacularly by the British government, John and I turned to civil society groups and our local MP for help. One by one, they failed us, too, seemingly too frightened to challenge the powers that be. In our case, the powers that be appeared to be the American government, which was in charge of security operations in northern Syria. We guessed that they were paying the Kurdish authorities to keep prisoners indefinitely where they were, as a way of shelving political problems. I recalled my Oxfam colleague who had refused to give me a character reference for my bail application, as this might "give Oxfam visa problems."

I recalled, too, a sinister incident related to me a few years earlier by another senior Oxfam colleague, who at the time also served on the board of a large international human rights organization. On the occasion in question, he and other senior executives from major charities had been called to a confidential meeting at the U.S.

embassy in London. Here they were told that they should play their part in the "war on terror" by reporting on any suspicious locals in the grassroots civil society organizations they were funding across the world. Since the U.S. didn't have convenient access to these local groups, charities should act as their "eyes and ears" on the ground. U.K. charities, it seemed, were now expected to report the U.S. State Department, just like everyone else.

The various charities and human rights organizations we contacted, and to whom our hundred or so friends and supporters wrote letters, gave us a variety of reasons why they couldn't help. Amnesty told us they didn't think public campaigning would be beneficial in Jack's case, although I heard privately from a well-connected friend that their senior management team had decided that the case was "too politically sensitive." Human Rights Watch in London said they did not take on individual cases. Prisoners Abroad could help only if the government was engaged with the case, as they gave only welfare, not consular, support. The Red Cross took our details through their Refugee Services and International Tracing department but were not able to give us details of any progress on our case, as their efforts to negotiate access to prisoners in Syria was highly confidential.

Our MP, Anneliese Dodds, attempted to get a response from Alistair Burt, Minister of State for the Middle East, with regard to government action on Jack's case. All she received were six, practically identical, letters from him, stating that the government advised against all travel to Syria. Her question in the House of Commons elicited the same response. Although we urged her to ask Jeremy Corbyn, a prominent supporter of the Kurdish democratic cause, to use his high-level Kurdish contacts to gain some movement on Jack's case, the only response we have ever received from the Leader of the Opposition — a supposed man of principle — has to date been deafening silence.

Sally Lane

Rojava/Kurdish representative response, July– August 2017

John, when I met him, was an earnest hippie who wore a red bandana to keep his flowing blond locks out of his eyes. He'd been a proponent of Murray Bookchin, an ecological anarchist, ever since he was a student. Bookchin's proposed principles of a decentralized political structure, based on equality, feminism, and grassroots democracy, had appealed to John's enthusiasms for environmentalism and organic farming and dislike of hierarchy and corporatism. Like many people on the left of the political spectrum, John had supported the Kurdish project to implement Murray Bookchin's ideas in a grassroots revolution, which, amongst other things, freed women from the shackles of traditionalism and offered the promise of a "beacon of democracy in the Middle East."

During the civil war in Syria, the Syrian Kurds had gained de facto autonomy in the northern part of the country after Assad withdrew his troops from the area to fight against rebel forces in Aleppo. The Kurdish Democratic Union Party (PYD) officially announced its regional autonomy in 2014, and the Constitution of Rojava (the newly formed territory) was drawn up as the legal framework to guarantee the social and democratic rights of its citizens in the three cantons, Kobane, Afrin, and Jazira. It seemed that the Kurds were determined to create, out of the ashes of war, a new and more just society, safe from the persecution they had endured historically as a minority group under the governments of Turkey, Iran, Iraq, and Syria.

Given its socialist utopian ideals, it is no wonder that the "Kurdish project" became the darling of the left in the Western world, and why political leaders like Jeremy Corbyn were keen to ally themselves with the Kurds' social and economic revolution. It also explained why the left didn't want any "inconvenient truths" about the Kurdish project spoiling the Kurds' idealized image or raising questions about the contrast between the aims of the Kurdish revolution and its actuality. Truths such as, Why were the Kurds holding Jack in appalling conditions on no charge, and with no access to a lawyer, against the principles of the Geneva Convention and of its own Constitution?

Early in July 2017, John was keen to meet with the U.K. representative of the Kurdish Democratic Union Party so that they could discuss both their mutual appreciation of Murray Bookchin and a way forward to secure Jack's release. A mutual friend managed to arrange a meeting. At first, the Kurdish representative was nervous, saying to John, "I shouldn't really be talking to you" (why not?), but during a four-hour meeting in a coffee shop in east London they bonded over organic farming, ecology, and producer-consumer cooperatives. John even offered his services as a wheat expert for the Kurdish project, just as our student generation in the 1980s had volunteered to assist the socialist project in Nicaragua, working as idealistic young labourers in the new agricultural co-operatives.

We knew that this representative had some influence with the British government, as he had met a few times with the U.K.'s Foreign Affairs Committee (FAC). Indeed, we had used this knowledge (gleaned from an obscure parliamentary paper on the internet) to give the lie to the British government's position that they had no diplomatic contact with the Syria Kurds. (The FAC's response to this was that occasional diplomatic contact was not the same as consular assistance.) In his coffee-shop meeting, John was assured that Jack would receive psychological and medical help while he was in prison, as we were extremely worried about his mental state. In his last messages to us on July 8, Jack had told us he was being tortured and had "decided to take matters into his own hands." We did not know what that meant but were terrified that he was intending to kill himself.

In light of the British government's apparent inability to find contact details for Kurdish officials in Rojava, John and I had done our own trawl of the internet. We'd chanced upon an urgent action report from Amnesty International, calling for the release of a Kurdish opposition activist, Suleiman Abdulmajid Oussou, who was being held by the Asayish (Kurdish police) in Qamishli, the same location Jack had given us. The description of the prison where Oussou was being detained also sounded remarkably similar, including the dangerously high temperatures, hardly any light, and lack of ventilation — in Jack's word, a "dungeon."

Attached to the bottom of Amnesty International's urgent action report were the contact details of the head of the Kurdish police, Ciwan Ibrahim, and the co-president of the PYD, Salih Maslem Mohamed, provided so that Amnesty's vast network of supporters could write to the Kurdish authorities to demand Oussou's release. Sure enough, these were the exact contact details of the authorities holding Jack. When we contacted Ciwan Ibrahim, we received a reply saying, "I hope you are all fine. The Asayish security apparatus in Rojava and North Syria had brought 'British Jack' during a special security operation. What happened was good, for we have Jack now and he is fine." It seemed baffling to us why Amnesty believed that public campaigning was appropriate for Oussou but not for Jack, particularly when Oussou was released the day after the urgent action report was dated. It was also bizarre that we could find out Jack's whereabouts while the British government was incapable of doing so.

Rescue plan, July–September 2017

In the summer of 2017, our biggest supporters — in the absence of any governmental, journalistic, or NGO support — was an independent film company called Amazing Productions. After the initial wariness we now had with all journalists, we soon came to realize that this film company was the genuine article: they were fully aware of the political situation on the ground in Iraq and Syria; already had contact with the relevant individuals in the U.K. and Rojava; had done their own investigations into Jack's activities and had found no evidence of violence or criminal activity; and of most interest to us, had a very useful "fixer" who had access to YPG and PYD contacts in the region. This contact was an ex-army officer who had left the military to make documentaries about conflict-ridden areas. During our meetings, we found him to be a softly spoken, intelligent, and articulate young man — more like a university tutor with muscles than an army officer.

In a series of communications optimistically entitled "Going to Qamishli," John and I and the film company planned our rescue mission to Rojava. Strictly speaking, this was John's and the film crew's rescue mission, since it was thought I would be more useful on the home front, and it didn't make sense for both of us to be shot, killed, or kidnapped. John would undergo "hostile environment training" for three days at the BBC in preparation for the trip. The first hurdle was obtaining his passport back from the police, who had seized both of our passports when we were charged. We were told that all that was required for this was an invitation from the Rojavan authorities, who had already given their permission for the film crew to gain access to Jack.

John and I latched onto this hopeful prospect with gusto. The Kurdish official who had granted permission for access, Sinam Mohammad, was the PYD European representative based in Berlin. We understood from Amazing Productions that she was keen to show the Kurdish project in a good light, and to demonstrate that the Syrian Kurds treated their prisoners well and in accordance with international law. This meant that we weren't unduly concerned at early delays to the trip, caused by the fact that Peter Taylor, a veteran BBC broadcaster in the Middle East, was making a program for *Panorama* about Turkey and didn't want to upset his documentary subjects by doing a program about their adversaries, the Kurds. There were other broadcasters Amazing Productions could pitch to.

Around this time, I was corresponding via Whatsapp with a female YPJ fighter who divided her time between working in the press office in Qamishli and fighting on the front line against ISIS. She had been provided to me as a contact by a friend of a very secretive contact, whose identity I never did find out, and became my only source of contact to Jack after all communication with him was terminated on July 8. She appeared genuine, having sent a few voice mails assuring me she would check on Jack's welfare, and told me that one of the prison guards was a childhood friend of hers and was able to pass on information about him. I told her that she and Jack had the same enemy in ISIS and that we didn't understand why his detainers were treating him so badly. Surprisingly, she related that Jack was well-liked by the guards (on July 31, she even told me Jack was "charming," a description echoed by a British female YPJ fighter some months later, who said he was "adorable" — neither adjective being one usually given to vicious ISIS fighters).

My relationship with her seemed highly ironic: here I was, worried for her welfare when she went off to fight against ISIS in Raqqa — just like any mother concerned about their offspring in a life-threatening situation — while her friends and associates were detaining our son. I was aware, of course, that she could simply have been an MI6 agent manipulating me, but I desperately needed to believe that there were individuals who cared about justice and human rights, even in a war situation, and was desperate to keep contact with someone who had direct access to Jack.

In mid-September, the usually upbeat senior producer at Amazing Productions rang me with a new, utterly dejected tone to his voice. Sinam Mohammad had revoked the permission to see Jack, and the rescue mission was off.

Summer job at Christ Church, Oxford University

As a pillar of the British establishment, there is no better example than Christ Church College at Oxford University, the only college in the country that hosts within its grounds its city's cathedral. One of the oldest and grandest colleges, Christ Church proudly boasts of having produced thirteen of Britain's twenty-seven prime ministers, including Gladstone, four times prime minister, whose ferociously glaring portrait hangs in the sumptuous dining hall. David Cameron, Boris Johnson, and George Osborne were all members of the infamous, hooligan Bullingdon Club, whose group photo is taken each year on the steps of Canterbury Quad, Christ Church.

In the summer of 2017, I needed a job, since the copy-editing work from my one remaining client had dried up (perhaps they had found out who I was?), and my leafleting job was not enough to hold body and soul together. So it was that I became a bowler-hatted "seasonal custodian" at Christ Church, responsible for protecting the immaculate college lawns from the tourist hordes that descended each summer to see the famous "Harry Potter" hall where Harry, Hermione, and Ron received their mail from swooping barn owls.

Being undercover as a charged local terrorist was not easy at Christ Church, particularly since looking out for terrorists was part of my duties. On my second day, I received "suspect package" training, and was told to look out for cars parked in unusual places and rubbish bags put out when it wasn't rubbish collection day. As the trainer explained, it wasn't always easy to spot a terrorist. (*You might even be sitting next to one*, I silently responded.)

It was after about a month that I was called upon to alert the authorities (the hall porter) about my suspicions about an unexplained object. At my post at Fell Tower next to the deanery, I noticed a small, strange, shiny dustbin, a bit like a miniature robot Dalek from *Doctor Who*, sitting outside one of the canon's houses, where it definitely hadn't been before. I daringly approached it, but when I saw a wire looped over the lid's handle, I decided I should seek back-up. No one I contacted via my hand-held radio seemed to know what the mysterious object was, so I duly reported it to the lodge. It was only at the end of the day that I found out the story behind the incident: apparently, one of the canons had had several summer parties involving rather a lot of alcohol and was too embarrassed to put the huge pile of empty bottles in the usual clear plastic bags left out for the cleaners, in full view in the quad. So it was that the small, silver dustbin had been ordered for him to hide his shame. Ironically, the plan backfired when a suspect-package-trained custodian shone a very public spotlight on it.

I ended the job in early September, knowing that sooner or later my identity would get found out. Sure enough, when it did a couple of months later, staff at Christ Church had split opinions about me. On one hand, the Archdeacon who lived in one of the college houses told me that he'd led prayers for me, Jack, and John in one of his cathedral services. On the other hand, one of the senior custodians said she hadn't been impressed that I'd had the gall to work there: her husband worked for the military, and he'd had to tell his contact at MI5 about me in order to pre-empt any possible trouble for him or herself. Quite what that trouble might be I didn't know, since all I had been doing was trying to earn a living while being me. To me, the two contrasting responses neatly summed up the British establishment: one half prays for you while the other half reports you to the authorities.

Campaigning for Jack's release, October–November 2017

By mid-October, John and I were frantic with worry. We hadn't heard from Jack since July 8, and his last messages had been so alarming we were starting to think that perhaps he had harmed himself and no one had thought to tell us. We also began to wonder if the reason that Sinam had called off the trip to Rojava was because he was no longer alive, or was not in a fit state to be seen.

It had been Jack's messages in June 2017 that had set me screaming to the FCO's emergency line:

> I think it might be too late when it comes to the whole mental situation. Yesterday I had what is universally considered a mental breakdown, it was actually very weird. I feel very strange now. Even the guards here were surprised.
>
> I'm sitting in my cell going insane. You wouldn't believe some of the things. The other day I was punching the wall because I was going insane and my hand was bleeding and I stopped, and this is how I remember it, and my left hand was bleeding and then I forgot about it and when I looked at my hand a few hours later, there was nothing there. I genuinely think I'm going insane. I didn't know humanity was this bad.
>
> When people come I don't even want to see their faces. Being alone with myself is the problem. When I'm alone with my own brain, my brain just generates crazy thoughts the whole time, I'm just sitting remembering how many people Ive lost, who has betrayed me, who tried

to get me killed, I'm thinking about all this stuff for hours a day, I don't even want to wake up. I'm vexed I woke up....

I don't want to ask about my wife. On TV here (I thought it would be a good distraction), but it makes it worse, I sit watching the photos of refugees, I keep hoping Ill see pictures of my wife. I hear about how many civilians get killed every day and there's nothing I can do. I'm sitting here in this flipping prison. You asked me why they're treating me like this. They know I'm not ISIS. They supposedly wrote me some report about how I'm not ISIS and they sent it to Britain, this was when they were doing negotiations with England, theyll put you in prison and lie to you. They leave you and forget about you. Then I told them they were liars. They didn't like that at all, so they started to treat me badly....

I can't even keep track of dates now. But someone told me Britain is coming and that is 3 months ago now. When did you speak to Canada and Britain? These guys just do what they want.

I'm not killing myself because of Islam. Because I know it's not a solution. And I know I have responsibilities that I will be asked about on the day of judgement.

Dad if the problem is that they don't want me in their countries, then tell them to let me go somewhere else. A desert island for example. Or somewhere like that where I won't annoy them

I don't want to blow anyone up.

Or oppress anyone.

I just have to leave this place or I fear I will lose my mind.

Because of Islam is why I'm sticking around.

If I ever did tell my story I would only ever tell the truth. I hate lying. You know if I didn't want to tell you something I would just avoid saying it, but now I wouldn't even do that, I just want honesty. Unless when I had to lie like when I was getting out of dowlah, or when I was in prison and I was trying to convince them I'm not against them. My hatred of lying has increased so much.

And then the messages on his final day of communication — July 8 — chilled us to the bone:

My health situation has got much worse. I won't be able to explain because I only have half an hour.

Now they don't bring me food. Since I last spoke to you, it's started happening. You can knock on this metal door for half an hour and they don't come. And when they come they're angry because you knocked the door.... And then they punish you. Ive actually been tortured, intimidated.

If Canada doesn't get out of this within a week I'm going to do things my own way.

What I'm going to do might result in me getting shot, but Ive made my decision....

How any official — let alone an entire official body responsible for British citizens abroad, such as the FCO — could read those messages and not feel an iota of concern, I had absolutely no idea. Jim Collins's assessment that "yes, it must be very distressing" went no way in describing our enraged helplessness. Since calling on the nonexistent compassion of officials was getting us nowhere, and the advice of Alan Semo, U.K. Kurdish representative, to exercise "quiet diplomacy" was proving equally futile, we decided, like Jack, to "take matters into our own hands."

Media attention, we had been told, would make Jack's situation worse. But we couldn't see how his situation could possibly get worse. He was in a dungeon with no contact with the outside world and no one working toward his release. The portcullis of the British government had decisively come down: no NGO would come near us, nor would the "Muslim community." It was not illegal to abandon a British citizen to their fate, and journalists were forbidden to present any information about our knowledge of Jack's innocence in case this prejudiced the trial against us. The unreality of the situation made me feel as if I was in some sort of computer simulation, or a Charlie Brooker dystopian film: any minute now the screen separating me from the laughing audience would be ripped down, and the real world would be resumed. (And if I really was in a computer simulation, I wanted to press the *Undo* button until I got to the part where I'd failed to hide Jack's passport so that none of this would have ever happened.)

John and I decided, therefore, that we had no choice but to conduct our own social media campaign. All of a sudden, from months of nothingness and inactivity, we were plunged into a whirlwind of petitions, posters, leaflets, Twitter and Facebook campaigns, international media, and radio and TV interviews.

What we didn't know at the outset of all of this was that, after the initial intoxicating flurry of our activity, the true extent of the power of the state would reveal itself. Backed up by the Murdoch and Lord Rothermere empires, which in turn are backed up by the power of the mob, unchallenged by a political opposition and civil society that daren't ally themselves with the possibility of terrorism — unproven or not; and reinforced by a conservative national broadcaster that sees its role as one of "protecting society," the present government was in no way threatened by two desperate parents from Oxford.

Staging a week-long fast on the steps of St. Paul's cathedral on October 19 at the launch of our social media campaign was a calculated move. First of all, we needed a stunt to capture the media's attention. Second, we wanted to show our solidarity with Jack in light of his appalling conditions in which the guards "forgot to feed him." Third, we needed a location where we were not likely to get arrested, since if that happened while we were still on bail, we would be straight back to Wandsworth and Bronzefield. This meant that my plan to chain myself to the balustrade outside the FCO was out. Tayab advised us not to use the words *hunger strike*, since this would demean the actions of prisoners such as those in Guantanamo, for whom hunger striking really was their action of last resort to highlight their unjust situation. If we weren't prepared to carry a hunger strike to the death, he said (we weren't), then our action needed to be called a "fast" instead.

By the day of the launch, we'd already released a petition explaining that Jack had "been disappeared" in a Guantanamo-style black site and had had no communication with the outside world in over three months. It was inconceivable in a technological age that the British government was unable to pick up the phone to speak to one of its allies — the Kurds — in the international coalition. We greatly feared for Jack's mental state, as he'd told us he knew he was going mad with "only his brain for company" and believed humanity had forgotten about him.

We knew that there were "black sites" all over the world, where Western governments indefinitely put people who were inconvenient for them. In June 2017, a joint Associated Press and Human Rights Watch report had established that there were eighteen such black sites operating in Yemen, run by the UAE, where over two thousand alleged unlawful enemy combatants were being held incommunicado in a secret network of prisons. A legacy of the War on Terror as instigated by George Bush, these sites were being run with the joint authority of the U.S., which obtained intelligence information about the detainees via interrogation sessions involving torture. To John and me, it was obvious why our timid MP felt so powerless in representing John and me as her constituents: the global forces at work were so much larger than herself.

During the week of our fast, John and I did indeed receive publicity for our cause — notably from international news organizations such as CNN and al-Jazeera, which didn't have to worry about the parochial U.K. contempt-of-court laws. The *Today Programme*, in contrast, had had to be pulled, since we'd apparently strayed too close to revealing what we knew about Jack's activities. *Russia Today* did a broadcast from the steps of St. Paul's, in which I rashly revealed — already feeling light-headed from the lack of food since the night before — that one of Jack's friends had told me that a group of them had been working "from the inside" against ISIS, and that it had posed great problems for them when the British government decided Jack was a terrorist. This provoked predictable scoffing from a Northern Irish pundit, who declared that it was nonsensical for the country to believe that Jack was some "latter-day James Bond." Not so nonsensical, it seemed, to believe that he was a vicious terrorist who deserved to be tortured.

The backlash to our campaign was more vitriolic and sustained that we could ever have imagined. Richard Littlejohn, editor at the *Daily Mail*, said we "could starve for all [he] cared," and that our son could "rot in a Kurdish jail until he pegs it, too." The hate comments that we received on our "Free Jack Letts" Facebook page were so severe and numerous that I was spending two hours a day deleting them, until I gave up and blocked the page to U.S. and British viewers.

John, similarly, was having a running battle with a Wikipedia warrior who had posted false allegations about Jack: John would correct these statements, the warrior would reinstate them, and the whole process would be repeated ad infinitum in an astonishing test of patience and determination on both sides. John and I also gained insight into how the "hate bots" work on Twitter and Facebook: one vile comment would be issued by a human about how we or Jack should be treated ("hanged, raped, starved," etc.), and then an automated "bot" would reproduce this message to tens of thousands of followers. Our pleas for justice and attempts to rally the forces of reason didn't stand a chance.

Mainstream media, as represented by the BBC, reinforced the vitriol of the tabloids. Told that we would have a chance to present the enormous difficulties faced by the parents of young people in Syria — and that the program would be a sympathetic portrayal, unlike previous coverage — we agreed to be interviewed on the BBC's new American-format news program *Beyond 100 Days*. It was only when we viewed the broadcast later that evening that we realized that we had been set up and stitched up yet again. At the end of the "debate" between Christian Fraser, the program's presenter, and us, Fraser concluded that the issue of returnees was "tough on parents, but tougher on governments, I think." He added, "There will be a lot of people who share fears of what sort of ideology are we importing if we bring them back, and how can we be sure if we rehabilitate them they won't offend again?"

My outraged letter to Ofcom — the regulatory body for communications — about this blatant bias exhibited by the BBC, which presented the personal views of the presenter as the final word on the subject, and which also presumed to know the ideology and prior offences of our son, did not result in the upholding of our complaint. Mr. Fraser, they said, was merely giving his "personal take" on the situation, rather than giving his personal opinion, although the distinction between the two was completely lost on me. In actual fact, it didn't come as a surprise to us that Ofcom decided in favour of the program: as I said to Tayab, the process of complaining to the BBC was "like asking a hangman not to execute you."

Similarly, our requests to the Muslim Council of Britain and local imams to circulate our petition for justice for Jack to their subscribers were politely acknowledged but not actioned. U.K. journalists, also, were very quickly scared off by the prospect of a £30,000 contempt of court fine — even *Private Eye*, the irreverent magazine that had been our best hope for any bold action. It seemed that the whole of civil society — NGOs, journalists, grassroots organizations — had combined with the weakness of the political opposition and the presumptuous hatred of most of the British public to ensure that the governmental line of "all returnees are guilty until proven innocent" would remain unchallenged.

Coincidentally, the brazenness of the government's intransigent stance against Syrian returnees became evident during the week of our campaign. Rory Stewart, Minister for International Development, stated on *BBC Radio 5 Live* that the "only way" to deal with British ISIS fighters in Syria is "in almost every case" to kill them because of the "serious danger" they pose to the U.K.'s security. The government dispassionately said his comments were in line with the U.K.'s stated position, not seeming to mind in the slightest that Stewart's comments went against every single rule of international humanitarian law — or domestic law, since we do not have the death penalty in this country. It also didn't seem to present a difficulty that Stewart was referring to all those captured on suspicion of being jihadis, including those locked up in prisons like our son, not just those active on the battlefield. This stated position was so extreme that we waited for the furious reaction from government opponents outraged at this trashing of the very basis of our civilized society.

Except it didn't come. Not a whimper of protest, for example, from Jeremy Corbyn, who supposedly always sought the peaceful, as opposed to the militant, solution. It appeared, in fact, that there were only two people in the entire country who were prepared to make a public stand against the government's position: one was Max Hill, the independent reviewer of antiterrorism legislation, who, a few days before Rory Stewart's outrageous statements, had commented that some individuals, for instance, teenagers who "naively" travelled from Britain to join Islamic State in Syria, "do not justify prosecution, and we should be looking toward reintegration and moving away from any notion that we are going to lose a generation due to this travel."

The other was Yasmin Alibhai-Brown, a professor at Middlesex University, who wrote in *inews* that she was horrified by Stewart's remarks. She pointed out that the people he was condemning "include truly evil ideologues as well as naive men and women, goodhearted folk who went to Syria to help President Bashar al-Assad's victims," and that, although Stewart was an educated man, he "seemed not to realise that he sounded like an enflamed Islamicist who wants to kill all Westerners who are not on side." Like us, she was also deeply perturbed by the lack of opposing voices to the government's unlawful stance.

When assessing the overall effects of our fast later on, we told ourselves that it had had an important symbolic effect. Fasting itself had been challenging. We'd only managed six fast days rather than seven, as both of us had started to feel very unwell. We'd been very strict about not cheating on our liquid diet of water only: when I'd been longing for a cup of tea on Day 3, for instance, my friend had shaken her head sadly and said that would be a matter "between me and my conscience." Needless to say, her disappointment in me meant that the tea bags stayed in the jar. What finally ended my own fast was a phone call from a CNN journalist. When trying to speak to her, I was unable to string a proper sentence together, having forgotten that the brain needs nutrients. Realizing it was a ridiculous situation that I was incapable of explaining Jack's plight when a journalist finally wanted to publicize it, I decided to break my fast with a large bowl of peas. The body is a strange thing: I instantly felt better and became a functioning human being once again.

The long-term effects of our campaign were more difficult to determine. On the face of it, the political context surrounding Jack's case seemed to have become even more entrenched. We'd received a barrage of hate, courtesy of social media; most of the broadcasters who'd interviewed us put out the message that Jack could be a danger to society; and a government minister and leading newspaper columnist had called for the extrajudicial killing of our son.

While it was true that almost two thousand people demonstrated their support by signing the petition calling for Jack to receive a fair trial in the U.K., the fact that we needed ten thousand for the issue to be raised in Parliament meant this wasn't nearly enough. Our consolation was that, at least if his parents were campaigning, Jack couldn't be considered "disappeared." However, given the weakness of social support for us, plus the total absence of political or diplomatic support, what on earth were we supposed to do next?

Chapter 30

Canada to the rescue?

A possible answer to our dilemma in getting Jack out came in the form of the Canadian government. John, Jack, his brother, and I were all dual Canadian British citizens. I myself had been dragged reluctantly from the suburbs of London to Canada as a teenager — loathe to leave behind my friends and everything I knew — by a father determined to move to a country where it was still possible to buy land and build your own house.

My Canadian citizenship was granted to me when I was in my early twenties, in a ceremony that I still remember vividly for its hilariousness, but also for its touching significance. I had dutifully studied for my citizenship test ("What is Canada's biggest export?" [wheat]; "What is the capital of Saskatchewan?" [Regina]) and was rewarded for my correct answers by being invited to the local court house for the awarding of our certificates. At the time, my parents and younger sister were living in a small town in southern Ontario close to the Michigan border, and the court house was no bigger than an average-sized living room. On this, my citizenship day, this room was packed with five rows of families of excited Russians, Armenians, Belgians, etc., all about to be welcomed as fully fledged

Canadians. A hush descended on the chatter when something tall, scarlet, and shiny was glimpsed by the door. To our astonishment, this turned out to be a real Canadian Mountie, in full regalia, complete with distinctive wide-brimmed hat. Before our eyes, this figure marched across the front of the small room, halted, saluted, and then proceeded to stand to attention throughout the entire ceremony. I was so moved at the fact that this cavalry officer, who surely should have been rescuing people from bear attacks or leaping across log booms to catch cattle rustlers, was taking time out to attend my citizenship ceremony.

Involving the Canadian government in Jack's case had been the subject of some debate between John, me, and our lawyers. If two governments were involved, postulated the lawyers, then each could claim it needn't act because the other party was dealing with the issue. However, John and I reasoned, since the British government was doing absolutely nothing, the Canadians couldn't make the excuse that their intervention was not required. John was a Canadian by birthright, not just by ceremony, and he was confident that his more sane and fair-minded government would do the right thing in negotiating Jack's release. Moreover, Canada had a written constitution that guaranteed the rights of its citizens, unlike Britain, whose unwritten constitution did not.

On June 27, 2017, it seemed as if our hunch was right. To our great excitement, a message from the Canadian high commission in London arrived, which led us to believe that our nightmare might soon be coming to an end.

"If we were able to negotiate your son's release," said this email message, "would there be a family member, friend or professional (e.g. doctor, psychiatrist) who could travel to stay with him while travel documents could be arranged and who could escort him to the final destination? You don't need to answer this question immediately, but may wish to begin to think about such things."

Happily, we started to plan who amongst our contacts could escort Jack out of his hellhole. Tayab? His GP? The Red Cross? Little did we know in our optimistic imaginings that over five years later, we would still be mired in frustrating non-conversations with the Canadian government about the extensive limitations that they, just like their British counterparts, faced in making the smallest step toward getting Jack out.

One of the first considerations, the Canadian government said, was that they needed Jack's consent to negotiate on his behalf, and they needed to speak to him directly. To us, this was stupid: Why wouldn't someone want to be released from illegal detention? Unfortunately, however, Jack was forbidden by his jailers to speak to anyone but his parents. When he'd spoken to the BBC journalist, Daniel Sandford, at the beginning of June 2017, he'd been punished by the harshest solitary confinement for over a month, during which he'd resorted to counting millipedes, punching the wall, and screaming at himself. Reports of this acute distress had provoked Global Affairs Canada (GAC), based in Ottawa, to say that the "Government of Canada takes torture allegations very seriously," and they had assured us that they were working with consular officials in Lebanon, Iraq, and Turkey to address the situation.

On August 24, 2017, I sent GAC Jack's transcribed messages to us from the past two months, with the passages referring to the Canadian government highlighted:

> I've been in solitary confinement for 2 months. But as a request for help tell them to get me out. If not Britain, then tell Canada to come and get me.
>
> If I'm not out in 2 days I'm going to do something crazy. I don't want to go crazy so I might have to solve this in another way. Where are the Canadians?

If the Prime Minister of Canada was saying
Let him out, they would as this lot absolutely
worship the West. The situation has got much
worse. My health situation has got much worse.
I won't be able to explain because I only have half
an hour.

Global Affairs Canada politely thanked me for sending these
messages — Canada's reputation for politeness is well-deserved —
but pointed out that, unfortunately, because Jack had inconven-
iently got himself apprehended by the Kurdish "People's Protection
Units," the YPG, and the YPG was regrettably a "non-state actor,"
there were "no formal processes or rules that govern detention or
release from detention in that context." They suggested that we have
weekly telephone calls where we could discuss our mutual efforts in
speaking to the relevant players involved. Meanwhile, they assured
us they were putting all the information and contact details we were
sending them "on file."

Inexplicably, we had gone from "planning on who should escort
Jack during his release" to being put "on file" in the space of a few
short weeks. Although the Canadians were purportedly "reaching
out to local groups," it seemed that their progress was excruciatingly
slow. Rojava's democratic experiment, where every single decision was
devolved down to the neighbourhood level, seemed to mean that no
one had responsibility for anything and nothing ever got done.

By chance, around this time in September 2017, I was sent
a manuscript to copy-edit entitled *The Handbook of Postcolonial
Politics*, which contained a chapter by a young Kurdish academic: "The Revolution of Smiling Women: Stateless Democracy and
Power in Rojava." Predictably, this chapter cited the burgeoning
woman's liberation movement as one of the defining successes of the
new autonomous region's social and ethical revolution. Thinking

about Jack's inhumane conditions, I could barely suppress my fury when I read the words I was supposed to engage with, while dispassionately correcting their grammar:

> Whenever I asked men [in Rojava] about their views on the women's movement, their answers expressed pride and happiness ... the very fact that men today are in a position in which they know that a commitment to gender equality is a precondition for the new social system ... shows that women's liberation established itself as an undeniable pillar of Rojava's revolution ...

The manuscript went on to explain how the new democratic laws of Rojava were drafted:

> In order to achieve a "moral-political society," the guiding principle for justice should be ethics rather than law ... the Social Contract was a result of countless discussions in the communities ... the communes and councils, women, different ethnic groups, religious leaders, and youth were consulted in the process.

"People can go to the tribunals," the chapter continued, "if problems could not be solved at the local committee level. These [tribunals] consist of a mix of lawyers, elders, and peace-keeping committees of ordinary citizens. Rather than legal expertise, people who can adequately represent people's interests are appointed as rotating judges."

I wanted to scream. Where within this utopian, women-led, peaceful, grassroots, decentralized justice system did it state it was permissible to incarcerate an innocent young man, who, according to your security forces, "has done no crime" but is gradually going out of his mind at the prospect of being held indefinitely until he dies of despair? Once I'd safely delivered my copy-edited chapters to the publisher, I asked as much of the young Kurdish author, who was based at one of Britain's prestigious universities. "I have loved ones who were killed by ISIS!" she said. "He's not ISIS," I replied. "In fact, he spoke out against ISIS." "Frankly, I have no obligation to get involved in such a messy and sensitive issue," she retorted. "I have no official capacity in Rojava and will not be involved. Do not contact me again."

If the Canadians were trying to deal with "rotating judges" and "local committees of ordinary citizens," it was no wonder they were making scant progress. We suspected, in any case, that all the talk of "reaching out to local groups" was a red herring. Everyone knew that the real power of the region lay with the Americans, who were funding and arming the Kurds in their fight against ISIS, and who were ultimately responsible for all security in northern Syria. It wasn't the neighbourhood women's institutes that were blocking negotiation attempts, it was the toddler in the White House.

From death row to ISIS suspects: Clive Stafford Smith enters the fray

When Clive Stafford Smith entered our lives, everything changed. All of a sudden, people started returning our calls, journalists pricked up their ears, and the Canadian legal establishment began to be interested in our case. In a hopeful development, the Canadian Broadcasting Corporation began to explore the idea of a trip to Qamishli, accompanied by Clive — a trip that had to be abandoned when Sinam Mohammad suddenly withdrew permission for a visa.

Clive was the young English lawyer and campaigner, educated at the elite Stowe private school and Columbia Law School in New York, who took on seemingly hopeless death penalty cases in Georgia and Louisiana and, against all odds, nearly always won. Later in his career, he had taken on "war on terror" cases and had helped secure the release of sixty-nine prisoners from Guantanamo Bay, including every British prisoner. He was hugely respected by activists and the establishment alike, and had received numerous awards, including an OBE in 2000 for "humanitarian services." He also had a prominent media profile, with his best-known documentary being *Fourteen Days in May*, produced in 1987, which documented the final days of his client, Edward Earl Johnson, who was executed in a Mississippi gas chamber. At the time, Clive had been only twenty-eight years old, and one of only a handful of lawyers working on death penalty cases.

John and I believed that if anyone could save Jack it would be Clive. While we had absolute faith in our lawyers, who had been working pro bono, or on minimum legal aid fees, around the clock for us for almost two years, they were bound by legal constraints in campaigning on our behalf, which in any case, was not their job.

In December 2017, Clive and Maya Foa, the director of Reprieve, flew to Canada to meet Canadian politicians and officials, including the consular officers whom we'd been dealing with, as well as journalists, our Canadian friends, and members of John's family (most of mine had by then emigrated to Atlanta, Georgia — strangely, a location that Clive was very familiar with, since many of his previous clients had been prisoners on Georgia's notorious death row).

An important part of meeting friends and family was to establish a "support package" for Jack when he arrived in Canada: it needed to be demonstrated that there were people willing to provide him with assistance with housing, finance, accessing psychological and medical care, and with emotional support after the trauma he had been through.

We had no idea of the state of his mental health, and the only clue we had to his current level of resilience were a couple of comments he had made in Kurdish detention while we were still able to communicate with him. One had been his statement from May 30, saying, "If some normal person was treated like this, he would become Deashi (ISIS) but Allah saved me from this," and another was his vow that he "would knock on every single door in Iraq" to find his wife. We needed to believe that his strength of character — tested to unbelievable limits already — and his absolute adherence to his faith, which did not condone suicide, would see him through.

"Tell Jack's parents he is probably no longer alive"

A breakthrough with the Canadian government occurred as the indirect result of what must surely be one of the most tactless and irresponsible comments ever made by a journalist. In early January 2018, one of David Rose's contacts — a female Irish journalist, whose name I don't know and don't care to — contacted David to tell him that she had recently interviewed some of her Kurdish contacts, who had told her that someone should "tell Jack's parents that he is probably no longer alive." David was understandably reluctant to be the person to do so, so he contacted Tayab so they could talk over what to do. Tayab, fortunately, is too sensible and too sensitive to deliver such spurious and half-baked news to us, so he and David discussed how they could investigate this latest bombshell further.

With typical boldness, David then did what no other journalist, politician, or consular official had thought of doing, which was to contact the Rojavan press office and ask for "proof of life." Jack's parents had not heard from Jack in six months, he said, and had no clue as to whether he was alive or dead. He himself, he explained, worked for the *Mail on Sunday*, whose sister paper, the *Daily Mail*, he added, was one of the most widely read newspapers in America (mostly, it has to be said, for the *Mail Online*'s "Sidebar of Shame," a gossip column, but the Rojavan Kurds weren't to know that). Unless he received immediate confirmation of proof of life, he would have no hesitation in publicizing the Kurds' treatment of prisoners in that week's Sunday paper.

Incredibly — given that we had been trying different approaches for months to be able to communicate with Jack — an answer was received the very next day, January 9, 2018. An unnamed press officer promised that David would be able to speak to Jack on his mobile number at twelve o'clock the following day.

That night we couldn't sleep, and the next day, the morning hours seemed to crawl. We knew that Syria was two hours ahead and weren't sure whether "twelve o'clock" had referred to Syrian time or U.K. time. When 10:00 a.m. our time came and went, we supposed the message must have meant U.K. time. However, when twelve noon came and went, and so did 1:00 p.m., 2:00 p.m., etc., we started to slump back into despondency. Clearly, we had been lied to and manipulated once again. I snapped at people who ill-advisedly crossed my path that day and, by 5:00 p.m., truly hated the world and everyone in it all over again. Then, suddenly, at 6:00 p.m., the phone rang.

It was the consular official I am calling *LC*, from Global Affairs Canada. She had just had an hour-long conversation with Jack. He was alive! Instead of allowing Jack to call David Rose, the prison authorities had put him in touch with the Canadian consulate. *LC* reported that Jack had spoken in a "strong voice" and had "expressed himself well." He was eating okay, with his diet including cheese, olives, and bread, and although there were things he couldn't say, he confirmed that he wanted to go to Canada, and even said to pass on the message to his mum and dad that "he was sorry."

The relief was so overwhelming that our depression instantly disappeared, and we contacted our close friends to say we were "floating on air" at the news. It wasn't until two weeks later that we learned more about *LC*'s conversation with Jack — which severely took the wind out of our sails — but for that evening, at least, we were happy.

Jack's messages, January 10, 2018

> LC:
>
> How are the conditions where you are?

> J:
>
> terrible but i can't explain
>
> [I'm] in a room fit for 5 people that's filled with 30 people
>
> i spent 35 days in a room about as tall as i am and half that in width
>
> please get me out of this place

From the transcripts of Jack's written and audio messages in his conversation with the Canadian government, we learned that although the food he was being given was adequate, he was given no exercise and in fact was rarely allowed out of his cell. Even then, time outside would only be for twenty minutes. The consequences of this terrified me: I had read a *Daily Mail* article from July 2017 that featured a shocking picture of emaciated prisoners packed together in one room in a jail south of Mosul. One Iraqi lieutenant described how many of these prisoners were infected with diseases and had health and skin problems because they were not exposed to the sun. Most of them couldn't walk, and their legs were swollen because they couldn't move. In some cases, prisoners had infected wounds and were returning to jail from hospital with legs or arms amputated.

Risks to Jack's safety also came from the other prisoners. "I don't feel safe in the room except when on one of the guard schedules," he said. The room "leader" hated him and apparently used the guards against anyone he hated. One of the other foreigners hated him because he had a beard. Although he stressed that "he didn't preach or anything," the only reason people hated him there "was because of his religion." It appeared that there was a mix of religions among the prisoners, including atheists.

The most gut-wrenching of Jack's messages were those that detailed how he had tried to kill himself in solitary confinement. When he had "only his brain for company," he had started to go insane and talk to himself. Because he thought that "dying was better than his mother seeing him insane," he tried to hang himself, but failed. This had happened, he explained, seven months earlier. I felt sick to think that this must have been just before his last conversation with us on July 8, when he'd said he "would take matters into his own hands" because he'd despaired of ever getting out of there. In our panic at the time, we had contacted the FCO, our MP, Amnesty International, etc., and all we had received was a collective shrug.

"The pen is lifted" comment from Jack's July 1, 2017, conversation suddenly made sense to us. We hadn't understood this at the time, but John had looked it up and discovered it came from a *hadith* written by the scholar Abu Dawood concerning the final judgment of the insane: "The Prophet (PBUH), said that the pen is lifted for three people and that one of them is the insane until he regains his sanity." The pen referred to meant the pen of the "one who records the sins"; therefore, this *hadith* meant that the sins of insane people were not recorded or, in other words, the insane were not responsible for their actions by virtue of their insanity. It was now clear that, although Jack was convinced that suicide was "un-Islamic" — as he'd stated to us many times before — he did believe it was permissible in cases of insanity.

My last assurance against Jack's taking his own life was thus breached. So it was that I reacted angrily when the Canadian government stressed their difficulties in trying to intervene on Jack's behalf, specifically citing the lack of Canadian official representation in Syria, an inability to travel there, practical communication challenges, and the lack of a "reliable interlocutor." They did, however, tell us they would do their best to get Jack a doctor: he had kidney stones, which gave him acute pain when he sneezed, and had a growing lump on his testicle.

"How can any parent read those messages and not be filled with anguish, desolation, and fury that no one is doing anything?" I said to Global Affairs Canada. And then, echoing the phrase Jack had used earlier, I continued: "If the Foreign Minister or Justin Trudeau were to make a call, something would happen ... all anyone does is tell us to be patient. Why should we be patient? He will die unless someone does something. Are we supposed to sit around and say — as the British consular official told us — 'At least you will know you have done all you could'? Would people say this if it was their own child?"

No reply was forthcoming. I had learned by now that my rants of this nature were treated by all those in authority — British or Canadian — with supreme condescension, as if they were merely the embarrassing tantrum displays of a two-year-old.

Chapter 31

Geopolitics and the borders with DFNS

The name "Rojava" for the semiautonomous region in northern Syria seemed to be slipping out of use. We noticed, for instance, that Sinam Mohammad, the European spokesperson for the region, had started to use "Democratic Federation of Northern Syria" (DFNS), in her official communications, instead. Her statement to the press on Jack's case in October 2017 claimed that, contrary to our assertion that Jack had been "disappeared," he was, in fact, in weekly contact with his parents. Since we hadn't had a word from him in nearly four months, this was blatantly untrue. Sinam also said that the Kurdish authorities were willing to hand Jack over to officials of the relevant governments, but that "so far there has been no official request from either Canadian or British governments." This assertion meant that either the Kurds or the Canadians were lying to us, since we had received assurances from the Canadian government that they were indeed working toward Jack's release. In the same press release, the Kurds similarly went on the offensive at our protest that Jack was being held without charge: they decided to charge him.

We wondered if the use of the term "Democratic Federation of Northern Syria" was intended to draw a distinction between the geopolitical aims of the Iraqi Kurds and those of the Syrian Kurds (the "wrong Kurds," as the consul in Erbil had explained to us). In September 2017, Iraqi Kurdistan had voted overwhelmingly (93 percent) for independence from Iraq. Iraq's prime minister, Haider al-Abadi, however, refused to recognize the referendum and sent troops to Kirkuk, an oil-rich region taken under Kurdish control after the defeat of ISIS forces there. The DFNS, however, despite having much in common culturally with Iraqi Kurdistan, was politically very different. Its ruling party — the PYD — did not espouse the conservative nationalism of the Kurdistan Regional Government (KRG) in Iraq, preferring the libertarian socialism of decentralized committees, gender equality, and people's tribunals. Crucially, the DFNS was not seeking independence from Syria, no doubt believing they could better achieve their aims by coming to an accommodation with Assad's government.

We were deeply skeptical that diplomacy between one of the G7 countries and one of their allies could not solve the problem of gaining access to Jack. We ourselves were aware of journalists and academics who frequently went to Qamishli as part of their day jobs, so the contention that Global Affairs Canada was unwilling to risk the personal safety of its personnel rang rather hollow. Clive declared he was ready and willing to go himself — not because he was particularly brave, he said, but because it was the right and logical thing to do.

Most importantly, in terms of political movement, it seemed that there had been a change of American policy as to how countries were expected to deal with their returnee foreign nationals. In June 2017, Brett McGurk, American top envoy to the coalition, had said that any "foreign fighter who came to Syria will die in Syria." However, by March 2018, James Mattis, U.S. defence secretary, was quoted as saying the countries of origin of fighters needed to come forward to claim them. "How [these countries] carry out that responsibility — there's a dozen different diplomatic legal or whatever ways, I suppose," he said. "There is not a one way forward.... It's being worked on. There's a number of things going on already to have some of them being repatriated to certain locations."

My own hope was that Trump, ever the manager of America's household budget, would cut the expense of stationing his government's troops abroad and pull them out of Syria sooner rather than later. And then, with no one to foot the bill for keeping them, the Kurds would have no choice but to release their prisoners for repatriation.

Chapter 32

Lead-up to Old Bailey trial

Bail variation hearing, March 15, 2018

In the battle to save Jack's life, I had almost forgotten about our upcoming criminal trial. A nasty reminder of it came on February 19, 2018, when Tayab sent us the prosecution's objections to our bail variation application. Our bail restrictions, which we had been adhering to for two years, were onerous and unnecessary and we wanted the court to change them. I now had a job for marketing research company Ipsos MORI as a door-to-door interviewer on social issues, which sometimes involved travel to neighbouring counties. Having to inform the CPS seven days in advance if I was staying overnight somewhere other than Oxford was becoming impractical. John's restrictions were more burdensome: he had to sign in at the police station every Monday, and since he had no passport, he was also prevented from attending any overseas conferences, which were important for his academic research. He also wanted to be able to visit his elderly mother in Canada: if he was going to prison for some years, it might be the last time he would see her.

The prosecution argued fiercely that our bail restrictions were necessary. If we had our passports, we might abscond to Canada and not return for our trial. Also, we might commit further offences by sending money to Jack, although the absurdity of this wasn't mentioned: since there was currently an electromagnetic force field around Jack that prevented anything or anyone getting to him, we would need some sort of superpower to teleport him a few quid. The prosecution's assessment of the risk we presented to society even included mention of our social media campaign in October 2017: "The defendants have embarked on a sustained campaign in both the U.K. and Canada to seek to gain government assistance to secure their son's release," they said. "This has included a 'hunger strike' and an online petition.... It is clear that the defendants' priority remains securing the release of their son, by whatever means."

It was difficult to comprehend a world in which it was considered a criminal offence to make attempts to save the life of your own child, including by peaceful protest. Why was the prosecution attempting to turn us into arch criminals?

The bail variation hearing took place on March 15, 2018, in the Old Bailey, presided over by our trial judge, Judge Hilliard, whom we felt we were getting to know quite well by now. The hearing was "in chambers," so he wasn't wearing his long wig. After weighing the evidence carefully, Judge Hilliard came up with a compromise: John would get his passport back so that he could visit his elderly mother and plead the case of his son with the Canadian government. I, on the other hand, would not be handed my passport back. The reason given for this was that Mr. Letts would be less likely to abscond to Canada and fail to surrender for his trial if his wife were still in the country. In other words, I was to be held as a hostage.

Although our lawyers expected me to be fuming at the sexism inherent in this judgment, I didn't care. It would be difficult for me to leave my job in any case, and John was much better at the media stuff than I was. He and Clive could now start preparing their Canada trip as soon as possible. Fixing a meeting with Canada's foreign minister, Chrystia Freeland, would be their top priority.

Supreme Court appeal, April 19, 2018

Our appeal challenging the legal argument behind our criminal case was due to be heard on April 19, 2018. This particular date was seared in my brain, as it was on an April 19 that I had been taken as a tearful fourteen-year-old by my family to begin a new life in the wilderness in Canada. Perhaps it would also become the date on which I wished I'd never made the decision to return to my birth country at the age of twenty-two.

The appeal was to be heard in the highest court in the land, the Supreme Court, which ruled only upon law of public importance. Our case — having been referred upward by the High Court and the Court of Appeal — had been permitted to be heard on the grounds that the wording behind Section 17 of the Terrorism Act was unclear and open to dispute. Our challenge centred on whether the wording of the legislation — "reasonable cause to suspect that the money would or might be used for terrorism purposes" — should be given an objective or subjective interpretation. Our lawyers contended that John and I were reasonable people who did not believe the money would be used for terrorism purposes (the subjective interpretation). The prosecution's argument was that any reasonable person, who had received external information from a source such as a police officer, that suggested the money might be used for terrorism purposes "ought to have known" not to send it (the objective interpretation). The fact that we sent money in order to save Jack's life, with the consent of our Prevent officer, was neither here nor there.

It is a rare highlight in a lawyer's or barrister's career for one of their cases to be heard in the Supreme Court. The outcome of such a case can have far-reaching consequences and change the wording of legislation. The two bundles prepared for the hearing were each several hundred pages long. I couldn't imagine how much our trial was costing — we must be well over the £3 million mark by now.

Despite the seriousness of the occasion, the childish part of me had been excited to think of entering the grandeur of the "chamber of secrets" at the court at the House of Lords, with its vast hall, tiered galleries, red velvet seats, and, of course, the raised golden throne from which the Queen delivered her speech during the State Opening of Parliament. I was somewhat disappointed to learn that the newly formed Supreme Court, after being hived off from the House of Lords in 2009, was now housed in a separate building opposite, on Parliament Square. The new building was the former Middlesex Guildhall, which Tayab assured me was still quite grand. Apparently, this decision to move the court was to make the judicial process seem a more democratic one. It was important, believed the law lords, to draw a distinction between Parliament and the judiciary or, in other words, to separate those who made the law from those who administer it. Moreover, it was mooted, there was a concern that the House of Lords had been "becoming more political in character."

The new democratic touches to the highest court in the land were evident in its architecture and its working practices. The judges were no longer seated on a raised dais, and in fact, had to look up to counsel rather than down. They were seated in a U-shape facing the defendants and the public gallery, and there was no dock, or wigs, or gowns. The court itself was open to the public during working hours (indeed, a whole party of schoolchildren traipsed into our hearing before leaving shortly thereafter, presumably bored). In addition, filming was allowed in the courtroom, a first for any court in the U.K.

It had been two years since John and I had first set foot in a court, for our criminal trial. We were living testimony that when the wheels of British justice are set in motion, there is nothing — not a juggernaut, meteor, or intergalactic laser beam — that can stop them.

We knew that much of the legal argument would pass over our heads, so as ever, we tried to assess what the five judges were thinking from their body language. Unfortunately, none of them gave much away. I had been pinning my hopes on one of them, Baroness Hale, who was the first woman to have been appointed as a law lord in the House of Lords in 2004. She looked pleasant and grandmotherly (I also read that she took her democratic duties seriously and had served as a celebrity judge on BBC's *Masterchef*). It was clear from her clipped and incisive questions, however, that she was not the cuddly sort of grandmother I remembered from childhood. The other judges were remarkably expressionless, although one of them seemed to be favouring the prosecution over the defence, nodding approvingly at their barrister's answers to his questions.

It was all over by lunchtime, even though the court had been booked for a full day. It would be months until we learned the judges' decision. This would have to be delivered to us, however, before the start of our criminal trial on September 6, 2018.

Chapter 33

Clive and John in Canada

On April 20, 2018, the day after our Supreme Court appeal, Clive Stafford Smith and John — with his newly acquired temporary passport — flew to Canada. The objective of the trip — as sanctioned by our trial judge, Justice Hilliard — was to plead Jack's case with Canadian officials, who were purportedly seeking to secure his release.

John and I were highly excited at the prospect of the trip, but its actual outcome — after two weeks of back-to-back meetings with Canadian officials — was utter frustration and despair. In the international game of snakes and ladders we were being forced to play, it felt as if we had gone up a couple of rows via a short ladder, only to plunge down an enormously long snake.

It soon became clear to Clive and John that Canadian government officials — as represented by Global Affairs Canada (GAC) — had put all their efforts into marshalling legal reasons why nothing could be done. Although a few NDP, Green, and Conservative MPs and Senators offered sympathetic support, the people who were in a position of actually being able to do something — i.e., the ruling Liberal government and GAC — had clearly banded together to concoct a watertight case for why Jack should stay exactly where he was. Not one Liberal MP agreed to meet with John or Clive, being either mysteriously suddenly out of town or "too busy."

The most absurd excuse provided by the GAC was that Jack should remain in detention because it was "too dangerous" to get him out. The only possible exit route via Iraqi Kurdistan could result in Jack's getting kidnapped or killed. (Even in a military vehicle with a military escort, we wondered?) And, continued the reasoning, Jack was not sufficiently *compos mentis* to give his consent to being rescued, given the danger involved. The Canadian government, therefore, had to take responsibility on his behalf.

Clive, John, and I had never heard such an inane, infuriating, pathetic absurdity in all our lives. Jack was not deemed capable of agreeing to his own rescue, but was considered capable of agreeing to be detained, with no external assistance or communication with the outside world indefinitely.

We suspected the dead hand of the British government in this outrageous state of affairs. Sure enough, Clive and John discovered via one of our close Canadian friends, a Toronto city councillor, that a Liberal politician from Toronto had privately admitted that despite Canada being a sovereign country, capable of making its own decisions, the British government would need to "sign off" on any proposed plan for Jack.

Enraged at this stonewalling, Clive wrote a series of furious letters to Lisa Helfand, Director General of Consular Operations at Global Affairs Canada, following his and John's dismal meeting with her team on April 26, 2018.

"I have to say that I have never been to a more dispiriting meeting in the 35 years I have done this work," Clive's first letter began. This from someone who is one of the primary legal negotiators in Guantanamo and represents prisoners on America's death row.

Please correct me if you think I am stating things incorrectly, but you said that the legal advice you were getting was that all options were not possible: first, while the Kurds would allow Jack to be released via Iraq, that option was too dangerous; second, you said that currently the Kurds would not allow Jack to leave via Qamishli Airport and anyway the option of going through Assad's control was too dangerous; and third, the Kurds would not allow Jack to go out through Turkey.

Thus, as matters stand, there is no option save to leave Jack to rot and eventually die there.

Clive then went on to propose solutions countering the Canadian government's stance that, although "they were working on Jack's case 24 hours a day," it was impossible for them to do anything.

We simply do not accept that Canada is such a weak and feeble country that, working with allies, Jack cannot be protected as far as Erbil Airport, whence we can take flights to various places including Dubai, Egypt, the Emirates, Jordan, and Turkey.

You said that your "lawyers" advise that Jack could not give voluntary consent to going in this direction. With respect, this is idiotic: do they really think he can give "voluntary consent" to staying in a torture prison in Syria *ad infinitum*? And if he truly were incapable of giving voluntary consent, his legal "next friends" can: they are his parents, who hereby give that consent....

As you know, the Kurds are transferring prisoners back to ISIS. This is being done in part because the Kurds have learned that Western countries are not fulfilling their duty to their citizens to secure their release, and they are stuck with a large number of refugees and prisoners. You say that you will ask the Kurds not to violate the principle of non-refoulement — although you seem to accept that they violate any number of other legal principles. Apparently you believe they will comply with your request — though they do not comply with any other request you make of them. If, God forbid, one day we see an ISIS YouTube video of Jack being beheaded, there will justifiably be consequences.

Clive's letter — like his subsequent five letters detailing the Canadians' failure to fulfill their legal obligations under the Convention Against Torture (CAT) and Cruel, Inhuman, and Degrading Treatment (CIDT) — was copied to Chrystia Freeland, Minister of Foreign Affairs, and the Senator and MPs who had expressed sympathy for our position. His impassioned approach — refreshingly free of legalese and containing nothing but common sense and a sense of moral outrage — we believed could not be ignored. As well as challenging the Canadian government's failure to engage with the practical solutions for Jack's release, Clive tackled their excuse that Rojava, or the Democratic Federation of Northern Syria, as it now wished to be called, was a "non-state actor" and therefore could not be held to account like "proper states." "They don't have laws like we do," our Global Affairs case officer had told us in one of our weekly and futile phone calls. In other words, Jack had stupidly made the mistake of being captured by the wrong people.

"The UN Convention Against Torture (CAT) is *jus cogens* and therefore applicable to the Kurds whether they signed it or not. To hold someone incommunicado is illegal.... This is also CIDT (Cruel, Inhuman or Degrading Treatment)," said Clive. "John and Sally have not heard from Jack since July 8, 2017, at 21:08 BST. That means that they have had no contact with him for more than nine months. Your office has heard from him once, as I understand it, on January 10, 2018. That is now more than 100 days ago.... There has been no proof of life. All of this is excruciatingly difficult for Sally and John."

Just like the British government, however, the Canadian government simply didn't care. They knew that there was no wide political or public support for Jack in Canada — even though we received much less partisan coverage there than in the British press — and therefore felt no pressure to respond to Clive's pressing legal and moral arguments. As Jack said in a Red Cross message that we received from him five months later, "the world hates me without even knowing me."

Global Affairs Canada's reply to Clive's letters — received six weeks after it was sent (because it inexplicably went into spam and for some reason had been attached as an easily overlooked image), merely stated the Kurds had provided assurances that "Mr. Letts was being cared for in the best possible way, given the difficult circumstances and resource constraints," which of course, meant absolutely nothing at all.

Realizing that he was flogging two dead horses — one British and one Canadian — Clive decided instead to negotiate directly with the Kurds. So it was that John and I prepared ourselves for a new round of promises, expectations, setbacks, and delays, this time delivered by another set of Kurdish military and political contacts, supposedly at a much higher level than before. This course of events — with the ultimate goal of Clive flying to Qamishli to visit Jack in person — was set for the summer of 2018, while John and I clung on hopefully at the sidelines, willing a breakthrough.

Chapter 34

Delegations to Rojava: Red Cross and the Labour party

Jack's Red Cross messages, May and July 2018

On May 10, 2018, we received Jack's first message to us in ten months, and only the second communication to the outside world from him in all that time (the other being his January 10, 2018, conversation with the Canadian government). It was delivered to us by our case worker at the London office of the Red Cross, which had been trying to gain access to his prison in Qamishli for over a year.

Seeing his handwriting with its characteristic flourishes gave us a massive and much-needed emotional boost. He was still alive! And was *compos mentis* enough to write us a heartfelt letter, which contained an apology for the distress he had caused us, as well as his realization that he had been wrong in believing he could go to Syria to make a difference.

"[In this period of a year], I feel as if I've a died a number of times ... I was stupid enough to believe I was leaving where I was to a land that fought Hitler to implement a free society that treats you as a human regardless of your race or religion. I was wrong. I sometimes hear English voices here and realise how easy it would be to take me from here to Turkey," he wrote. "Please remember me as a good person who wanted to steal from the rich to give to the poor."

Jack added that he had finally managed to find a book to read in the prison, about the Second World War; indeed, his Red Cross case worker said he practically related the contents of the entire book to her during her visit. This was the Jack we remembered — passionate, intense, and utterly well-intentioned, and this was the true picture of the boy the British and Canadian governments were determined to shield from the world. Much of his message was censored — with vast blocks of text simply removed — which the Red Cross said was information that was not allowed, being of a "non-family" nature. They warned us that we could share no information that might jeopardize their access to the prison, by containing material that the Kurds would not want publicized.

We knew from Clive's correspondence with the Red Cross in April 2018 that the charity's assistance could extend to the issuing of emergency travel documents (since many refugees often had no passports or travel documents after fleeing a war zone). Importantly, Syria, as run by Assad, was a country that accepted the validity of an ICRC (International Committee of the Red Cross) travel document for exit purposes. All that was required for this process to be put in motion was for the Canadian or British government to request the prisoner's release from the detaining authority. (When Clive had asked the Canadian government to request emergency travel documents for Jack, he had received the reply that since no travel was currently planned for Jack, there was no reason for the government to request these documents. A catch-22 that only government lawyers determined to do nothing could possibly dream up.)

During the summer of 2018, it became evident that we had no choice but to pin all our hopes on Clive's getting to Qamishli. In July, we discovered we had lost the Supreme Court appeal, which meant that our trial would not be dropped as we'd hoped, and that objective evidence, without any *mens rea* on our part, would be all that was required to convict us. As an additional blow, in June I had been fired again after a three-months' employment in the Politics Department at Oxford University after one of the Canadian graduate students had "recognized me." In hopeful anticipation of Clive's visiting him, I gathered messages for Jack from his former schoolfriends:

"My brother, I don't know where to start. Everytime I think of you I feel like crying, wallahi I miss you like crazy. Best believe I ain't never forgotten you bro, and I pray with all my heart that I will see you again, and i know that inshallah I will see you again akhi," read one message.

"Make sure you keep headstrong like you've always been, me and others are doing everything we can to help you. I have never forgotten about you and never will, you're one of my closest brothers and no bullshit in the media or anything else will change that," read another.

I knew that Jack's friends meant everything to him, and that their messages would bolster his spirits immeasurably.

A second Red Cross message from mid-July gave us hope that Jack was holding on, trying to make the best of his situation — even performing "Nazi/Allies" comedy routines with his German cellmate to pass the time — but it was clear he was losing hope that any government would come to rescue him: "No government believes I am human ... with inherent worth and deserving of a second chance.... If I ever leave this place, I don't want to hurt a single person, not after what I've seen, and after realising how violence can consume people and strips them of their humanity." Not sentiments you would expect from a jihadi, but Jack was right in his assessment of his situation: no government had an interest in correcting the established narrative about him, particularly when the upcoming trial of his parents depended on it.

Labour party visit to Qamishli, and Sajid Javid, Home Secretary, April–July 2018

Between April and July 2018, two things happened that gave the lie to the Canadian and British government's position that it was "too difficult" or "too dangerous" to negotiate with the Kurds for the release of Canadian or British prisoners in northern Syria.

The first was a trip by Labour party officials at the beginning of April 2018 to Qamishli, where Jack was being held. One of these officials was Lloyd Russell-Moyle, MP for Brighton Kemptown, and another was Lord Maurice Glasman, Labour peer. The stated aim of the trip was to express solidarity with the Kurds in the face of threats from Turkish forces, particularly in light of the Turkish army's seizure of the Rojavan town of Afrin in March 2018. "We're here for a long-term relationship with you, where we can support you against all the people who are trying to destroy your liberty," said Maurice Glasman. Russell-Moyle said they would share news of the trip with "our parliament and with our people," and that he hoped for "better scrutiny of arms sales to Turkey."

Unfortunately, neither politician thought to try to visit Jack Letts, British prisoner from Oxford, incarcerated without any access to the outside world, and situated less than a mile from where this congenial meeting with his captors was taking place. (Our MP said later that if she had known about this trip, she would have asked her party colleagues to advocate on Jack's behalf, which rather begged the question as to why she — the only British MP to have a constituent detained by these particular Kurdish hosts — wasn't in the loop.)

Interestingly, the route the Labour officials took to get to Qamishli, as reported by local Kurdish news, was the Semalka crossing, which connects the Kurdistan region and Rojava. If you look up images of the Semalka crossing, you will see that it consists of a short concrete strip spanning a river no more than 150 metres wide. This — according to Canadian officials — was the route that was much too dangerous to escort Jack across, even with a couple of tanks and some military personnel.

The other lie by the British government, exposed in a leaked letter to the *Daily Telegraph* in July 2018, was that British officials were unable to contact the Kurdish authorities, as they "had no consular assistance" in the region and the Kurds were "non-state actors." The letter in question had been written by Sajid Javid, U.K. Home Secretary, to Jeff Sessions, U.S. Attorney General, and had stated that he and his officials were ready to extradite to the U.S. two British prisoners — suspected ISIS fighters, nicknamed the Beatles — who were being held in Rojava. In a breach of long-standing U.K. policy against the death penalty, Javid stated that, in this case, he was not seeking a death penalty assurance and also that U.S. courts were better placed to handle "foreign fighter" cases "because of the risk of legal challenge in the U.K." According to Javid, it would be easier to convict the men in the U.S., where intercept evidence was allowed, and where there were additional charges for terrorism offences not available under U.K. law.

For me, despite the horror of a cabinet minister secretly plotting to send Britons (who had been stripped of their British citizenship) to their certain deaths, I was secretly heartened that someone,

somewhere — presumably a senior civil servant, since Javid's letter
had been officially circulated to only a select few, including the
Foreign Minister, Boris Johnson — had believed they could not
stand by and let this happen. Hence, they had acted according to
their conscience and had leaked the letter to the *Daily Telegraph.*

My panicky email to the Foreign Office asking for assurances
that Jack wouldn't be extradited to the U.S. or sent to Guantanamo,
produced a reply from Consular Special Cases saying, "The U.K.
Government's priority is to ensure where crimes have been committed individuals face criminal prosecution in the most appropriate
jurisdiction, following due legal process" (more bureaucratic gobbledygook that says nothing at all). However, there was, at least, an
addition within the reply, which stated, "Our position on the detention facility at Guantanamo Bay is that it should close." Perhaps, I
thought, someone should inform our Home Secretary of that fact,
and while they're at it explain the illegality of simply making up
policy on the hoof and sending people to their deaths without thinking of informing Parliament or, indeed, anyone else.

Jack's welfare, summer–autumn 2018

As a mother, like all mothers, I had spent every day from the day
Jack and then *E* were born keeping them alive. Making sure they
were well-fed, warm, sheltered, happy, had friends, were doing well
in school — all those normal things every parent does — had occupied a vast proportion of my day. In the usual course of things,
children grow up and parents find other things to occupy their
time. With Jack, the reverse was true. Even though he was now in
his early twenties, my anxiety over his day-to-day welfare resembled
that of a new mother with an infant. Yet, though my nurturing in-
stinct had gone into overdrive, I had no outlet for my fears. When

I tried to imagine what he was doing at any particular moment, my mind had nothing to feed on, apart from his disconsolate and censored Red Cross messages. Was he was going out of his mind with boredom and inactivity? Was he being bullied by his cellmates? Was he suffering from the diseases of confinement and poor hygiene, such as infections, skin diseases, and muscle wastage? When was the last time he'd had a shower? These thoughts didn't stop at night, either; so, my thoughts would churn in a loop as I tossed and turned, or got up at 4:00 a.m. to write another stroppy or anguished letter to a government minister, knowing that all I would get in reply would be "we have no consular access in Syria ..."

One of the stipulations governing the Red Cross's visits to detention centres was that their officers would not report on the conditions endured by prisoners, for fear of jeopardizing either their famed neutrality or access to the people they were trying to help. While I could accept this intellectually, I couldn't accept it emotionally. Their delegates had seen my son, they knew how he looked, if he was thin, or depressed, or was losing the use of his legs through lack of exercise, but they couldn't tell me any of this. "Can't you even tell me the good stuff?" I asked plaintively. "Like if he's being fed properly, or he ever gets out of his cell? Just so I don't have to think about it every second of the day." The reply was always that Jack was able to tell us things himself in his letters to us, as long as these things didn't breach the censorship rules (which of course they did).

Similarly, I found it agonizing to have to sit in court while our preparatory hearings were going on, having to listen to the prosecutor speaking for four hours non-stop on how legislation was designed to protect society, and that there was no evidence to show our son had been in danger while in Raqqa. I wanted to shout out, how would she feel if her children were parachuted to the most dangerous city on earth, and then she metaphorically had her arms chopped off so that there was nothing she could do about it?

I had been cautioned by our lawyers not to interject in court and not to direct my anger at the prosecutor, since she was just doing her job. Instead, I had to just squirm in my seat, force myself not to walk out, and direct hate vibes at the back of the prosecutor's be-wigged head. Hate produces extremism and radicalization, and the British government was doing a very good job of turning one usual-ly mild-mannered, middle-aged book editor — described as "prim and proper" by one of her best friends — into a ball of fury. And if that was how I felt, imagine if I were a Syrian or Iraqi, who had grown up seeing their friends and relatives bombed, killed, muti-lated, with their limbs blown off, all because international powers were determined to fight proxy wars in a gigantic power play in an oil-rich region. Rage, I imagine, must spread through generations.

Chapter 35

"Duress" is not a defence

Trial, Old Bailey, September 6, 2018

Our criminal trial on Thursday, September 6, 2018, did not get off to a good start. "If they are still there on Monday, I will have them fined, and/or arrested with a view to imprisonment," was Judge Hilliard's opening salvo. The miscreants he was referring to were our little band of supporters — thirty or so friends who had made the early morning trip up to London — who had been demonstrating outside the Old Bailey with banners and placards.

"It is simply unacceptable that jury members should be subjected to emotive demonstrations of the kind currently taking place outside this courtroom," said the judge. "Doing what any parent would do to save their child is not funding terrorism," he read out, quoting one of the banners (which summed up our situation rather neatly, I thought). "It needs to be conveyed to these demonstrators that they will be fined according to the value of court time lost, due to the necessity of empanelling another jury which has not

been influenced by seeing these banners on their way into court."
He then looked up meaningfully at the public gallery, where some
of our friends were now sitting. "I don't know if there are members
of this demonstration who are currently in attendance at this court
room, but if so, this needs to be conveyed at the earliest opportunity. Also, if members of the press have already made public photographs of this demonstration, these photographs will need to be
immediately withdrawn, or will be considered to be in contempt
of court."

The rows of journalists to our left instantly began tapping away
on their mobile phones, no doubt typing "Retract! Retract!" to
their editors, for fear of being fined the contempt-of-court charge
of £30,000.

John and I felt flummoxed and crushed before our trial had
even started. We stood no chance if the judge was already politically biased against us. As we were exchanging alarmed glan-
ces in the dock — a modern dock this time, as, thankfully, our
trial would not be in notorious Court 1 — Henry Blaxland, John's
new and reputedly fearsome barrister, stood up and stated, "There
is a thousand-year-old tradition of protest in this country, your
Honour." Good old Henry, we thought. Someone to break through
the general obsequiousness of the British court to say what needed
to be said. The judge, however, was unmoved by Henry's observa-
tion, and merely reiterated his former position.

Our friends, and some of the journalists we had got to know
fairly well by now, were shocked by the judge's stance. One of our
friends — a veteran campaigner and well-known photographer
of the Newbury bypass protest of the 1990s — had the idea of
turning up the next day with a tongue-in-cheek placard saying,
"Sorry, judge." Another expressed the opinion that standing silently
with a completely blank placard would make the same point more
poetically.

One well-known writer friend of John's, Colin Tudge, expressed his outrage to our campaign manager, Ingrid, in the absence of any opportunity to air his views more publicly in print:

> If the government and/or the police want to convict someone who is up for trial at the Old Bailey, like a serial killer or a child molester, then people are apparently free to protest to their hearts' content all the way down Fleet Street if they choose, banging on the police van, shouting abuse — whatever. But if the powers-that-be sense that a jury might acquit a person that they are anxious to put down, for whatever reason, then suddenly the judiciary becomes hyper-sensitive, and barriers go up, with threats of draconian sentences for contempt of court for anyone who dares to utter a squeak. How can that be justified? ... We really should get angrier than most people do most of the time.

Yes, indeed, we thought.

It was only as the pretrial arguments progressed, when the judge appeared to be giving due consideration to our defence's position, that we gained a little more faith in the man himself. Perhaps, we reconsidered, his banning of the protest really was his attempt to strip the case of its political elements in order to concentrate solely on the law. (Although this, of course, disregarded the fact that our case had been politically charged from the outset, right from when Detective Inspector *T* told us that the decision to charge us or not would be made "at ministerial level.")

In one crucial aspect of our preparatory hearings, i.e., the admissibility of the "duress" argument, the judge even gave a strongly worded judgment in our favour.

The prosecution had argued that the defence of duress — in our case, that we had acted out of necessity in order to save our son's life — should not be available for any terrorism offence. The prosecutor had even argued, as mentioned previously, that there was no evidence that Jack had been in any danger in Raqqa and had required rescuing. Henry Blaxland — who was rapidly becoming another of our heroes — demolished both of these arguments, which had been presented in extremely long and laborious detail, in five minutes flat. "Duress as a defence is available for every offence on the statute book, except murder," said Henry, as the judge enthusiastically nodded in response. "And Jack was in Syria, your Honour. With regard to the danger he was in, I think that is all that needs to be said on the matter."

One aspect of our trial framework, which filled me and John with strange optimism, was the possibility of getting Jack back to the U.K. as a witness in our trial. We had thought of this as a potential line of approach before — one of the stated objectives of Clive's trip to Qamishli had been the securing of Jack's witness statement — but the thousand and one practical details that had so far defeated this approach meant that no progress had been made. This time, we hoped, the notion of Jack appearing as a witness would be entered into a legal framework — where British officials would, ironically, be finally accountable to the law — and, most importantly, it would be a way of getting our son back.

What our defence required — in this aspect obviously most exciting to John and me — was actual proof that the British government had actively blocked attempts to gain access to Jack and/or to obtain a witness statement from him. This would demonstrate "abuse of process" by the Crown and could be grounds for having our case thrown out. Evidence of the government's abject failure to do anything — as amply demonstrated by the infuriating

Foreign Office letters to us — was not enough to demonstrate active blocking.

Ironically, from the prosecution's point of view, Jack was not required as a witness to prove their case against us. Whether he was a terrorist or not was immaterial. Jack could have been soaking up rays on a beach in Costa Rica for the past four years, and John and I could still be found guilty if it was demonstrated we'd had the slightest notion that he might be a criminal, rather than a beach bum. In the end, the upshot of this latest legal argument was a repetition of what had happened when our criminal trial was first aborted nearly two years ago, i.e., a further appeal was lodged at the High Court (this time by the prosecution to appeal against the judge's decision on duress) and a further delay to the trial itself; this time to April 2019, three and a half years after we were arrested. The most senior judge in the country, Lord Leveson, would preside over the duress argument appeal, as it was deemed to be a "complex and important issue."

We believed that, by deliberately stalling, the prosecution was playing games to delay having to provide disclosure on the British government's communications with Jack's detainers. They may have even had to disclose that there hadn't been any communication at all.

The politics of our case appeared to be growing ever wider. This, I'm sure, was no comfort at all to Jack, who was rotting in his cell while the legal ramifications spun miles away in a sort of perpetual vortex — as if on a separate planet entirely.

Chapter 36

Jack becomes a Canadian election issue

On October 16, 2018, Jack unexpectedly became a headache for the Canadian prime minister, Justin Trudeau, when the question of his release became an election issue. Trudeau was running for re-election in 2019, and the Conservative government had spied an opportunity in Jack's case to attack the Liberal leader for his supposed "soft on terrorism" policies. So it was that the political problem of Jack being repatriated to Canada took centre stage at Prime Minister's Question Time in the Canadian Parliament, with the Conservative leader, Andrew Scheer, deriding Trudeau for "proactively reaching out" to Jack, "a known ISIS fighter," while his fellow MPs shouted and jeered in support.

The bizarreness of the issue suddenly being propelled into the spotlight after a year and half of being shunted into the sidelines was not lost on me and John. In Britain, we had not been able to raise even a flicker of political interest, our MP still apparently unable to elicit the attention of Jeremy Corbyn, and the government too busy shooting itself in the head over Brexit to give time to anything else.

Global Affairs Canada had done their best to keep a lid on the whole affair by trying to convince us that Jack was safest "staying where he was." Over the summer of 2018, they had even started to adopt the language of the British government by saying that "Canada has no consular presence in Syria and has not done so since 2012. There is therefore very little we can do to assist": i.e., they had not even bothered to invent their own excuses. It was clear that Britain was putting pressure on the Canadian government to fall in line with the British policy of admitting no returnees whatsoever.

In Parliament, Trudeau was clearly caught on the back foot. Although his government had recently gone cold on Jack, transcripts (sent by me to a Canadian journalist) had appeared in the press, showing that Global Affairs Canada had asked Jack several months beforehand if he would like to come to Canada, and if he wanted their assistance. Without referring specifically to Jack's case, Trudeau merely replied that his government took "with the utmost seriousness, the threats posed by travelling extremists" and emphasized that the Canadian government had at its disposal a "full range of counterterrorism tools."

What had galvanized this unexpected situation was an article in the *Guardian* by Bethan McKernan on October 6, which had quoted Canadian diplomats as saying Jack "might be repatriated to Canada." Kurdish officials, claimed the article, had engaged in promising negotiations to hand over an estimated eleven Canadian citizens, including women, children, and at least one highly ranked fighter, but "Ottawa recently backed out of the agreement ... without giving reasons." This statement certainly chimed with our experience of Global Affairs Canada officials telling us in January 2018 that they were "diligently working on Jack's release," but then telling Clive in May 2018 that unfortunately, all release options were "impossible."

Faced with the transcripts, Trudeau could not deny his government's involvement. However, neither did he want to concede to Scheer that he was going against the public's wishes by inviting a "known ISIS fighter" to Canada, particularly when that individual was a British citizen and only a Canadian "by convenience." Clearly, Trudeau was facing a dilemma that John and I needed to help him resolve, while ensuring that the resolution was in our favour. I couldn't quite believe that we were influencing an election in one of the G7 countries, but our situation was already so unreal, this latest episode just seemed to be another bizarre twist.

In a clever move, John seized on the one issue that would reverse Scheer's advantage and force him onto the defensive. "If Mr. Scheer has any evidence that our son is a 'known jihadi fighter,' he has a duty to report this information to the Canadian and British authorities," John wrote in an open letter to all Canadian MPs, which was also sent to select Canadian journalists. "No such evidence has ever been passed to us, or to our lawyers in the U.K." Scheer's response to this, as shown in CBC's webcast, that "he stood by his statements" was markedly free of the smug bellicosity that had accompanied his previous performance in the House of Commons. Clearly, it wasn't only Trudeau who wasn't in full possession of the facts of Jack's case.

Complicating — and humanizing — the debate surrounding the Canadian detainees in Syria was the fact that only three of them were suspected fighters. The rest were women and children. And these "non-combatants" — including one mother with three children, aged one, four, and five — were living in tents and facing a harsh winter, where disease, cold, and overcrowding would soon combine to create life-threatening conditions. Even Andrew Scheer would not be able to say that these children posed a threat to Canadian security, and as Clive said, it was "hard to imagine why a government with any sense of decency would not bring them home."

A factor bitterly dividing Canadians on the detainee issue was the recent case of Omar Khadr, a Canadian citizen who had been held in Guantanamo for ten years — between 2002 and 2012 — after being captured at the age of sixteen following a firefight at an outpost in Afghanistan. In 2017, Khadr successfully sued the Canadian government for its role in his mistreatment at the U.S. military prison in Cuba — including its interrogations of him after his subjection to torture techniques such as sleep deprivation, being shackled in prolonged stress positions, and extreme physical force.

Clive himself had visited Omar Khadr in Guantanamo in 2006, at which meeting Khadr told him that the confession for which he was incarcerated — i.e., that he had thrown a hand grenade that had killed a U.S. Army Sergeant — had been obtained under duress. The resulting compensation payment of $10.5 million given to Khadr in July 2017 — together with an apology from the Canadian government — provoked vehement, mixed reactions from the Canadian public.

The Conservative Canadian view, as represented by our current detractor, Andrew Scheer, was that it was "disgusting" that the Canadian government had handed over millions to a convicted terrorist. The Liberal government, on the other hand, said the settlement had been necessary because of clear violations of Khadr's Charter rights by Canadian officials. Trudeau followed up this apology with the principled and laudable statement, "The measure of a society, a just society, is not whether we stand up for people's rights when it's easy or popular to do so, it's whether we recognize rights when it's difficult, when it's unpopular" — a sentiment which seemed to encapsulate everything John and I had been fighting for over the past year and a half.

Inevitably, the Canadian public and politicians compared Jack's present case to that of Omar Khadr. In the comments section of newspapers and social media, John and I were portrayed as money-grabbing opportunists who merely wanted to get our hands on millions of dollars of Canadian taxpayers' money, and who weren't even really Canadian to boot. ("Which would you prefer? A million pounds or your son tortured?" is what I wanted to say to these commentators but chose not to inflame them.) Our attempts to say publicly that we had no intention of claiming compensation, we just wanted our son back, either weren't publicized, or were criticized by our own Canadian supporters, who told us that by declaring this in advance, we were throwing away our only potential source of leverage against the Canadian government.

The conclusion of Jack's case being debated in the Canadian Parliament was an agreement by the Liberal government — determined by a vote of 280 to 1 — to an opposition motion calling for a federal strategy to bring Canadian ISIS fighters to justice. A plan for this had to be devised within forty-five days of the date of this agreement, October 23, 2018.

Seven days later, John hit the headlines with his presentation on Jack's illegal detention, which he gave on Parliament Hill in Ottawa. A press conference had been arranged in conjunction with Families Against Violent Extremism (FAVE), a small charity headed by Alexandra Bain, a religious studies professor at St. Thomas University, New Brunswick. Standing at a podium in front of a colourful rank of the banners of each of Canada's ten provinces, and flanked by the spotlights of all of the country's main news outlets, John looked impressively presidential as he delivered his passionate plea.

"I want everyone here to know what we know — that Jack worked with others in the religious opposition to ISIS in Raqqa. He condemned ISIS on social media, and he wants to spend the rest of his life living peacefully and bearing witness against ISIS," he announced, as the cameras flashed and whirred. "For three years we have not been allowed to talk about our case, or counter lies that have been printed about Jack, because of contempt of court rules. In fact, I expect the British authorities to arrest me on my return to the U.K. because I'm violating this ban. Unfortunately, I do not have any other choice than to speak out because I love my son and I think he's innocent."

As it turned out, John also needed to speak on behalf of the relatives of the other Canadian detainees, who had been lined up to speak but had cancelled due to fear of repercussions in their own local areas. Unlike us, a lot of them had experienced forms of harassment such as bricks through their windows and were understandably wary of going public. However hard we were finding things, it seemed that other families, who were Muslim, were suffering in much more overt and violent ways.

The day after the press conference, John flew back to the U.K., eager to find out if Clive's proposed trip to Rojava had taken place in the meantime. Fortunately, he wasn't arrested as feared. We both hoped that his going public for a second time (after our disappointing social media campaign a year ago) would finally yield positive results rather than the hate, indifference, and continued governmental inertia we'd experienced to date.

Chapter 37

Finally, contact

On December 19, 2018, we received a glorious message from Clive, saying he had just spent two and a half hours with Jack — the first time in nearly five years that someone we knew had had direct contact with him. The warden present at their meeting — a decent guy, according to Clive — had allowed the allocated visit time of an hour to be extended. Jack was in good spirits, and Clive had "really liked him" (effusive for Clive, I thought). Perhaps, unbelievably, Jack's boyhood charm had survived his horrendous experiences.

After several false starts, which had included six postponed flights and innumerable broken promises, we had despaired of Clive ever getting to see Jack. The most recent Kurdish excuse for delay had been that their general was unfortunately otherwise engaged, having had to rush off to Damascus for talks on Democratic Federation of Northern Syria (FNS) regional autonomy. Although Clive had been able to visit the women and children in the Rojavan camps in his October trip, he had been unable to see Jack, and had received no explanation why not.

At long last, this time round we were able to pose all the questions we'd aimed at the Red Cross but which had received no answers. How was he? (In good health and good spirits.) How were his conditions? (Harsh, but he is managing.) How does he look, what about the state of his teeth, hair, skin? (He doesn't look gaunt, and the last three look okay.) Does he have any knowledge of the outside world? (He seems to be informed; perhaps there is a TV in the cell.) How does he spend his time? (Not sure, but he has read the one book in the prison four times.) Is he losing hope? (He believes his two governments have given up on him, and his Kurdish captors never now speak of release.)

Under our further intense questioning, Clive revealed more of what Jack was currently going through, as well as his previous experiences under ISIS. He was being held in a space the size of a large living room with thirty-seven other prisoners, including Tunisians, Chechens, and Germans. Each of them had about half a metre to sleep in, was rarely, if ever, allowed out of the cell, and had had no hot water for nearly two years. I imagined fights breaking out between the cellmates in such appalling conditions, but Clive hadn't asked about this. He had been concentrating on getting a witness statement from Jack, for the purposes of his and our defence.

We learned that the statements Jack had made to the BBC only a month before — in his first external contact in seventeen months — were invalid, as the interview had been conducted under duress with several of his detainers present. The answers he had given, Jack explained, had been exactly the same as those he'd given during his previous three-hour interrogation sessions, which had employed "enhanced" techniques. In other words, he had delivered the statements he knew his interrogators wanted to hear and which wouldn't elicit severe mistreatment. Included within this was the statement that his parents knew he was going to Syria — something so patently false I wasn't worried anyone would believe it.

Importantly, Jack was also able to explain to Clive that the disturbing Facebook messages attributed to him had actually been written by others using his account (something we'd always suspected). He provided Clive with the names of the individuals concerned.

For John and me, this cast serious doubts on the role of the BBC in its information gathering. Not only had they conducted an interview under dubious circumstances, they had also immediately given the tape to the Crown Prosecution Service and refused to give a copy to our defence lawyers. Clearly, there had been some agreement between the BBC, the British government, and Kurdish authorities for the BBC to gain access to Jack to obtain information, which they then passed on to the British government without notifying his parents or lawyer. This information had been elicited from Jack without a lawyer present yet was being held by the CPS as evidence. Why should the BBC have information about my son that I didn't? Why was a public broadcaster doing the work of a public prosecutor?

For much of its history, the BBC has been fondly referred to in Britain as "Auntie," and, until recently, it was rare to hear a bad word about it. However, I was discovering during this period that my own perspective on this particular national treasure was being irrevocably altered. I was gaining an understanding of how the interconnections between government, security services, and our public broadcaster mesh to project a desired governmental narrative. Before being an unwilling participant in this process myself, I was about as far removed from being a conspiracy theorist as you can get. Now it seemed a question of just opening my eyes a little wider.

Most of Jack's stories, as related to us by Clive, were extremely difficult to hear. During his numerous imprisonments by ISIS, he had been starved (on one occasion, eating only bread and tomato paste for eight days), and held underground in brutal solitary confinement. Several times, he had been threatened with being sent to

ISIS's "re-education camps." During his Kurdish detention, he had not only tried to hang himself, he had also tried to slit his wrist (as he proved to Clive by showing him the scar).

It was no wonder that during this month of December I felt increasingly alienated from my Oxford neighbours, who were in the grip of Christmas conspicuous consumption. One neighbour in particular demonstrated how middle-class do-gooding can completely miss the point when she phoned me in response to an angry open letter I'd posted on our *Justice for Jack* website:

"Just a few words of advice," said the neighbour.

> I thought you should know that my husband and I agreed that your post is not likely to get support from people who might be persuaded to help you — it's just too emotive and not succinct enough. Just for comparison purposes, last week I wrote a forceful letter to Oxford City Council about a housing development in Headington, and my husband suggested I tone it down a little so that it would be taken more seriously by the authorities. Perhaps you could do the same with yours? Also, your sentence saying that you would like to stand outside the Foreign Office and shout "Murderers" is not helpful, and unfortunately means I won't be able to send your letter on to my Quaker friends.

Feeling the blood boiling in my head, I knew that middle-class politeness was going to desert me in a big way. Sure enough, my mouth started to act before my brain took control, and I found myself contemptuously declaring that her Headington housing development was in no way comparable to my son's life-threatening situation and hung up before she could say anything further. My small circle of friends had just got even smaller. For several minutes afterward, I was so spitting mad I didn't know what to do with myself. Seriously, getting Jack out of his hell-hole and me out of the ignorant, smug, self-satisfied enclave of Oxford's middle classes could not happen a day too soon.

A final comment on Clive's visit with Jack — a voice message I received out of the blue a couple of days after Clive's return to the U.K. — helped calm me down. The sender's number was unknown, and the message opened with "please forgive the cold calling." Introducing himself as a security adviser in the Middle East, the sender explained that he had just looked after Clive in Rojava and had spent over an hour with Jack. He wanted to tell me what a "kind, clever, bashful, and decent young man" Jack was. Since John and I had spent the best part of four years trying to convince an unreceptive world of this, his comment — unexpected, from the tough environment of the security business — felt like an immense validation.

Chapter 38

FCO Disclosure

January 2019

Around this time, as the farce of our trial continued and Jack's incarceration lengthened, I became bolder on Twitter.

"British & Canadian govs try to establish whereabouts of Jack Letts. Location info from BBC, MI5, MI6, Red Cross, Kurdish authorities clearly not enough for them. Try looking behind the sofa?" was one daring missive (as I anxiously awaited arrest for contempt of court).

"When I asked the Foreign and Commonwealth Office why they couldn't pick up *bleep* phone, they sent me a leaflet on rude and abusive behaviour. Exactly how polite are you supposed to be when they are trying to murder your son?" was another.

My increasing daring coincided with an event of major import: the arrival in the post, on January 15, 2019, of FCO disclosure information. John had asked this via a Freedom of Information request with the help of Reprieve so long ago — over a year before-hand — that we had forgotten all about it.

Suddenly, the reason for our global pariah status became clear from the disclosed FCO document, dated July 19, 2017.

"The parents have stated that there is a possibility their son may die given his reported treatment. They have also indicated that he may self-harm or commit suicide. Mr. Letts senior has said that a media campaign is a possibility highlighting HMG's inactivity. *Currently press coverage and public opinion is not sympathetic to the Letts family or Mr. Letts' predicament.*" (emphasis mine)

It was official: John and I were possibly the most unpopular couple in the whole of the U.K.

Based on this analysis, the FCO concluded they should continue "to deploy our standard lines to both the family and their legal representatives," as specified in "Option 1," i.e., "that we continue to inform the family that we are unable to provide consular assistance, that we cannot contact the PYD or YPG in relation to this matter, and that Mr. Letts could seek consular assistance should he present himself in a neighbouring country."

The foreign secretary — at the time, Boris Johnson — was, we found out, completely in agreement with this Option 1. We would never know what Option 2 was, since the censor's black pen had obliterated it, and Option 3 had been the feeble suggestion to "refer them to another EU country" — very amusing, given Brexit.

In other words, our complete ostracism from society, and the blocking of our attempts to breach the brick wall surrounding us on all sides, had been sanctioned from the very top. The government were satisfied they could stonewall us forever if they wanted to, since the public simply didn't care.

Other nuggets of revelatory interest were to be found scattered within the bundle of 130 or so documents.

"We are happy to meet [the Letts family] (as long as they are polite!)" stated one FCO message of November 23, 2017 — since being polite is obviously paramount when questioning inaction in the face of torture allegations.

"I am slightly worried their intention might be to highlight perceived inequalities/inconsistencies in consular assistance by directly comparing Letts' case to [blanked out by censor's pen] and using [blank] case ... as an argument for HMG to upgrade our consular policy in Syria," continued this memo.

"How do we balance our obligations on mistreatment with our policy of not providing assistance?" was one FCO concern of June 27, 2017.

By treating it as not an obligation at all was the clear answer, since the Letts family was so unpopular that, fortunately, governmental obligations did not apply to them.

It was from another snippet that I learned of Jim Collins's touching concern for his assistant's welfare when she'd been alone in a lift with me at the FCO headquarters on King Charles Street.

"Sally stormed out of the meeting room and left the building, delivering some unkind comments to [blank] along the way."

Gosh, how distressing this must have been for "blank" — my question as to how she could possibly bear to do her job, when her job was to do nothing? Our complaints to her about our son's being locked in a dungeon, banging on the wall for food until his hand bled, were clearly nothing in comparison to the unkindness I had visited upon her.

The lesson of all this, I presume, is that this is how the Empire was won. While the natives are being slaughtered around you, my son, always make sure that your manners never falter and the creases in your spotless white suit are firmly pressed. The entrails of the British Empire must never be on display; it's the image that counts.

Chapter 39

Jack's prison interview and Shamima Begum

On February 22, 2019, Jack made his first-ever public appearance on the world stage. Filmed being led out of a prison back room by a guard in a black balaclava, deposited on a wooden chair in front of harsh television lights, he proceeded to answer tabloid-style questions posed by Rohit Kachroo, ITV journalist.

It had been five years since we had last seen him, and we'd had no idea what to expect. It was painful to see how thin and bewildered he looked, and heart-breaking to hear that what he missed most about Britain were people, particularly his mother ("I know that sounds toddlerish," he said, with his characteristic rueful grin). If possible, he said, he would like to put in a request for a phone call home. A reasonable enough wish, one would think, but it seemed the government was quite happy for him to address the world, but not at all happy for him to speak for five minutes to his own mother.

One consolation was that at least his appearance wasn't dreadful: it looked as if he still had his teeth; his hair was short, and he was clean-shaven. I counted his fingers when his hands gestured close to his face: they were all still there. His manner of speech was that of the boy we remembered: eloquent, considered, and expressive. There was no evidence of the religious maniac who had addressed us from Raqqa, which convinced us even more that during his time there he had been playing to the gallery to stay alive.

Saying he "didn't want to start a new life with a lie," he answered the questions as honestly and directly as he could. What touched me most about this preamble to his responses was his belief that he was going to be given a chance of a new life, despite all the indications otherwise. Answering a question on his response to the Paris attacks, he tried to put his thoughts into context, from when the attacks first occurred to now. At the time, he said, he had just seen a young girl burn to death in the street from a coalition bomb and had thought that Europe would now get an understanding of the awful reality of that. Now, he said, he understood that the people targeted in Paris had nothing to do with this situation of war.

I knew — as indeed happened — that the print media would focus on his first comment and ignore his subsequent explanation. His response to "If you could request one thing of the government, what would it be?" was similarly ignored. In typical Jack fashion, he'd replied, "I would request that the women and children could be released from the camps. There are children dying there. If I have to stay here for another two years for this to happen, then I will." Surely it couldn't just be us, his parents, who thought these were not the words of a vicious jihadi fighter. His comment about "another two years" also gave me some comfort: this, surely, was an indication he was not about to try to kill himself again, having found a purpose in keeping himself alive.

The timing of Jack's interview was linked to two major events involving the fates of foreign nationals in Syria. One of these was the rescue from Camp Roj, Syria, of two Trinidadian brothers — Ayyub, seven, and Mahmud, eleven, Ferreira, on January 21, 2019. The boys' repatriation to Trinidad and reunification with their mother had been organized by Clive, and made possible by Roger Waters, former Pink Floyd guitarist, who had flown the boys out of Erbil in his private jet. Nearly five years beforehand, the boys had been kidnapped by their father and taken to ISIS territory, and then, after their father's death — so the story went — had been abandoned at the side of the road by their Belgian stepmother during their attempted escape to Turkey. (The latter part of this story is disputed, as subsequent reports maintained that their stepmother had, in fact, been captured by the YPG and taken, blindfolded, to one of the Syrian camps.) Thus, in one cleverly planned action, Clive and Roger Waters had proved that the pathetic stance of Western governments that "there was nothing they could do" about the fate of their nationals in Syria was a lie, and a dereliction of their duty.

The second event caused a much bigger splash in the U.K. newspapers, involving as it did British national, Shamima Begum, from Bethnal Green, a working-class area of London, who had gone to Syria as a fifteen-year-old with two of her friends. Thrust into the limelight of the world's media as a seemingly unrepentant ISIS bride, Shamima polarized the nation between those who believed she had been a groomed, naive teenager who deserved a second chance and those who believed she and the infant she was about to give birth to should be left to rot in Syria. Public opinion was outraged that she showed no remorse, although it wasn't clear what exactly she should show remorse for, since all she had done while in ISIS territory was keep house and look after her children, both of whom had died. The vitriol that poured out of ordinary citizens was shocking to behold. If this was the strength of feeling of the mob against a brainwashed teenaged girl, what hope was there that the vicious juggernaut of public opprobrium against Jack would ever be converted into respect for international law and human rights? Our pleas to be listened to were like the squeak of a mouse amid the roar of a thunderstorm.

Sajid Javid, Foreign Secretary, who had replaced the deliberately inactive Boris, clearly thought so, too. Responding to the public's thunderstorm roar, he made a clear bid to win political points by standing firm against a traumatized teenager, and six days after her interview with Anthony Loyd of the *Times*, summarily revoked Shamima's British citizenship. She could go to Bangladesh, the country of citizenship of her parents, he proclaimed, conveniently ignoring the fact that Bangladesh hadn't been consulted on the matter and subsequently announced it didn't want her.

After her *Times* interview, Shamima received death threats from some of the ISIS women, reportedly in response to her denigration of the caliphate. Shamima herself explained that she'd had to moderate her criticism of ISIS during the interview itself, highlighting the contextual error in taking any of her comments at face value.

Her explanation certainly chimed with our experience of Jack's bizarre and disturbing comments made during his time in Raqqa, compared to his normal-sounding conversation while he was in Kurdish territory. Leaked lawyer gossip informed us that it was a call from the British government that had requested Shamima be moved to another camp for her own safety, which rather demonstrated the government's ability to act when it wanted to.

Inevitably, press commentators made comparisons between Shamima's and Jack's cases, focusing mainly on the difference in their races. "Why was the citizenship of the brown girl revoked when that of the white boy wasn't?" was the main thrust of resentment from Shamima's supporters.

I tried to explain on Twitter that in no way was Jack being treated from a position of privilege: having two citizenships could, in fact be counterproductive, since each government maintained that the other should bear responsibility, with the result that neither did. Also, I surmised, it was likely that the U.K. government was hindered in stripping his citizenship since the action could be seen as contempt of court in the case against us, his parents. No doubt it was only a matter of time before it would happen to him, too.

All of the press interviews of ISIS suspects conducted around this time — in the aftermath of ISIS's last stand in the small town of Baghouz — were orchestrated by Western governments desperate for their suspect nationals to incriminate themselves publicly. In this way, it could be demonstrated that in no circumstances should these devils incarnate ever be allowed back to their home countries. Sending in journalists, and compelling Kurdish officials to let them into the camps, in no way seemed to impinge on government officials' assertions that they themselves were unable to visit the camps because of the "risk to life."

Journalists joked that their governments believed they had special press jackets that protected them against bullets. Others played the situation for laughs, showing pictures of female ISIS suspects throwing water at the press, captioned, "Ready to go back to their home countries?"

The worst of these journalists took the advice of "terror experts" who instructed them that the most important thing was to "get the dunya" of the suspects they interviewed, particularly if they only had a few minutes with each one. "Dunya," they explained, was the network of individuals who had facilitated the suspect's entry into Syria. In other words, the prime role of the journalist was expected to be that of a prosecutor: extracting a confession, uncovering accomplices, condemning the interviewee's actions, and ensuring that the penalty would be their permanent exile in any country other than their own.

BBC's Quentin Sommerville even seemed to imply that ISIS's evil ideology was so potent, it had somehow managed to insinuate itself into the bloodstream of its offspring: "They [ISIS] brutal-ized, traumatized, and corrupted their own children, and that hateful ideology will live on long after the caliphate has ended," he intoned in his broadcast from the burgeoning displacement camp near Baghouz as a group of mute and emaciated toddlers stared back, blank-eyed, at the camera. Many of these children were orphans. It was difficult to countenance a world in which the emotion broadcasters such as Sommerville were attempting to provoke at the desperate plight of these innocent, bereft souls was not pity, but fear. What country could possibly call itself civilized, I raged uselessly on Twitter, if it declared itself afraid of trauma-tized three-year-olds?

This simplistic, prejudicial journalistic approach, moreover, took no consideration that very little was known about the thousands of desperate, hungry, injured women, children, and men traipsing out of Baghouz. As David Milliband, CEO of International Rescue Committee, said on March 14, 2019, "The only thing we know for sure about them is that they lived under the control of ISIS.... The IRC knows from our experiences helping people who fled Mosul and Raqqa that it's incredibly dangerous to escape ISIS territory. People either have to risk crossing an active frontline as a battle rages around them or they have to pay an exorbitantly high price to be smuggled long distances."

Exactly what we had been saying for years. In a battle between Milliband and Javid for the soul of the nation, who was going to win? For us, it really was a contest between David (same name acci-dental) and Goliath, and — grandiosity aside — between the forces of good and evil. Despite the good people on our side — Tayab, Clive, David Rose, our friends and family, and Jack's schoolfriends, a core group of whom were busy tweeting, making videos, and signing petitions — we still seemed to be running in deep, sticky mud and getting nowhere.

One thing was clear. Public opinion would never be on our side. Richard Kerbaj, Murdoch, Trump, Alistair Burt, Javid, FCO, a weak Labour party, Brexit, populism, Twitter, and general Islamophobia had all made sure of that. The only thing that was going to work was legal action against the British government. Before we could even think of launching that, however, we had a criminal trial to get through.

Chapter 40

The trial

Old Bailey, May 22 to June 21, 2019

Watching courtroom dramas on TV, I'd always been convinced that I would never be one of those unwitting individuals who do not see the trap hidden beneath the prosecutor's treacherous, leading questions. You could see their strategy a mile off, I reasoned. No one would fall for that.

In the dock, however, things look very different. You are a hapless victim in the grip of a trained assassin practised in the art of uncovering your weak spots, then plunging in for the kill. My prosecutor was an ambitious young woman with owlish eyes that fixed upon her victim with a terrifying glare. ("Do they teach you that glare in barrister school?" I asked of Tim, my razor-sharp yet friendly barrister, who, unlike most Eton/Oxford-educated barristers in the Southeast, grew up on a council estate in the North. "She's a method actor," he told me, reassuringly.)

During my four days of cross-examination in the dock, however, I wasn't nearly as composed and confident as I'd imagined I would be. The stress of facing an expressionless jury, the imagined cynicism of their reaction to my inadequate responses, the emotional strain of having to relive Jack's dangerous experiences in Raqqa, and the knowledge of the high stakes involved in inadvertently saying the wrong thing, all combined to make me shaky with nerves ("Perhaps Ms. Lane could be given a sweater?" the judge kindly intervened at one point.) On the worst occasion — while being interrogated about Jack's strident religious social media messages — I disintegrated like cardboard in water. Although I was convinced of my own innocence — why was I even in the dock when all I'd been doing was trying to reason with my own child and help him leave a war zone? — I'd suddenly found myself at a complete loss when asked to explain Jack's Facebook comment that his "brand of Islam was in no way similar to David Cameron's." Where to start with a question like that? As I floundered and trailed off with various attempted responses, the prosecutor knew she had scored a major hit. The jury foreman, my friend in the gallery told me later, sniggered and elbowed his friend at my gaping-fish distress. By lunchtime on this second day of cross-examination, I felt sure we were going to prison.

John, I knew, would be eaten up with frustration at being forced to watch my evisceration from behind his Perspex cage. The decision had been taken by the defence that our case should be as apolitical as possible, concentrating on the rights of parents to save their child, and not on the civil war situation in Syria. John was much more overtly political than me, reasoned our barristers, and there was a risk he would get into long, haranguing debates with the prosecutor. This wouldn't go down well with the jury, they believed, and advised that John not take the stand. Instead, they would play his ninety-minute police interview, in which he'd argued with great depth and eloquence his belief in Jack's innocence, and how he would be the first to condemn his son if he had any evidence he'd done anything wrong.

Fortunately, after lunchtime on the day of my poor showing, I managed to rally. This time I was on surer ground: the police had behaved dishonestly in giving us permission to send Jack money to escape Syria, and then changing their mind two days later. Although DI *T* had said during her testimony at the beginning of the trial that the wording of the advice sheet had been very clear, I begged to differ. On the contrary, I asserted, the advice had been that, although the police did not authorize the sending of monies to Jack Letts, they "could not prevent us from sending it," and prosecution of us was only a "possible outcome." The decision of whether to send it or not rested with us. As I explained on the stand, given the choice between preventing Jack from being beheaded as a deserter and possibly getting a criminal conviction, we knew what we had to do. We believed most parents would do the same.

By this time, the jury had heard the testimony of the whole lineup of prosecution witnesses: Jack's friend *M*, who said Jack had broken with the Oxford prayer group and had gone on his own religious path; the same prayer group's leader, *A*, who said he'd warned John that Jack was going to Syria but that John had refused to believe him; *Z*, the youth Prevent leader who'd given us advice in the early days; Shiraz from the International Centre for the Study of Radicalisation at King's College London, who said he'd told us not to send money, and that if Jack was in Syria he "must be a fighter" even if he wasn't on the college's database of fighters; and the seven or so police officers from SECTU who'd been involved in our case and who had given, then rescinded, permission for us to send money to Jack for his escape.

In my opinion, the lineup of police witnesses appeared a shifty bunch with a lot to hide. Cross-examination of their evidence by our barristers revealed that they had altered statements (for instance, DC *N*, saying in one statement that "neither John nor I would concede that Jack was a fighter," but then in a statement two weeks later that "Sally conceded that Jack might be a fighter, but John did not"). Our Prevent police officer appeared nervous and unsure of the dates on which key events occurred, despite the documentary evidence of her notebook. Disappointingly, she even denied saying in an unplanned meeting with us in early December that she would pass to her superiors our request to send Jack money and get back to us. "I would have written that in my notebook if that were true," she said. "Particularly if some sort of feedback was required." All John and I could do from our incapacitated position in the dock was shake our heads in disbelief.

And then, of course, there was the testimony of Hanif Qadir, our ex-"not-so-friendly-after-all" fixer, Prevent officer, and "intervention" leader.

Our barristers were given extra time to cross-examine Hanif, as his testimony was so confused and self-justifying that it warranted a "bad character" line of questioning (something only allowed in certain legal circumstances). Hanif was a police informant, established our barristers, who had assured us that our communications with him were confidential, but then reported everything back to his contacts at the Metropolitan Police and SECTU, with an extra twist of his own. He'd assured us he was getting high-level clearance through his contacts in the security services to allow us to send money to Jack, but then vehemently denied this when questioned by the police. Despite telling us Jack would be an asset to his charity's deradicalization work when he returned to the U.K., he'd informed the police that Jack could be a danger to the country and that his return should be blocked. He'd also taken on deradicalization work from the Home Office while being suspended as an intervention provider. On the stand, he expressed his sense of deep grievance that all his Home Office funding had been taken away as a result of his involvement in our case, and lost his temper several times at what he said were unfair attacks on his credibility.

All in all, the ragtag assemblage of prosecution witnesses didn't seem to amount to much, and it seemed hard to believe that we would be found guilty on the strength of statements by the very experts we had gone to for advice, including the police. Surely, the jury would be able to see this.

Predictably, the press had a field day with the prosecutor's narrative, and each day of the first week of the trial we were treated to the media's lurid details of how we'd been blinded to our son's monstrous nature. In contrast to the lacklustre presentation of the prosecution witnesses, there was high drama to be found in Jack's messages themselves, with the height of the prosecution's case being Jack's supposed Facebook threat to behead a former schoolfriend. "Parents funnelled money to terrorist son despite knowing his beheading wish" screamed the headlines. It didn't matter that we disputed this statement came from Jack himself for a multitude of reasons, i.e., 1) we had reason to believe his account had been hacked, which we had commented on at the time; 2) Jack confirmed when he was out of ISIS territory that his account had indeed been used by "many different people, some of whom were extremists," who had "got his password from a guy he'd stupidly trusted"; 3) around the same time, I had received a message sent from Jack's private account informing me that Jack was dead — something I knew to be false, with the message itself demonstrating the fact that someone else clearly had access to Jack's account; and 4) the shocking beheading statement had immediately followed a Facebook comment from Jack's account beneath a photo of a group of British soldiers, stating the writer would like to "perform a martyrdom operation in this scene." I doubted this latter comment had come from Jack as I'd had a phone conversation with him a couple of weeks beforehand in which he'd said that suicide bombings were *haram* (forbidden): "Allah gives life, it is not for individuals to take away," had been his explanation.

Unfortunately, although I tried to explain these points on the stand, they were not reported by the press, and this alleged comment of Jack's continued to dominate the trial. As horrific as the comment was, it still seemed to me only fair that Jack should have a chance to explain it himself, particularly since John and I ourselves regularly received similar disgusting comments on social media, describing how we or Jack should be murdered, raped, or have our own heads chopped off. Ultimately, threatening us with fourteen years in prison or keeping Jack in inhumane conditions for two years did not seem to me to be a proportionate response to a disputed social media post.

The highlights of the trial — as agreed by us and all our supporters — were the closing speeches of Tim and Henry, our barristers, who by now felt like our dearest friends. In breathtaking, virtuoso performances, they laid bare the dishonesty and corruption at the heart of our case. We had been betrayed by the police and the government whom we had gone to for help; we were devoted parents who had done everything they could to save the life of their child; we were ordinary, decent people who had worked for charities and social causes all their lives and who had been living through a nightmare not of their own making.

In his summing up, Henry described the effect of our trial on the law itself. Tall, thin, and austere in his black gown, he resembled, I thought, a seventeenth-century cleric, or perhaps a heron about to scoop its prey. "These parents are supportive of the battle against terrorism," he said, directly addressing the jury as they listened with rapt attention (in contrast to the inattention they had mostly exhibited up to that point). "But this prosecution does absolutely nothing to further the prevention of terrorism. In fact, it runs the risk of undermining the fight against terrorism because it runs the risk of bringing the law into disrepute. This prosecution is completely inhumane to the point of being cruel. These parents have to all intents and purposes lost their son. They are having to deal with that. They are having to deal with the trauma."

Absurdly, I felt immensely proud of both Tim and Henry after their speeches. Tim was "like a TV lawyer," I told him, and Henry was like "the character out of *To Kill a Mockingbird*." ("Don't say that," said Tom, Henry's junior. "That didn't end well.") When the jury retired to consider their verdict, I hoped it would be these barristers' performances that remained uppermost in the jurors' minds.

In the end, the jury deliberated for nearly twenty hours. As we sat in the dock impassively awaiting their verdict, I realized there is something uniquely terrifying about the pregnant-with-possibility pause that occurs moments before the response to the crucial question, "Have you, the jury, reached your decision?" Particularly when the jury foreman is a burly, aggressively tattooed skinhead, who wears Union Jack T-shirts and poppies in his lapel, and sniggers during your evidence. Strangely, hearing the word "guilty" out of said foreman's mouth felt monstrously wrong rather than terrifying. Although the judge had already indicated in his concluding statements that any guilty sentence would not be custodial, the shock was still there, along with the confusion of how this could have happened.

As the papers later noted, the verdict drew gasps from the gallery (and I noticed our friend Ingrid wiping away a tear), but John and I displayed no reaction at all, perhaps because we had been instructed by our barristers to remain dignified, no matter what.

The jury's conclusion was that John and I were guilty of Count 1 — i.e., sending £223 to Jack's friend in Lebanon, who could help him buy glasses (ironically, this was the charge I hadn't originally been arrested for, which was only added on to the charge sheet later). We were not guilty on Count 2 — sending Jack money to escape Raqqa. For Count 3 (the payment sent when the Count 2 payment was blocked), the jury could not reach a decision, meaning we were deemed not guilty by default.

The discrepancy in verdicts, we and our lawyers believed, was due to the fact that the defence of duress was applicable to Counts 2 and 3, but not to Count 1. All in all, it seemed an incredible waste of taxpayers' money that a now estimated £6 million had been spent to convict two parents for £223. The judge's sentence was a fifteen-month custodial sentence, suspended for twelve months.

Our emotions were as mixed as the verdict. We were immensely relieved not to be going to prison. On the other hand, we knew that a terrorism conviction would mean we would have financial, legal, travel, and employment problems for the rest of our lives. I knew that I would never again be able to visit my brother and sister, who lived in the U.S. But the important thing was that we were free: contempt of court was a thing of the past and we could now put all of our energies into campaigning for the release of our son.

Epilogue

September 2022

In the summer of 2021, I had a horrible, vivid dream that Jack was as emaciated as a Belsen victim and was clutching my arm in a desperate grip. He was blaming me for not feeding him. I awoke gasping for breath. I knew that the dream characterized my enduring fear and guilt, as well as overwhelming feelings of powerlessness, derangement, and despair.

It is now just over three years since our trial's verdict in August 2019. In that time, I have put several thousand miles of clear, blue ocean between myself and that Perspex defendants' box at the Old Bailey. It feels now, as I sit in my rabbit-hutch apartment in central Ottawa, that although so much is different, so little has actually changed.

Jack is still imprisoned in northeast Syria, and we remain ignorant of his welfare and his fate. After seven months of not knowing if he was still on this earth — the Canadian government reportedly unable to give us this information — we received word from our reliable contact at Channel 4, who had heard from a BBC producer in Iraqi Kurdistan, that as of the beginning of July 2021, he was indeed still alive. There was no news of his physical or mental state.

John and I are still campaigning for his release, with the campaign focus having shifted to Canada after the U.K. government removed Jack's British citizenship in August 2019. In January 2020, we gained a Canadian lawyer, who agreed to institute a judicial review of the Canadian government's refusal to repatriate a group of twenty-six Canadian citizens: fourteen children, eight women, and four men, including Jack. After a dispiriting two-year period in which it seemed that our Canadian legal team was prioritizing the "easier cases" of the women and children to the exclusion of the more arduous cases of the men, we hired the energetic Barb Jackman, who immediately set to work preparing a defence specifically for Jack within the overall group action.

Tayab — who has become our friend, mentor, brother, adviser, and mediator — is still battling away on our behalf. In May 2021, he submitted a complaint to the UN special rapporteur on human rights, Fionnuala Ní Aoláin, which was based mainly on the evidence Jack was able to provide us with during the early days of his captivity in 2017. In August 2022, we received the long-awaited and welcome news that the UN decided to take up the complaint, and in two strongly condemnatory letters — one to the U.K. government and one to the Canadian government — expressed their profound concern that these two Western powers were flouting their obligations under article 3 of the Universal Declaration of Human Rights (i.e., the right to life), and under article 12 of the International Covenant on Economic, Social, and Cultural Rights ("ICESCR"), which guarantees the right of all people, including prisoners and detainees, to the highest attainable standard of physical and mental health. To date, neither government has responded to the UN special rapporteur to explain what steps they are taking to safeguard Jack's rights in compliance with their international human rights obligations.

After the Foreign Commonwealth Office told me there was no point in talking to them, now that Jack was no longer British, I decided in December 2019 to emigrate to Canada. A mere three months later, I cashed in my pension and put my possessions into two suitcases, leaving a few boxes behind at John's farm. John said that when he had wrapped up his grain business, he and *E* would likely follow in a couple of years' time.

I haven't lived in Canada for nearly forty years, and it is somewhat of a shock to start afresh on my own in a place where most of my reference points are completely out of date. Luckily, friends from my college days have been able to help orient me in the process of living and working here once again. Being on the no-fly list as a result of our conviction under the Terrorism Act, I'd had to take a cargo ship across the ocean. My arrival in Halifax had been a close call: just one day after we docked, the Canadian government closed the border due to the new and strange pandemic that was suddenly rampaging across the world (of which we had been unaware, as we'd been nine days at sea with no internet access). The fact that I had narrowly and fortuitously scraped through the government's border control in order to start a new life must mean something, I thought.

Every single day, I envisage Jack beside me once again: having leisurely breakfasts together, going for hikes in the vast and beautiful Canadian wilderness, gently catching up on the horrors that have befallen him. Tayab has told me there is no evidence for him to be charged with any crime and for him to be further locked up in a Canadian prison, so I believe there is justification for my imaginings.

It will take a long time for Jack to recover, I know. And I'm prepared. Over and over, I picture the scene when I first see him again: him, cracking a smile and telling me how much I've aged.

And me, telling him that that's what happens when your first-born jumps on a plane to go to a war-ravaged inferno and puts in motion a living nightmare in which you expend every breath trying to get him back again.

But that is the image that sustains me. And this is the year that I have silently pledged to myself that it will finally come true.

Acknowledgements

The strange and harrowing journey on which my first-born has sent me has occasioned unexpected encounters with a diverse array of remarkable people who have helped me in countless and often extraordinary ways. Without them, I would not have survived intact. I wish to acknowledge them here, as I am truly grateful to them for demonstrating to me the best of what it means to be human.

Tayab Ali, to whom this book is dedicated, has been our life raft in a turbulent sea and a true friend. Whatever the circumstances, he has been a source of integrity and sound judgment, applying his quicksilver brain to each new predicament that assails us. His legal team — many of whom feature in this book — formed our initial small band of human rights warriors: Itpal Dhillon, who was the first to read an early draft of this book and encouraged me to continue; Anna Renou, whose Antipodean directness provided welcome strength in fraught police interrogations; Ravi Naik, who is a street fighter in a suit; Tim Moloney, whose charm and ease of manner belie his formidable powers of debate; and Henry Blaxland, who, despite his austere exterior, made an emotional court plea on our behalf about the very nature of justice.

Our English friends and supporters have accompanied John and me at every step of the way, offering their help with a generosity of spirit, which we have been grateful to accept. Ingrid, who has opened up her heart and her home to us for over twenty years, has been like a second mother to both our boys. Jo B., who rallied her numerous friends and allies to join our cause, has been a constant inspiration and source of strength. Jackie, whose loving kindness exists alongside a mischievous sense of humour, has been at my side throughout all my joys and tribulations since we were both eleven years old.

Others who have supported us in myriad ways — all of whom are too numerous to mention — include Tom Wainwright and Richard Thomas, Donald O'Neal, Tania Wickham, Sally Bayley, Cathy Porter, Claire-Marie O'Grady, Liz Halsey, Deborah Glass-Woodin, Adrian Arbib, Elise Benjamin, Nikki Marriott, Nikhil Widdows, Gill and Simon, Colin and Ruth, Martin and Hanik, Darshna Soni and Simon Stanleigh, Lowkey, Tim Adams, Martin Stellman, Campbell MacDiarmid, Azadeh Moaveni, Brian Cathcart, Crispin Blunt, MP, Dennis Harrison, Stig, Lydia Goymer, John Rowley, Michael Simkin, Gill Collins, Maggie Piggott, Jill Fuller, Britte Thorenwaite, Naimeh Baidoun, Jan Bailey, Irina Hoffer, Jane Powell, Nikita Bernardi, and Kate Lonsdale. I also particularly wish to mention Jack's friends Mazen, Safa, Maimoun, Liban, Curtis, Mariam, and Sarah, who never gave up on him, and whose love for him has sustained me all these years.

Esther Whitby, whose literary brilliance intimidated me as a young and nervous editorial assistant at André Deutsch in the 1980s, became one of our biggest supporters, giving us access to her vast old girls' network and encouraging me in my own writing. I remain indebted to her steadfastness, insight, and kindness.

Clive Stafford Smith, who believed in Jack and his innocence and has stated in a public forum that "Jack is no more a terrorist than my grandmother," has been confronting government repression and brutality in all its worst forms for decades, yet has managed to maintain a truly admirable and indefatigable energy in pursuit of the truth.

The fearless reporting of investigative journalists David Rose and Simon Hooper has meant that parts of Jack's real story were revealed to the world while the rest of the media remained mired in lies.

Cage U.K., who have been leading the struggle against discrimination and prejudice aimed at Muslims since 9/11, have been instrumental in seeking justice for Jack. Cerie Bullivant and Fahad Ansari tirelessly and valiantly promoted Jack's and our case to an unsympathetic public, bringing on board the rest of their team, including Moazzam Begg, a former Guantanamo Bay detainee. I am particularly grateful to Moazzam for speaking to the absence of justice in Jack's case in our Ottawa online repatriation conference, as hosted by Canada's International Civil Liberties Monitoring Group.

Alongside Cage are my stalwart Twitter followers, whom I'd like to thank for keeping me going in the face of online venom levelled at me and my family. "The Londonistani" — whose identity I still don't know, but who is featured in the epigraph to this book — was my first Twitter follower and gave me the courage to speak the truth about my son. He revealed to me a uniquely Muslim world, where traditional religious values can exist alongside an acerbic and distinctively British wit, together with an acute, non-Eurocentric analysis of world politics.

There are many brave, creative, principled Canadians I want to thank for their efforts in sustaining me in my new life in Ottawa. Pamela Walker, who first housed, fed, and counselled me in my first three weeks in the country — and who declared me "the world's most disappointing terrorist" — proceeded to introduce me to everyone who could help me in my quest for Jack's release. Among her many friends and contacts were Monia Mazigh, who has always been ready to lend her unique and energetic inspiration; Bill Skidmore, whose commitment to global justice survived his retirement as a human rights professor at Carleton University; and the academic Nadia Abu-Zahra, who spoke so eloquently at our protest on the steps of the Prime Minister's office.

Several other friends helped me transition back to living in Canada after spending forty years in the U.K. The Geller sisters — Leah and Diana — ensured I survived my first winter by providing me with copious newcomer advice and a supply of warm clothing. Rose, Lori, Alison, Randy, Paul, Gill, and MJ — my friends from college days — showered me with gifts, recommendations, and Zoom calls. New friends, comrades, and supporters, who continue to restore my faith in human nature, include Aro Braithwaite; Ed Broadbent; Barb Jackman; Farah Saleem; Tim McSorley; Xan Dagenais Guertin; Elizabeth May, MP; Heather McPherson, MP; Joel Harden, MPP; Alex Neve; Sam Laprade; Scott Neigh; Nafeesa Mohammed; and Ottawa's finest political agitators, the Raging Grannies.

One person who deserves a paragraph of his own is Matthew Behrens, who has been a transformative influence in so many ways. I apologize in advance to his partner, Laurel, who has to deal with his being compared to a divine being by the disadvantaged souls he chooses to support, but it is true to say that he has lifted me from despair to hope in our campaign to save Jack. A brilliant writer, orator, performer, strategist, legal authority, and political organizer, he has applied his genius to our cause, with no motivation other than to right the wrongs of political persecution and outrageous injustice. I am indebted to his energy, power, and humility.

Others who deserve particular mention are my sister, Julie, who has lived our journey of hope almost as closely as John and I have, and who has lent her considerable artistic skills to the campaign; our younger son, referred to in the book as *E*, who has acquired a wisdom beyond his years as a result of our family upheaval, and has grown into a perceptive, kind, and thoughtful young man; my wonderful and dedicated agents at Curtis Brown, Jethro Thompson and Bea Menendez, who never lost faith that this book would find a home; Russell Smith, my editor at Dundurn Press, who tolerated (most of) my Britishisms and made the bold decision to take on my story; Laurie Miller, whose sensitive and intelligent copy-editing I greatly appreciated; Farida Deif and Letta Tayler at Human Rights Watch; and Justin Mohammed at Amnesty Canada, who promote human rights against intransigent governments every day of their lives.

Finally, I want to applaud the dedication and steadfastness of other family members and advocates, who have supported our collective struggle to free our children and grandchildren from arbitrary detention. They number in their thousands from many different countries, but I especially want to pay tribute to Narcos Lingistir, Abandoned Trinis, Deerslippers, Kimberly Polman and her sister, Kamalle Dabboussy, Bea Eriksson, and Natascha Mikkelsen. Our hearts are united in bringing our loved ones home.

About the Author

Photo by Aro Braithwaite

Sally Lane was born in London, England, and emigrated as a teenager with her family to Toronto, Canada, in 1977. She gained a degree in French and History at the University of Western Ontario. Much of her adult life was spent in Oxford, England, where she worked as a copy editor and charity fundraiser while bringing up her two boys with her husband, John. She has been campaigning for the return of her son from Syria for eight years.